Bed & Breakfast Homes Directory

West Coast

7th Edition

Bed & Breakfast Homes Directory

West Coast

7th Edition

by

Diane Knight

 KNIGHTTIME PUBLICATIONS

Watsonville, California

Graphic Artist, Sondra Prull
Edited by Suzy Blackaby
Front cover photo by Steven Buxton
Back cover photo by Raymond Miller
Maps by Eureka Cartography, Berkeley, California
Desktop publishing by Raymond Miller

Printed and bound in U.S.A. by Griffin Printing, Sacramento, California

Library of Congress Catalog Card Number: 90-642605

ISBN 0-942902-08-4

As we have slowly added more and more B&Bs in the Pacific Northwest to *BED & BREAKFAST HOMES DIRECTORY*, the emphasis has evolved from mostly California B&Bs to a more balanced West Coast guidebook. In light of this shift, we have organized the book differently this time. California, Oregon, Washington, and British Columbia are now independent sections, each of which is introduced by a map that may be used to locate towns in which to find B&Bs. Selected towns may be located alphabetically within each section.

I must again address the controversy over the issue of guidebook authors charging B&B owners to be listed. Knighttime Publications *does* charge a listing fee of two times the average double rate charged by the B&B. While this may seem on the surface to be a questionable policy, a deeper look should put readers' minds at ease.

Every effort is made to seek out and include only those B&Bs that meet our criteria of cleanliness, comfort, hospitality, and value. I am one of the few bed and breakfast guidebook authors who actually visits each B&B and describes it from firsthand experience. The listing fee is accepted only after the B&B is visited and approved. Any B&B that is judged to be out of line in any of the above-mentioned areas is not included. Further, I do not list any B&B that I would not personally be pleased to stay in.

In addition to the expense of visiting every new B&B and occasionally re-visiting old ones, there are the substantial expenses of actual publication of *BED & BREAKFAST HOMES DIRECTORY*. In short, it would not be possible to produce the book without the income derived from the listing fees.

Readers, be assured that you are my foremost concern. The integrity of this book must remain high so that you will continue to buy and use it, and so that I can continue to do the work I love. No compromises are made in its creation.

B&B hosts have agreed to honor published rates for our readers at least until the end of 1992. In order for these rates to be honored, be sure to mention that you found their B&B in the current edition of this book. Some hosts offer a special discount to readers, as noted; you must have a copy of this edition to obtain the reader discounts.

Your feedback regarding your experiences while using this book is strongly encouraged. Comments and suggestions -- as well as inquiries about being listed as a B&B establishment in a future edition -- should be addressed to me at 890 Calabasas Road, Watsonville, CA 95076.

As your travels take you to some of the places and people that have touched my heart, I wish you the joy of serendipity.

We are continuing the feature begun in 1988; that is, the addition of a listing of recommended restaurants for each state or province covered in *BED & BREAKFAST HOMES DIRECTORY*. This is not intended to be a comprehensive listing of good restaurants, nor does it contain extensive information about each one. It offers some assistance in finding suitable places for lunch or dinner as you travel through unfamiliar territory. You will have to call or drop by the establishment that you're considering to find out more about it.

I have selected many of the restaurants from my own happy dining experiences. I must admit that part of my motivation in compiling the listings is the marvelous convenience of having at my fingertips the names, addresses, and phone numbers of an excellent assortment of wonderful restaurants spanning the U.S. and Canadian west coasts. I have found myself using the listings constantly since the last compilation. The Dining Highlights have been substantially revised and expanded in this edition.

In addition to choosing restaurants myself, I've also asked hosts to name those in their areas that they can recommend without hesitation. Each was personally selected by someone who has had firsthand knowledge of it over a period of time. Restaurants range from a simple taco stand in Santa Barbara to a world-class restaurant in Sooke, B.C., and prices vary accordingly. There was no charge to restaurants for a listing.

Criteria for selection were good quality ingredients, careful preparation, a pleasant atmosphere, and (most important), superior value. The majority of restaurants included are gems -- really wonderful little places that tourists would be unlikely to discover on their own. While most offer good food at reasonable prices, some "splurge" restaurants are included -- and judged to be well worth the cost.

Although most of the restaurants have proven track records, no guarantees are possible. Your feedback on these recommendations is encouraged.

I want to emphasize that the number of restaurants listed for any given town is simply a product of information available to me. For example, since I live near the San Francisco Bay Area, my personal knowledge (as well as that of friends and colleagues) of its restaurants is much greater than that of, say, San Diego or Los Angeles. I apologize for the resulting lopsided coverage.

The B&Bs in this directory are, in most cases, strictly private homes, not commercial establishemnts. While some small, owner-occupied inns are also included, they are still the *homes* of the people who operate them. As a guest, remember to act with the same courtesy and consideration that you would expect of a guest in your own home.

Most *B&BHD* hosts don't consider themselves innkeepers. They are not in business full time -- and therein lies some of the appeal of being treated "like family." There may be occasions when hosts can't accommodate you because they'll be on vacation, or because Great Aunt Martha from Omaha will be using the guest room.

In many cases, daily maid service and room service are not provided. This varies a great deal from one B&B to the next, but, generally, the smaller and less expensive accommodations do not offer such services. However, it is at this type of B&B that you are likely to encounter the spontaneous personal favor at just the right moment.

A number of B&B hosts will accept only cash or traveler's checks in payment for accommodations. Over time, though, more and more hosts are accepting credit cards. This information is now included in the second paragraph of each description for your convenience. Be sure to verify what forms of payment will be accepted *before* your visit.

When reserving accommodations in B&B homes, it is very important to agree upon your time of arrival with the host. There is always some flexibility, but arrival time should be discussed. If it appears that you will be later than planned, it is only considerate (and most appreciated) that you call and let your host know.

Room rates include at least a Continental breakfast. In many cases, the rate includes a full breakfast; in a few situations, there may be an extra charge (as noted) for a full breakfast. If anything more than a Continental breakfast is served, it is so stated in each listing.

Many hosts look forward to having guests join them for a family-style breakfast. In some cases -- if the guest unit is totally separate and has cooking facilities -- the host(s) will simply leave the ingredients for breakfast so that guests may prepare it at their leisure. There are hosts who will be glad to serve you breakfast in your room, or even in bed. Morning may find you at a table of your own, or perhaps you'll breakfast at a large table with other B&B guests. As in many aspects of B&B travel, the accent is on *variety*.

For each listing:

The first line tells either the name(s) of the host(s) or the name given to the B&B and the phone number to call for reservations.

The second line gives the mailing address of the B&B to use if you're writing for reservations.

The third line, in parentheses, indicates the general location of the B&B. You should get specific directions from your host.

Next you'll find a descriptive paragraph about the B&B. It often tells something about the unique qualities of the home itself, the setting, the host(s), points of interest in the area.

The second paragraph indicates whether there are indoor pets and gives the host(s) preferences, such as "no smoking" or "children welcome." These appear in a consistent sequence in each listing. They are given only if the host(s) have indicated a specific policy on the subject. The paragraph also lists facilities or features available to guests, such as "laundry" or "hot tub."

Available transportation is sometimes indicated, as well as the host(s) willingness to pick up guests at a nearby airport (largely for the benefit of private pilots).

The following code refers to the headings at the end of each description:

ROOM
Refers to a guest unit. The unit may be a room in the B&B home, an adjoining apartment, or a separate cottage near the home. Each letter (A, B,...) designates one guest unit, whether it has one, two, or more rooms.

BED
Number and type(s) of bed(s) given for each guest unit. This means total beds per unit. **T** = twin, **D** = double, **Q** = queen, **K** = king

BATH
Shd means you'll share a bath with the host(s). **Shd*** means the bath is shared by other guests, if present. (You may have it all to yourself, especially midweek or off-season.) **Pvt** means the bath goes with the guest unit and is shared by no one else. It may be across the hall, but it is all yours.

ENTRANCE
Main indicates you'll use the main entrance of the home. **Sep** means there is a separate entrance for guests.

FLOOR
The floor of each guest room is indicated by number in most cases. **LL** means lower level, usually with steps down. **1G** means a ground level room, with no steps.

DAILY RATES   **S** refers to a single (one person); **D** refers to a double (two persons); **EP** refers to the rate charged for an extra person (above two) traveling with your party (generally, when there is an extra bed of some sort in the guest unit). Most of the rates quoted will have a local tax added. When this information is available, a plus sign (+) has been used by the **EP** rate. Some stated rates **include** the tax.

Example:

ROOM	BED	BATH	ENTRANCE	FLOOR	DAILY RATES
					S - D (EP) +
A	1K	Pvt	Main	2	$60-$65 ($10)

Room (or unit) A has one king-sized bed, a private bath, uses the main entrance to the home, is on the second floor. One person will pay $60; two persons will pay $65; an extra person will pay $10. A local tax will be added.

NOTE TO TRAVELERS IN CANADA: Many Canadian B&Bs must charge a Goods and Services Tax (**G.S.T.**), which is fully refundable to travelers upon leaving Canada. Hosts will assist with procedure.

AC = Air Conditioning; **VCR** = Video Cassette Recorder; **BART** = Bay Area Rapid Transit (in San Francisco Bay Area).

HOW TO ARRANGE A B&B VISIT

1. Try to plan your visit as far ahead as possible. This helps to ensure you'll get to stay at the B&B of your choice. Notify your host(s) immediately of any change in plans.

2. Call your host(s) for reservations before 9 p.m. Be sure to allow for the time difference if you're not on Pacific Time.

3. Carefully check details about the B&B you're considering before calling or writing. Confirm with your host anything that's not clear to you. Ask pertinent questions!

4. Check what form(s) of payment your host(s) will accept. Ask if a deposit is required.

5. Agree on time of arrival.

Hosts listed in *BED & BREAKFAST HOMES DIRECTORY* have agreed to honor rates stated in the directory until the end of 1992.

The information contained in these listings has been prepared with great care, but we cannot guarantee that it is complete or in all cases correct. It is the user's responsibility to verify important information when making arrangements.

CALIFORNIA

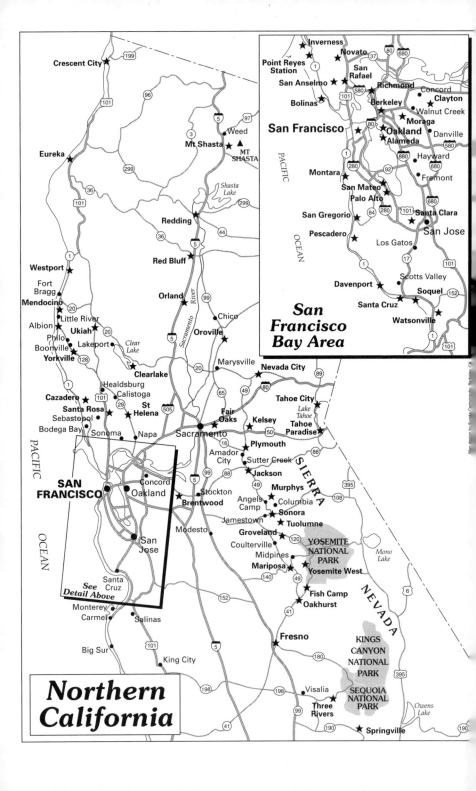

San Francisco Bay Area

Inverness
Point Reyes Station
Novato
San Rafael
San Anselmo
Richmond
Concord
Clayton
Bolinas
Berkeley
Walnut Creek
Moraga
San Francisco
Oakland
Alameda
Danville
Montara
Hayward
San Mateo
Palo Alto
Fremont
San Gregorio
Santa Clara
Pescadero
San Jose
Los Gatos
Davenport
Scotts Valley
Soquel
Santa Cruz
Watsonville

PACIFIC OCEAN

Northern California

Crescent City
Weed
Mt Shasta
MT SHASTA
Eureka
Shasta Lake
Redding
Red Bluff
Westport
Orland
Fort Bragg
Chico
Mendocino
Oroville
Little River
Albion
Ukiah
Philo
Boonville
Lakeport
Clear Lake
Yorkville
Marysville
Nevada City
Clearlake
Healdsburg
Calistoga
Tahoe City
Cazadero
St Helena
Lake Tahoe
Santa Rosa
Fair Oaks
Kelsey
Sebastopol
Tahoe Paradise
Bodega Bay
Sonoma
Napa
Sacramento
Plymouth
Amador City
SIERRA
Sutter Creek
Jackson
SAN FRANCISCO
Concord
Murphys
Oakland
Stockton
Brentwood
Angels Camp
Columbia
Modesto
Jamestown
Sonora
Tuolumne
San Jose
Groveland
Coulterville
YOSEMITE NATIONAL PARK
Midpines
Mono Lake
Santa Cruz
Mariposa
Yosemite West
See Detail Above
Monterey
Fish Camp
Carmel
Oakhurst
NEVADA
Salinas
Big Sur
King City
Fresno
KINGS CANYON NATIONAL PARK
Visalia
SEQUOIA NATIONAL PARK
Owens Lake
Three Rivers
Springville

PACIFIC OCEAN

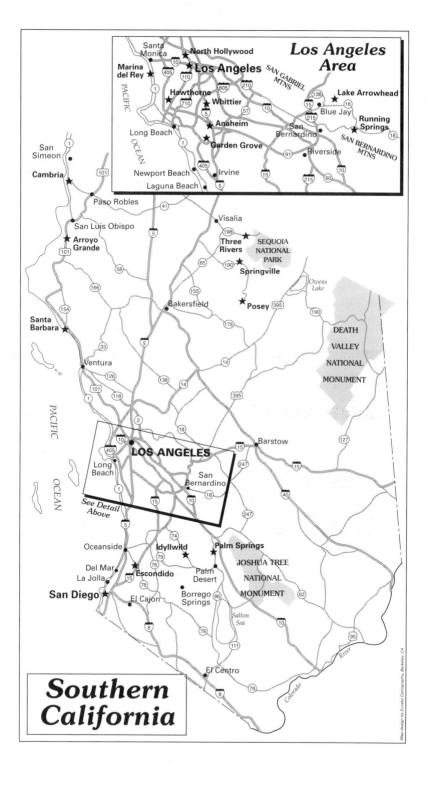

Los Angeles Area

Santa Monica
North Hollywood
Marina del Rey
Los Angeles
Hawthorne
Whittier
Anaheim
Garden Grove
Long Beach
Newport Beach
Irvine
Laguna Beach
PACIFIC OCEAN
SAN GABRIEL MTNS
Lake Arrowhead
Blue Jay
Running Springs
San Bernardino
Riverside
SAN BERNARDINO MTNS

San Simeon
Cambria
Paso Robles
San Luis Obispo
Arroyo Grande
Santa Barbara
Visalia
Three Rivers
SEQUOIA NATIONAL PARK
Springville
Bakersfield
Posey
Owens Lake
DEATH VALLEY NATIONAL MONUMENT

Ventura
LOS ANGELES
Long Beach
San Bernardino
Barstow
See Detail Above
PACIFIC OCEAN

Oceanside
Idyllwild
Palm Springs
Del Mar
La Jolla
Escondido
Palm Desert
JOSHUA TREE NATIONAL MONUMENT
San Diego
El Cajon
Borrego Springs
Salton Sea
El Centro
Colorado River

Southern California

Map design by Eureka Cartography, Berkeley, CA

Jan Christensen-Heller & Sidney Heller   **(510) 521-5075**
1421 Bay Street, Alameda, CA 94501
(West end of island in San Francisco Bay; access from Oakland)

This superbly renovated older home bears the look of understated but unmistakable class, both at first glance and in every interior detail. The tasteful environment grew from the hosts' appreciation of Indian and Oriental art, much of which was gathered in their travels. Rugs, antiques, sculpture, paintings, wallhangings, and various objets d'art exist in true aesthetic harmony, filling every room with the tranquility of the mildly exotic. The entire second floor comprises the guest quarters where one party at a time enjoys a spacious, unusually comfortable living area with a free-standing wood-burning fireplace, a full kitchen, a bathroom, and a choice of three very appealing bedrooms. It's easy to make oneself completely at home in the top-notch accommodations offered by the Hellers.

Dog in residence; no pets or children; expanded Continental breakfast; TV/VCR and phone in guest quarters; FAX machine and exercise equipment available; tennis courts nearby; swimming pool available at yacht club; great area for walking; bus, BART, and ferries nearby; ample street parking; German and Spanish spoken.

ROOM	BED	BATH	ENTRANCE	FLOOR	DAILY RATES S - D (EP) +
A	2T	Pvt	Sep	2	$75-$85
B	1D				$75-$85
C	1D				$75-$85

The Wool Loft   **(707) 937-0377**
32751 Navarro Ridge Road, Albion, CA 95410
(Ten miles south of Mendocino)

The Wool Loft's setting overlooking the sea reminds me of some B&Bs in Ireland or Scotland. Sheep graze in nearby fields; the family garden and henhouse contribute food to the table. Jan and Sid offer three cheery guest rooms with private baths in the main house to guests who prefer traditional bed and breakfast; one of these (B) is a newer room with wonderful river and ocean views. The Wool Loft itself (A) is a separate accommodation. It's a spacious studio apartment with queen-sized bed, fully equipped kitchen, bath, wood-burning stove, and huge windows that afford magnificent vistas. Quiet and cozy seclusion on the famous Mendocino coast is yours if you choose The Wool Loft.

No pets, children, or smoking; gather eggs for breakfast if desired; deck and fireplace in main house; firewood provided in Wool Loft; off-street parking. Two-night minimum; three-night minimum on holiday weekends. Special weekly rate for Room A, $600; no breakfast served during week. *Open weekends for B&B (Friday-Sunday only)*. Brochure available.

ROOM	BED	BATH	ENTRANCE	FLOOR	DAILY RATES	
					S - D	(EP) +
A	1Q	Pvt	Sep	2	$100	
B	1Q	Pvt	Main	1	$85	
C	1Q	Pvt	Main	1	$65	
D	1Q	Pvt	Main	1	$65	

Anaheim Bed & Breakfast　　　　　　　　**(714) 533-1884**
1327 South Hickory, Anaheim, CA　92805
(Off Santa Ana Freeway)

Anaheim is the obvious headquarters for anyone planning to visit Disneyland or the convention center, both less than a mile away, or Knott's Berry Farm. Many people also find the location ideal for visiting beaches, L.A., as well as points to the south and east. Disneyland's nightly fireworks can be viewed in summer from the back yard of this suburban home. Margot Palmgren's home exudes a friendly welcome that puts visitors at ease right away. She speaks German fluently and loves meeting people from all over the world. You'll be in good hands with Margot; she knows the area intimately and can give you a real insider's view of things...for example, she remembers when the Knott family ran a little fruit stand nearby -- and the day Disneyland opened!

No pets or smoking; TV in each room; AC in Room A; ceiling fan in B and C; AC and fireplace in den; full breakfast; ample street parking; good public transportation and airport connections.

ROOM	BED	BATH	ENTRANCE	FLOOR	DAILY RATES S - D (EP) +
A	1D	Shd*	Main	1G	$30-$40
B	2T	Shd*	Main	1G	$30-$40
C	1D	Shd	Main	1G	$30-$40

The Guest House   **(805) 481-9304**
120 Hart Lane, Arroyo Grande, CA 93420
(Off U.S. 101, seventeen miles south of San Luis Obispo)

Homesick New Englanders, look no further than The Guest House at Arroyo Grande. It was built in the 1850s by a sea captain from the east and bears an unmistakable resemblance to the homes he left behind. Present owners Mark Miller and James Cunningham have kept the flavor of old New England alive in the house. Stenciled wall designs, American primitives, Oriental rugs, and family heirlooms add to the mellow, inviting atmosphere. A crackling fire in the hearth and comfortable places to sit make the living room a haven for easy conversation. The afternoon social hour often takes place in the bay-windowed sun room with French doors that lead out to the garden. Breakfast is appropriately hearty fare, served in the sun room or out in the garden. For traditional Yankee hospitality at the sign of the pineapple, The Guest House is a classic.

Cat in residence; no pets, children, or RV parking; full breakfast; afternoon refreshments; city park in turn-of-the-century village of Arroyo Grande; many antique shops in town and wineries in surrounding countryside; off-street parking.

ROOM	BED	BATH	ENTRANCE	FLOOR	DAILY RATES	
					S - D	(EP) +
A	1Q	Shd*	Main	2	$45-$60	($10)
B	1D	Shd*	Main	2	$45-$60	($10)
C	1D	Shd	Main	1	$45-$60	($10)

Briarhill Lodging   **(510) 644-1420**
6815 Bristol Drive, Berkeley, CA 94705
(Up hill from Ashby/Claremont area)

What Dr. Elizabeth Broadhurst appreciates most about her lovely pale pink home is its combination of the ridgetop canyon setting (newly seeding after the fire) with returning wildlife, arresting views across San Francisco Bay, and the wealth of cultural, recreational, and gastronomic opportunities nearby. Perched high in the Berkeley hills, the home has a light, lively ambiance highlighted by interesting artwork and Oriental rugs. A retired professor and author who enjoys people, good books, the arts, and travel, Dr. Broadhurst generously shares her home with one set of guests at a time. Two corner rooms at the back of the house share a full bath and can accommodate from one to four people comfortably. Workspace, a private telephone, a FAX machine, a typewriter, a TV, an iron and ironing board, and other conveniences fill a host of needs one might have while enjoying hospitable lodgings in this unique and fascinating locale.

Dogs and families welcome; full breakfast; extensive network of hiking trails nearby; San Francisco, twenty minutes away; popular upscale mecca below the Claremont Hotel for shopping, coffee house dallying, dining, and people watching just downhill; bus and BART nearby; off-street parking. Brochure available. *Re-opening after re-constuction expected by fall 1992.*

ROOM	BED	BATH	ENTRANCE	FLOOR	DAILY RATES S - D (EP) +
A	1D	Pvt	Main	1	$40-$60
B	2T				$40-$60

One-Fifty-Five Pine   **(415) 868-0263**
P.O. Box 62, Bolinas, CA 94924
(Between Stinson Beach and Point Reyes National Seashore)

When nothing else will do but a private abode in clear sight of the ocean, One-Fifty-Five Pine is a good choice. The red frame cottage is set just above the Pacific, only a three-minute walk from the beach. Viewing sunsets off Duxbury Reef is big-time entertainment here. Inside, the warmth from the large stone fireplace inspires contentment. The knotty pine interior includes a living room, two bedrooms, a bath, and a multi-windowed kitchen/dining area across the back. The cottage is well suited to families and groups of four. When two couples travel together and cook some meals in, the value can be budget pleasing. Spectacular vistas, fresh ocean air, the nearby beach, and fireside snuggling enhance the feeling of complete escape that can be found at One-Fifty-Five Pine.

No pets inside; smoking outside only; no RV parking; ingredients for full breakfast in well-equipped kitchen; futon bed available; off-street parking. Inquire about midweek, off-season discounts.

ROOM	BED	BATH	ENTRANCE	FLOOR	DAILY RATES
					S - D (EP) +
A	2D	Pvt	Sep	1	$125 ($15)

19

Thomas' White House Inn   **(415) 868-0279**
P.O. Box 132, Bolinas, CA 94924
(Between Stinson Beach and Point Reyes National Seashore)

The magic and mystery of Bolinas lies in its refusal to go the way
of so many other seaside communities that nurture tourism at the
expense of the natural environment. Bolinas is not easy to find; it's
been said that if you want to find it, you will. Its startling beauty is
nowhere more apparent than at this marvelous bluffside inn overlooking the Pacific.   Just to breathe the fresh air here, to savor the
panorama of blue sea, Stinson Beach, the foothills, and Mount Tamal-
pais, feels like a privilege. The New England-style home of Jackie
Thomas is a crisp white with red trim. It has two stories and, at the
top, an observation deck. Two large, artfully appointed bedrooms and
a half-bath comprise the second floor. The first floor offers a full bath
with an aviary for zebra finches, a living room with a fireplace
accented by Mediterranean blue tile, a sun porch, and an open country
kitchen with dried flowers hanging from the beams. From bedrooms,
common rooms, and from the beautifully cultivated grounds, the view
is omnipresent -- just as it should be.

No pets; no smoking on second floor; expanded Continental breakfast; off-street parking.

ROOM	BED	BATH	ENTRANCE	FLOOR	DAILY RATES	
					S - D	(EP) +
A	1Q	Shd*	Main	2	$95	($10)
B	1D	Shd*	Main	2	$85	($10)

Diablo Vista (510) 634-2396
2191 Empire Avenue, Brentwood, CA 94513
(Just east of Antioch, off Lone Tree Way)

This elegant ranch-style home is set on two acres of fruit and nut trees, with a view of Mount Diablo in the distance. It's an hour from San Francisco and ten minutes from the Sacramento River Delta. For hikers and cyclists, Black Diamond Regional Park, with its many trails and historic sites, is only four miles away, as is Contra Loma Lake for swimming, windsurfing, and fishing. Brentwood is famous for its many "U-Pick" fruit and vegetable farms, and maps are available from hosts Dick and Myra Hackett. Their main guest room (A) is located at one far end of the house. This huge room has its own entrance, bath, kitchenette, small library, TV, stereo system, and AC/heating units. Subtle colors, Oriental rugs, custom-made window cushions, and American antiques create a harmonious, soothing effect. Room B is a cozy room with twin beds; the bath is a few steps down the hall. Guests in this room enjoy reading or relaxing in the sitting room of the main residence. Take a swim in the pool, soak in the hot tub, sip a drink in one of the two gazebos, or relax in the lovely garden. Hosts have thoroughly searched out the best restaurants in the area, a boon to those of us who take our dining seriously.

No pets; children over eight (swimmers) welcome; smoking outside only; TV; stereo; swimming pool; hot tub; jogging and biking trails surround property; plenty of parking; some Spanish spoken.

ROOM	BED	BATH	ENTRANCE	FLOOR	DAILY RATES S - D (EP)
A	1Q	Pvt	Sep	1G	$45-$50
B	2T	Shd	Main	1G	$35-$40

21

PineStone Inn By The Sea   **(805) 927-3494**
221 Weymouth Street, Cambria, CA 93428
(Overlooking Moonstone Beach)

From this new Victorian-style inn you can watch sunset and moon-rise, hear the sounds of the surf, or take a walk on the beach. The lower floor is just for guests. The foyer is carpeted in mauve and attractively painted light green using a stippling technique. The carpeting and stippling are carried into one pink guest room and another that's blue. Each has a full private bath, a gas fireplace, cable TV, and a sliding glass door to an individual garden patio. The quiet, relaxing rooms are as pretty as can be. On the second floor, there is another room for guests with a small private deck. Hosts Frank and Barbara Banner welcome people to enjoy the gorgeous view in the lounge by the large stone fireplace, in the dining area, or on the front deck. Their warm hospitality includes generous buffet breakfasts, afternoon refreshments, and anytime-coffee, tea, or chocolate. A sterling location plus all the comforts of home make staying at Pine-Stone Inn By The Sea a total pleasure.

No pets, smoking, or children; kitchen privileges; walking distance to Cambria village shops and restaurants; off-street parking.

ROOM	BED	BATH	ENTRANCE	FLOOR	DAILY RATES S - D (EP) +
A	1Q	Pvt	Main	1	$70-$75
B	2T or 1K	Pvt	Main	1	$70-$75
C	1Q	Pvt	Main	2	$70-$75

SeaEscape (805) 927-3112
340 Weymouth, Cambria, CA 93428
(Just east of Highway 1)

For an overnight stay while traveling the California coast or a weekend getaway, Cambria makes a wonderful stopping place. Just seven miles south of Hearst Castle, two blocks from Moonstone Beach, and within walking distance of charming Cambria village, Duane and Miriam Benell enjoy semi-retirement at their SeaEscape. The guest room of this lovely home is on the ground level, and the living-dining area is on the upper level with a view of the ocean. Having greatly enjoyed B&Bs abroad, hosts are pleased to extend hospitality to foreign visitors traveling in California. Though the Benells divide their time between Cambria and Whittier, B&B is available most of the year with *advance reservations* by calling (805) 927-3112, (310) 695-5431, or writing 12002 Beverly Drive, Whittier, CA 90601.

No pets or smoking; one or two children OK; full breakfast; small RV parking; TV and fireplace upstairs; off-street parking. Room B used only for people in same party as Room A. Advance reservations *essential* year-round for Hearst Castle tours.

ROOM	BED	BATH	ENTRANCE	FLOOR	DAILY RATES S - D (EP)
A	2T or 1K	Pvt	Main	1G	$40-$50
B	1Q		Main	1G	Inquire

Seaview Through the Pines   **(805) 927-3089**
570 Croyden Lane, Cambria, CA 93428
(East of Highway One, in pines overlooking coast)

The large, contemporary, cedar home of Audrey and Bill Mankey is perched on a hillside in the pines with a broad-range view to the sea. The entire lower level is a guest accommodation -- a clean, inviting place to unwind and settle into. The apartment has a full, well-stocked kitchen; a living room with a sitting area, cable TV and VCR, a fireplace, and a table for dining; a full bathroom; and a bedroom with an ocean view through the open doorway. A door from the kitchen leads to a private deck with a hot tub, a hammock, chairs, and view. Guests find refreshments upon arrival, plus a host of helpful information and a menu describing the wonderful breakfast choices. Neutral tones add to the tranquil environment, and it's obvious that everything, from bed to sofas to chairs, was built for comfort. Nestle into a beautiful world all your own at Seaview Through the Pines.

No pets; infants and children over thirteen welcome; no smoking; full breakfast; off-street parking.

ROOM	BED	BATH	ENTRANCE	FLOOR	DAILY RATES	
					S - D	(EP)
A	1Q	Pvt	Sep	LL	$85	($15)

Whispering Pines   **(805) 927-4613**
P.O. Box 326, Cambria, CA 93428
(1605 London Lane, off Ardath)

For many, discovering Cambria is an added bonus to visiting the magical Hearst Castle at San Simeon. The quaint coastal town retains its homespun charm even though it becomes more arty and sophisticated each year. In a lovely, tranquil area just a short drive from the old Cambria village is Jack and Ginny Anderson's multi-level contemporary home with views of rolling hills and pines -- Whispering Pines, that is. Guests may retreat to the total privacy of a deluxe, tri-level apartment with its own entrance and a hot tub just outside. Light, immaculate, and tastefully decorated, the unit consists of a living room with TV and VCR, dining area, kitchenette, full bath, and large loft bedroom. A tantalizing choice of breakfast entrees is offered, along with the luxury of delivery to your quarters. Simply put, Whispering Pines is a great little hideaway on the central coast.

No pets; smoking outside only; no RV parking; full breakfast; off-street parking. Hosts also operate Bed & Breakfast Homestay, a reservation service listing $55-$85 rooms and apartments in the area. **KNIGHTTIME PUBLICATIONS SPECIAL RATE: 10% discount with this book. Brochure available.

ROOM	BED	BATH	ENTRANCE	FLOOR	DAILY RATES S - D (EP)
A	2T or 1K	Pvt	Sep	2 & 3	$75

House of a Thousand Flowers   **(707) 632-5571**
P.O. Box 369, Monte Rio, CA 95462
(Five miles east of Jenner-by-the-Sea)

It's obvious right away how the House of a Thousand Flowers got its name. Greenery, including fuchsias and other blossoming plants, bedeck the house and infuse it with cheer. Host Dave Silva takes pride in the family home that is now a remote country haven for harried city folk in need of escape. He and his border collie, Annie, greet guests upon arrival. (It's been said that this is the only B&B run by an old man and his dog; Dave says the dog is the one with the class.) The house is set high on a bluff above the Russian River and has two cozy guest rooms on its lower level. Each has its own deck, separate entrance, and access to an enclosed, plant-filled spa. Look toward the sea and you may witness the magical effect created as fingers of fog move through the redwoods. The main floor is also yours to enjoy, with grand piano, extensive library, and dining room where Chef David serves his famous omelettes. Coffee is ready by your room in the morning, and breakfast is served at your convenience. Discover a little slice of paradise at the House of a Thousand Flowers.

Dog and cat in residence; full breakfast; afternoon refreshments; rollaway bed available; spa; river and ocean activities, good restaurants and wineries nearby; off-street parking; credit cards (V, MC). Brochure available.

ROOM	BED	BATH	ENTRANCE	FLOOR	DAILY RATES	
					S - D	(EP) +
A	1Q	Shd*	Sep	LL	$90	($15)
B	1Q	Shd*	Sep	LL	$80	($15)

The Farm House at Clayton   **(510) 672-8404**
7 Alef Court, Clayton, CA 94517
(Off Ygnacio Valley Road near Concord Pavilion)

Surrounded by immaculate, well-tended grounds and hilly terrain just minutes from the renowned Concord Pavilion is the inviting, blue, country-style home of Marilyn and Charles Kistner. They have created a lovely suite on the second floor for guests. The spacious, carpeted bedroom is done in striking navy blue contrasting with crisp white wicker, eyelet lace, and an unusually attractive handmade quilt. There's a sitting area with a fireplace, a bathroom with a Jacuzzi tub for two, and a deck with a view over rooftops and trees. The game room, featuring a fireplace and pool table, as well as the sunny, many-windowed country kitchen and adjoining brick patio -- indeed the whole house -- are the guests' to share. With excellent dining spots and the Pavilion just five minutes away and the Concord BART station a mere ten to fifteen minutes away, The Farm House at Clayton is a convenient yet hidden discovery.

No pets or children; smoking outside only; full, home-cooked breakfast and afternoon refreshments; TV/VCR; AC; five minutes from Mount Diablo State Park (hiking, picnicking) and Oakhurst Golf Course; good airport connections; off-street parking; airport pickup (Buchanan). Brochure available.

ROOM	BED	BATH	ENTRANCE	FLOOR	DAILY RATES
					S - D (EP)
A	1Q	Pvt	Main	2	$85-$95

Big Canyon Bed & Breakfast   **(707) 928-5631**
P.O. Box 1311, Lower Lake, CA 95457
(Seigler Springs, at foot of Cobb Mountain)

    The remote and woodsy mountain setting makes Big Canyon Bed & Breakfast a perfect place to escape to the quiet, natural world that inspires true relaxation. The Cape Cod-style home has two spacious rooms for guests on its upper floor. One (A) has its own entrance, woodstove, skylight, and kitchenette, while the other (B) has a cozy alcove window seat. The entire floor makes an ideal family or group accommodation. In the immediate surroundings you may enjoy identifying spring wildflowers, gazing at bright stars, and finding Lake County diamonds. Or take a twenty-minute drive to the lake and get into the swim of things. The casual country atmosphere of Big Canyon is conducive to doing simply whatever you please.

    Smoking outside only; AC; (main) kitchen privileges; double sofa bed in Room A (no charge for use); off-street parking. **KNIGHT-TIME PUBLICATIONS SPECIAL RATE: Two nights for the price of one Sunday-Thursday with this book. Brochure available.

ROOM	BED	BATH	ENTRANCE	FLOOR	DAILY RATES	
					S - D	(EP) +
A	1Q	Pvt	Sep	2	$65	
B	1Q	Pvt	Main	2	$65	

The Forbestown Bed & Breakfast Inn   **(707) 263-7858**
825 Forbes Street, Lakeport, CA 95453
(One block from Clear Lake in downtown Lakeport)

Jack and Nancy Dunne are pleased to own Lakeport's first bed and breakfast inn. The 1869 home was built when the town was known as Forbestown. Expert restoration has given the beautiful old home all its original charm. Each of the four luxurious guest rooms is a tasteful creation named after a historical figure of the Forbestown era. (A colorful cast of characters, I might add!) American oak antiques and designer fabrics highlight the decor, and gentle strains of music add to the calm elegance within. Outside, a secluded garden beckons one to relax in a lounge chair or to take a dip in the inviting pool or spa. Hosts can help with arrangements for visiting a gold mine, geothermal steam wells, wineries, and fine restaurants; water recreational equipment may be rented nearby. A rare glimpse of Lake County history coupled with splendid hospitality await you at The Forbestown Bed & Breakfast Inn.

No pets; no children under twelve; smoking outside only; full breakfast; afternoon refreshments; AC; ample street parking; credit cards (V, MC, AE); airport pickup (Lampson Field). Off-season rates for business travelers. Brochure available.

ROOM	BED	BATH	ENTRANCE	FLOOR	DAILY RATES S - D (EP) +
A	1Q	Shd*	Main	1	$95
B	1K	Shd*	Main	1	$105
C	1Q	Pvt	Main	2	$95
D	1Q	Shd*	Main	2	$85

Muktip Manor   **(707) 994-9571**
12540 Lakeshore Drive, Clearlake, CA 95422
(South shore of Clear Lake)

The home of Jerry Schiffman (affectionately known as Muktip
Manor) has a peculiar, Early California charm of its own. The living
quarters are all on the second floor, with doors opening onto a
wrap-around veranda.   Located opposite the lake, it affords good
views and a small, private beach.   The guest unit consists of a
bedroom, living room, kitchen, and bath. While not luxurious, the
decor is delightfully eclectic. Jerry is a former actor. (Look for him
on reruns of *Streets of San Francisco;* he always played a cop or a
corpse.) Occasionally he enjoys an evening sail in his catamaran with
guests who so choose. Whatever your particular pleasure might be,
there's a host of activities to choose from: boating, windsurfing,
swimming, canoeing, fishing, rock-hunting, and wine-tasting at Lake
County wineries. The lifestyle at Muktip Manor is casual, unpreten-
tious, and laced with humor -- a thoroughly engaging combination.

Dog and cats in residence; no children; pets welcome ($5 extra);
full breakfast; TV; kitchen; large deck; canoe available; launch ramp
and public fishing piers nearby; ample street parking; airport pickup
(Pearce). Animal lovers preferred. $5 discount per day with *current*
edition of book.

ROOM	BED	BATH	ENTRANCE	FLOOR	DAILY RATES S - D (EP)
A	1D	Pvt	Sep	2	$50

Shelby's Happy House   **(707) 994-2554**
P.O. Box 2079, Clearlake, CA 95422
(Two blocks from Clear Lake on Shelby Lane)

Shelby, a special niece of John and Sharron Lucich, dubbed their home "a happy house," so they honored her when they named their B&B. Inside and out, it inspires a smile. The endearing blue Cape Cod-style home is filled with charm and country comfort. There's a pink confection of a bedroom with a private bath on the main floor. An upstairs bedroom with a canopy bed is decorated in white eyelet and navy blue. The large living room with a fireplace and a restful atmosphere is as inviting as the lovely patio out back. It is an easy walk down to water's edge where you can picnic at delightful Redbud Park. Or spend the day sampling Lake County wines in tasting rooms that operate nearby. Enjoy a contented holiday in this hospitable setting near California's largest natural lake.

No pets; smoking outside only; full breakfast; off-street parking; airport pickup (Pearce Field).

ROOM	BED	BATH	ENTRANCE	FLOOR	DAILY RATES S - D (EP)
A	1Q	Pvt	Main	1	$75
B	1Q	Shd	Main	2	$65

Pebble Beach Bed & Breakfast   **(707) 464-9086**
1650 Macken Avenue, Crescent City, CA 95531   **1(800) 821-9816**
(Across from state beach)

Experience an out-of-the-way surprise at this lovely home situated near a beautiful stretch of coastline you might not otherwise discover. Pebble Beach Bed & Breakfast is a quiet and gracious place. Watch sunsets from your room, relax in the guest lounge area, catch up on work at the desk and phone, or join Margaret Lewis for music (from an extensive collection of CDs) and a glass of wine. The entire second floor is for guests, with two main guest rooms, a lounge, a bath, and an extra bedroom for an additional person in a party. It's only steps to that gorgeous beach, and Redwood National Park is within a few minutes' drive. Whatever brings you to this northwest corner of California, you'll remember it fondly after a stay at Pebble Beach Bed & Breakfast.

No pets; children by special arrangement; smoking downstairs only; full breakfast; lounge with telephone, desk, and refrigerator; cable TV in each room; off-street parking. Third bedroom is $20 for extra person in party.

ROOM	BED	BATH	ENTRANCE	FLOOR	DAILY RATES S - D (EP) +
A	1K	Shd*	Main	2	$75
B	1Q	Shd*	Main	2	$65

New Davenport Bed & Breakfast   (408) 425-1818
Davenport, CA 95017   426-4122
(Nine miles north of Santa Cruz)

The New Davenport Bed & Breakfast is located in one of Davenport's original old buildings, just across the Coast Highway from the
ocean. Four bright, comfortable rooms, furnished with antique beds
and oak dressers, are available to B&B travelers. Delicious breakfasts
are served in the sitting room and next door at the New Davenport
Cash Store (pictured).   Breakfast, lunch, and dinner are served
throughout the week. Weekend festivities often include live music and
a lively crowd. This landmark also houses a pottery, gift, and craft
gallery. The New Davenport is an ideal getaway from the Bay Area.
Though the trip is short, there's a wonderfully remote feeling about
the place. And when you don't have to spend hours driving, there's
much more time for fun.

No pets; no smoking in rooms; off-street parking; credit cards (V,
MC, AE); bus service from Santa Cruz. Additional rooms available
on the second story of the main (Cash Store) building, most with
ocean views; some family rooms available. Rates range from $85-
$105 for two. 30% midweek discount in winter. Brochure available.

ROOM	BED	BATH	ENTRANCE	FLOOR	DAILY RATES S - D (EP) +
A	1D	Pvt	Main	1G	$55
B	1D	Pvt	Main	1G	$65
C	1Q	Pvt	Main	1G	$70
D	1D	Pvt	Main	1G	$65

Halbig's Hacienda   (619) 745-1296
432 South Citrus Avenue, Escondido, CA 92027
(East of town, off Valley Parkway)

The Halbigs came to Escondido in the fifties and the town literally grew up around them. The home that they built by hand sits on a knoll, removed from the hustle bustle, with wonderful views of the surrounding mountains. Fruit trees dot the property. Long verandas, adobe brick construction, and hand-hewn wooden doors recall the days of the early California ranchos. Two rooms are available for bed and breakfast guests. Escondido makes a good base for exploring San Diego's back country, fishing in nearby lakes, dropping by the Wild Animal Park, or paying a visit to Lawrence Welk's village and dinner theater. Beaches are only twenty minutes away, and San Diego thirty-five. Enjoy a quiet, country-like atmosphere on the edge of town when you visit Halbig's Hacienda.

Children and pets welcome; TV; off-street parking; some Spanish spoken.

ROOM	BED	BATH	ENTRANCE	FLOOR	DAILY RATES S - D (EP)
A	1Q	Shd*	Main	1G	$40
B	1D	Shd*	Main	1G	$35

Camellia Cottage   (707) 445-1089
1314 I Street, Eureka, CA 95501
(Convenient to downtown and Old Town attractions)

Light, airy rooms with splashes of vibrant color make this fully refurbished home seem larger than it is. A garden-like environment with a country French flavor was fashioned both inside and out by retired history professor Peggy Staggs. As one enters the front door, bright floral themes against a white background delight the eye and convey a cheery sense of welcome. Guest rooms are especially stylish and comfortable. Several bed sizes, private or shared baths, or even a large suite can be arranged. A fenced garden surrounds a back porch with a swing -- a charming spot to spend a sunny afternoon. The artistic, informal atmosphere of Camellia House gives it all the appeal of a carefree summer day.

No pets; no children under eleven; no smoking; full breakfast; fireplace in living room; TV/VCR available; off-street parking. Discounts for extended stays. Room B or C with private bath, $85. *Closed December 20 to March 1.* Brochure available.

ROOM	BED	BATH	ENTRANCE	FLOOR	DAILY RATES S - D (EP) +
A	1D	Pvt	Main	1	$70
B	1K	Shd*	Main	2	$75
C	2T or 1K	Shd*	Main	2	$65

An Elegant Victorian Mansion   (707) 444-3144
1406 C Street, Eureka, CA 95501   442-5594
(Convenient to downtown and Old Town attractions)

"An Elegant Victorian Mansion" -- that's what a local newspaper reported in 1888 when this Queen Anne-influenced Eastlake Victorian was being built for two-term Mayor and County Commissioner William S. Clark. The prestigious home, restored in every exquisite detail by owners Doug and Lily Vieyra, offers a glimpse of history, luxurious accommodations, and bountiful hospitality. Three individually decorated guest rooms feature beautiful antiques and artwork and enough amenities to make one feel totally pampered. Guests are invited to use the library, parlors, and sitting room as they wish. Lily's talents in the garden rival her skills in the kitchen; her roses are beautiful, as are palate-pleasing breakfasts and ice cream sodas. She and Doug want to bring alive the most gracious aspects of living at the turn of the century, to be a civilizing influence in an all-too-fast-paced world. They succeed marvelously.

No pets; no children under fifteen; no smoking; full breakfast; Finnish sauna; massage available; TV/VCR; stereo; off-street parking; French and Dutch spoken; credit cards (V, MC). Corporate and winter discounts. Brochure available.

ROOM	BED	BATH	ENTRANCE	FLOOR	DAILY RATES S - D (EP) +
A	1Q	Shd*	Main	2	$60-$65
B	1Q	Shd*	Main	2	$70-$75
C	1T & 1Q	Pvt	Main	2	$90-$95 ($30)

Old Town Bed & Breakfast Inn (707) 445-3951
1521 Third Street, Eureka, CA 95501
(Third near P, east end of Old Town district)

Built in 1871, this historic home is one of the few remaining Greek Revival Victorians in the area. It was the original home of the local lumber baron until he built the Carson Mansion. Then it was moved to its present location, just a block and a half from the Mansion. Hosts Leigh and Diane Benson have kept the spirit of the past alive by furnishing the inn with antiques of the period. They've added their own whimsical touches, such as a teddy bear on each bed and rubber ducks and bubble bath for the clawfoot tubs. The result of their labors is the quintessential bed and breakfast inn. After a stroll around Old Town, relax by the fireplace in the Raspberry Parlor. Complimentary afternoon tea or wine and award-winning chocolates by the bedside await you. In the morning, sample one of Diane's country breakfast creations such as Eggs Derelict or Lumber Camp Breakfast Pie and homemade biscuits. Old Town Bed & Breakfast Inn's warm atmosphere and convenient location will make your stay in Eureka a memorable experience.

Cats in residence; no pets; children over ten welcome by arrangement; full breakfast; afternoon refreshments; off-street parking; credit cards (V, MC). Extended stay and business traveler discounts.

ROOM	BED	BATH	ENTRANCE	FLOOR	DAILY RATES
					S - D (EP) +
A	2T or 1K	Pvt	Main	2	$85-$95
B	1Q	Shd*	Main	2	$65-$75
C	1Q	Shd*	Main	2	$65-$75
D	1D	Pvt	Main	2	$70-$80
E	1Q	Pvt	Main	1	$95-$105

A Weaver's Inn (707) 443-8119
1440 B Street, Eureka, CA 95501
(Convenient to downtown and Old Town attractions)

Weaver Dorothy Swendeman and her husband Bob are the proud owners of one of Eureka's fine turn-of-the-century homes, built in 1883. Surrounded by a profusion of gardens and a picket fence, the inn has an authentic warmth created by old Victorian colors, hand-crafted artworks, antique furnishings, and gracious, caring hosts. As a guest, you're invited to experiment with the looms, use the spinning wheel by the fireplace, enjoy sweet repose in a garden setting, or simply make yourself at home wherever you choose. Beautifully appointed accommodations include one room with a Japanese soaking tub in the bath, another that's perfect for a solo traveler, and an elegant suite. In the formal dining room or the sunlit porch, the Swendemans try to serve breakfast fare that "you won't get at home" -- just one aspect of their generous hospitality.

Children and pets by arrangement; smoking outside only; full breakfast; sofa bed also in suite; fireplace in living room; piano in parlor; Japanese garden retreat; croquet on the lawn; credit cards (V, MC, AE); off-street parking. Brochure available.

ROOM	BED	BATH	ENTRANCE	FLOOR	DAILY RATES S - D (EP) +
A	1Q	Pvt	Main	2	$70
B	2T or 1K	Shd*	Main	2	$65
C	1T	Shd*	Main	2	$45
D	1Q	Pvt	Main	2	$85 ($15)

Riverview Bed & Breakfast   **(916) 961-1994**
3926 Ridge Street, Fair Oaks, CA 95628
(Overlooking American River)

Just twenty minutes from downtown Sacramento via Highway 50, the village of Fair Oaks is a largely undiscovered vacation spot. It has the charm of another era but functions as a lively community in the present. There's an interesting assortment of antique shops, restaurants, and an amphitheater offering summer Shakespeare as well as other plays and musical performances. Within a short walk is Riverview Bed & Breakfast, a spacious bluffside home overlooking the American River. One guest accommodation is a huge bedroom with a sitting area, a large private bath, a fireplace, and a private deck overlooking the river. Another attractive bedroom has a sloped ceiling, a river view, and country furnishings. If you're eager to be out and about, amble down to the historic bridge and the American River Parkway where walking, jogging, and cycling are popular. Rafting and fishing enthusiasts find the lure of the river irresistible. Educator Karen Blake invites you to make her home your own while discovering the pleasures of Fair Oaks for yourself.

Dog in residence; no pets; smoking outside only; full breakfast; TV in Room A; TV available for Room B; AC; good book collection in library; off-street parking.

ROOM	BED	BATH	ENTRANCE	FLOOR	DAILY RATES S - D (EP)
A	1Q	Pvt	Main	2	$70-$75
B	1D	Shd	Main	2	$50-$55

Karen's Bed & Breakfast Yosemite Inn   **(209) 683-4550**
P.O. Box 8, Fish Camp, CA 93623
(Off Highway 41, two miles from south entrance to Yosemite)

Nestled in the trees in a quiet and lovely setting, this inn was built with special attention to the needs of guests visiting Yosemite and environs. Each room, delicately decorated in either soft pink, blue, or peach, is fully carpeted, has a full ensuite bath, individual temperature control, and woodland view. Guests have their own entrance and a sitting room with a woodstove and stocked teacart all to themselves, but they are also welcome to enjoy the main living room for visiting or for watching TV or videos. Full breakfasts by candlelight are featured at Karen's. She helps guests to sort out all the options Yosemite offers in each glorious season; also close at hand are Bass Lake, the Mariposa Grove of Giant Sequoias, and the unforgettable Scenic Narrow Gauge Railroad excursion route. Nearby dining experiences range from simple to grand. All the elements of a perfect holiday await you at Karen's Bed & Breakfast Yosemite Inn.

Cat in residence; no pets; smoking outside only; full breakfast; TV/VCR; off-street parking. Brochure available.

ROOM	BED	BATH	ENTRANCE	FLOOR	DAILY RATES S - D (EP) +
A	2T	Pvt	Sep	2	$85
B	1Q	Pvt	Sep	2	$85
C	1Q	Pvt	Sep	2	$85

The Country Victorian   **(209) 233-1988**
1003 South Orange Avenue, Fresno, CA 93702
(Southeast downtown area)

When the Robinson family built this home in 1900, it was a country farmhouse located outside the city limits. A residential neighborhood has since grown up around it. Howard and Nancy English are only the second owners of the home, and they feel a strong connection to its past. When they bought it in 1977, it still held many of the original family's belongings. Some of these photos, furnishings, and mementoes can be seen throughout the interior, and Nancy has added collections of her own. Some newer touches have made the home more comfortable, but nostalgia remains the key ingredient. Three accommodations serve B&B guests -- an upstairs room with lots of charm and two luxurious suites. The upstairs suite has a king-sized flotation bed; the downstairs suite has a queen-sized Murphy bed. Your hosts are long-time residents; they can guide you to many local points of interest.

No pets; smoking outside only; TV in each room; pool table; indoor spa; Fresno Zoo (third largest in California) and many lakes in area; Kings Canyon/Sequoia National Park, one hour away; Yosemite, two hours; enclosed and off-street parking. Brochure available.

ROOM	BED	BATH	ENTRANCE	FLOOR	DAILY RATES	
					S - D	(EP) +
A	1Q	Pvt	Main	1	$50	($10)
B	1K	Shd*	Main	2	$50	($10)
C	1D	Shd*	Main	2	$40	($10)

Hidden Village Bed & Breakfast   (714) 636-8312
9582 Halekulani Drive, Garden Grove, CA 92641
(North Orange County)

   With handy access to three attraction-packed counties (Los Angeles, Orange, and San Diego), Dick and Linda O'Berg's home is a
harmonious blend of several motifs: New Orleans Colonial architecture, Hawaii-like gardens, and Victorian-flavored decor. Linda is an
accomplished weaver/artist who has lovingly combined wicker, handmade quilts, antiques and collectibles, brass and wooden bedsteads,
wallcoverings and wainscoting, and her impressive doll collection to
create an atmosphere of great warmth and comfort. Visit her weaving
studio and admire her lovely creations, unwind in the luscious private
garden, or make yourself at home in the cozy TV room with fireplace
and videos. The master king guest room upstairs even has its own sun
deck, TV, and fireplace. Enjoy a full breakfast served indoors or in
the peaceful garden setting. At Hidden Village, everything a business
traveler or vacationer might need has been anticipated.
   Smoking outside only; full breakfast; bus stop nearby; minutes
from Disneyland, convention center, and beaches; off-street parking;
van pickup from local airports. Brochure available.

ROOM	BED	BATH	ENTRANCE	FLOOR	DAILY RATES	
					S - D	(EP)
A	1K	Shd*	Main	2	$55	($10)
B	1K	Shd*	Main	2	$55	($10)
C	1Q	Pvt	Main	1	$55	($10)

Jim & Eugenia Colucci   **(209) 962-7019**
P.O. Box 516, Groveland, CA 95321
(Off Highway 120 enroute to north entrance of Yosemite)

Groveland is a great off-the-beaten-track location on the way to Yosemite. The Coluccis' home is an ideal stopover, but it is also utterly relaxing and could keep one entertained for days. The chalet-style house is set in the pines above a private community lake offering all kinds of water recreation. It has a 180-degree, fifty-mile view toward the mountains of Yosemite. No street lights and very little traffic ensure a good night's rest in one of the comfortable guest rooms. A large loft bedroom with a private bath overlooks the living area; a good-sized room on the main floor has an extra sofa bed and a uniquely appointed private bath. The open, airy feeling of the interior is perfectly suited to the Alpine surroundings. An old clawfoot bathtub in the living area has been cleverly adapted into a wonderful place to settle in with a good book. While breakfasting under the gazebo on the deck, guests may observe deer feeding close by. Eugenia's Mexican breakfast is a popular specialty, and Jim's French toast is another favorite. These generous, easygoing hosts have a definite knack for making people feel at home.

Pets and children welcome; full breakfast; day bed extra in Room A; AC; tennis courts, pool, and lake within walking distance; inquire about parking; Spanish spoken; airport pickup (Pine Mountain Lake).

ROOM	BED	BATH	ENTRANCE	FLOOR	DAILY RATES S - D (EP)
A	1K	Pvt	Main	2	$40-$60 ($25)
B	1K	Pvt	Main	1	$40-$60 ($25)

43

Duarte Bed & Breakfast   **(310) 644-3795**
4625 West 131 Street, Hawthorne, CA 90250
(Convenient to LAX, I-405, and beaches)

Long-time resident Maxine Duarte is accustomed to welcoming back guests who consider her place home when they travel to the L.A. area. The ambiance of her clean and neat contemporary dwelling has an international flavor with a Latin accent. Two accommodations are offered: a large master suite with a private bath and a TV; and a smaller room with a fold-out foam sofa, a TV, and a shared bath. In the enclosed veranda at the back of the house, three feathered friends -- a cockatiel and two parrots -- reside in cages. Downstairs on the lower level, there's a room with gym equipment and laundry facilities that guests are free to use. Just outside, a garden patio is also available. A relaxed, generous spirit marks the hospitality at Mrs. Duarte's. She'll give you a key, and you may come and go as you please -- just like home.

Children welcome; full breakfast; refrigerator and microwave available; restaurants, tourist attractions, and beaches (Manhattan, Hermosa, Redondo) nearby; good public transportation and airport pickup or shuttle; ample street parking; Spanish spoken.

ROOM	BED	BATH	ENTRANCE	FLOOR	DAILY RATES S - D (EP)
A	1Q	Pvt	Main	1	$45
B	1Q	Shd	Main	1	$35

Wilkum Inn (714) 659-4087

P.O. Box 1115, Idyllwild, CA 92549
(In mountains above Palm Springs at 26770 Highway 243)

That at-home feeling greets you as you enter Wilkum Inn. The warmth of pine, lace curtains, quilts, an organ, a large river rock fireplace, and cozy places to sit makes you want to don a bathrobe and curl up with a good book. The guest rooms are comfy and full of personality, too. One is on the main floor; others on the second floor include the Eaves, a two-room suite. Need a totally separate space where you can hole up in wooded seclusion? Try the inn's most private quarters: a self-catering unit with its own entrance, kitchen, and loft. Wherever you stay, you'll be surrounded by trees and mountain vistas. And for your culinary pleasure, innkeepers serve an expanded Continental breakfast that might include crepes, Dutch babies, cheese-stuffed French toast, or *aebleskivers*.

No pets or smoking; some robes provided; complimentary beverages and snacks; hiking trails, a rock climbing school, Idyllwild School of Music and Arts, and good restaurants nearby; off-street parking. $5 extra for one-night stays in A-D. Two night minimum for E. Brochure available.

ROOM	BED	BATH	ENTRANCE	FLOOR	DAILY RATES S - D (EP) +
A	1D	Pvt	Main	1	$70
B	1Q	Pvt	Main	2	$75
C	1Q	Shd*	Main	2	$65
D	2T or 1K	Shd*	Main	2	$55-$70
E	1Q	Pvt	Sep	2	$85

Moorings Bed & Breakfast   (415) 669-1464
P.O. Box 35, Inverness, CA 94937
(Just north of village at 8 Pine Hill Drive)

Tucked into a hillside overlooking Tomales Bay, there's a haven of gracious living -- Moorings Bed & Breakfast -- home of Lee and John Boyce-Smith. Although they are passionate about traveling themselves, Lee and John enjoy sharing their unique life style with one set of guests at a time. The light-bathed interior is a handsome blend of Oriental rugs, polished wood, fine paintings, and heirloom furnishings. These -- plus a crackling fire in the hearth, classical melodies in the air, and nature's untamed beauty all around -- offer a wonderful contrast of civility and wildness. A suite for guests includes a lovely, open-beamed bedroom in white and blue, a bath, and a small sitting room with sofa, chairs, and TV. Bedroom and sitting room open to a private deck with table, umbrella, chairs, and chaises. Surrounded by the magnificent Point Reyes National Seashore, Moorings Bed & Breakfast is a place to savor the Good Life.

No pets or children; smoking outside only; full breakfast; TV; extra bed; deck; street and off-street parking; German spoken.

ROOM	BED	BATH	ENTRANCE	FLOOR	DAILY RATES	
					S - D	(EP) +
A	1Q	Pvt	Main	1	$70-$75	($25)

Rosemary Cottage   **(415) 663-9338**
75 Balboa Avenue, P.O. Box 619, Inverness, CA 94937
(Just south of village and west of Sir Francis Drake Boulevard)

A wall of windows overlooks a dramatic sylvan scene -- a sunlit wooded gulch that is sanctuary to many wild birds of the Point Reyes National Seashore. You lie on the deck at night and marvel at stars that never seemed so bright before. A romantic French-country cottage is your own private hideaway; luxuriate in its seclusion and the beauty surrounding it. Designed and built by owners Suzanne and Michel, Rosemary Cottage is about fifty yards through a forest from their home. It has many handcrafted details, a wood-burning stove, a full kitchen, and space that will comfortably sleep four. Under an old oak tree, the large deck overlooks an herb garden. It is a marvelous setting for alfresco meals. Settle into quiet relaxation or take off to enjoy the beaches, hiking trails, and prolific wildlife of the Seashore. Rosemary Cottage is near it all -- in a world of its own.

Families welcome; full breakfast; off-street parking; Spanish spoken. $35 extra for one-night stay on weekend.

| ROOM | BED | BATH | ENTRANCE | FLOOR | DAILY RATES |
					S - D (EP) +
A	1Q & 2T	Pvt	Sep	1	$115 ($15)

Terri's Homestay   **(415) 663-1289**
P.O. Box 113, Point Reyes Station, CA 94956
(83 Sunnyside Drive, Inverness Park)

High atop Inverness Ridge in a remote, "above it all" location adjoining Point Reyes National Seashore is Terri Elaine's comfortable redwood home.   Here guests have plenty of space and privacy in quarters that include a large bedroom with a sitting area, a private bath, separate entrance, wood-burning stove, deck access, and an amazing view over ridges of Bishop pine toward the sea. Guatemalan artwork and fabrics add zest to the natural environment.   Feel like exploring?   Take a 45-minute hike to the top of Mount Vision for a rewarding panorama; spend some time on secluded, bluff-lined beaches; see how many different species of wildlife you can spot. In the evening, enjoy a soak in the outdoor spa.   To round out a thoroughly relaxing holiday, schedule a massage by Terri, who practices a variety of disciplines.   This quiet, sunny spot offers an array of pleasures you won't soon forget.

Dogs on premises; children and outdoor dogs welcome; no smoking; no RV parking; expanded Continental breakfast; antique piano, CD player, and futon in room; small charge for use of spa; massage by appointment; ample street parking. Inquire about midweek, off-season, and extended stay rates.

ROOM	BED	BATH	ENTRANCE	FLOOR	DAILY RATES
					S - D (EP) +
A	1Q	Pvt	Sep	1	$90-$100 ($15)

Ann Marie's Country Inn   (209) 223-1452
P.O. Box DN, Jackson, CA 95642
(Central Jackson at 410 Stasal Avenue)

The old-fashioned flavor of the Mother Lode in the early days is captured in this small country Victorian in the heart of Jackson. The 1892 home has the fancy exterior woodwork, gabled bay window, and front porch typical of the time. In cool months, the fire of the wood-burning stove warms the cozy parlor, dining area, and open country kitchen. Full of antiques and collectibles, the house has one guest room inside -- The Doll Room. It houses host Alberta Thomas's collection of dolls, which she acquired in Europe as a child; the bathroom has a hand-painted clawfoot tub. Set among trees to the rear of the property is The Cottage -- a quaint, wood-frame structure with Dutch doors. It has deep carpeting, a fancy brass bed, and a small, pot-bellied stove. From the inn, explore the town on foot, have dinner close by, and get a feel for living in the colorful town of Jackson.

Cat and dog on premises; children welcome; smoking outside only; full breakfast; AC; street parking; major credit cards. Midweek rates, $10 less. Brochure available.

ROOM	BED	BATH	ENTRANCE	FLOOR	DAILY RATES S - D (EP) +
A	1D	Pvt	Main	1	$75-$85
B	1Q	Pvt	Main	1	$90-$100

The Wedgewood Inn   (209) 296-4300
11941 Narcissus Road, Jackson, CA 95642   1(800) WEDGEWD
(Six and one-half miles out of Jackson, off Highway 88)

Just ten minutes from bustling Jackson but hidden in a forested setting, The Wedgewood Inn comes as a heady discovery. The stunning Victorian replica is endowed with treasures collected over a lifetime by Vic and Jeannine Beltz. They have lovingly arranged each antique, collectible, family heirloom, objet d'art, handmade Victorian lampshade, and work of stained glass in its perfect place to create a rich haven of turn-of-the-century charm. Each romantic guest room has a distinct character expressed by colors, fabrics, furnishings, and nostalgia pieces. Three rooms have clawfoot tubs, balconies, and wood-burning stoves. A parlor grand piano carved in Austria graces the living room while beautiful tapestries enhance the formal dining room. Jeannine varies the table settings and the elaborate breakfast specialties that guests savor each morning. Vic and Jeannine offer a gracious welcome and a most comfortable stay in their dream-come-true, The Wedgewood Inn.

Cocker spaniel (Lacey) in residence; no children; smoking outside only; full breakfast; AC; terraced garden park with pathways, rose arbor, gazebo, fountains, hammocks, and croquet; off-street parking; credit cards (V, MC, D). Lodging in Carriage House, $110. Brochure available.

ROOM	BED	BATH	ENTRANCE	FLOOR	DAILY RATES S - D (EP)
A	1D	Pvt	Main	2	$70-$80
B	1Q	Pvt	Main	2	$75-$85
C	1Q	Pvt	Main	3	$80-$90
D	1Q	Pvt	Main	2	$85-$95
E	1Q	Pvt	Main	2	$90-$100

Windrose Inn   **(209) 223-3650**
1407 Jackson Gate Road, Jackson, CA 95642
(Just north of downtown area)

When you cross the footbridge over the creek that runs in front of this turn-of-the-century Victorian farmhouse, it is indeed like stepping into another era. Old-fashioned gardens and fruit trees abound on the lovely grounds, and places to take it easy include a wide porch, a gazebo, a hammock by a fish pond, and a patio under an arbor. Each of the inn's attractive rooms is an individual creation. The Deco Room has a stylishly modern look and an oversized bathroom; The Wicker Room is a vision of seafoam green and peach with white wicker furnishings; The Brass Room, done in tones of rose, has a romantic brass bed. Experience a bit of gold rush history without even leaving the inn (which you'll be reluctant to do anyway): From the solarium adjoining the kitchen, observe the century-old, hand-dug Chinese well that once served the nearby Kennedy Gold Mine and the schoolhouse across the road. Other historic sites, foothill wineries, and fine restaurants within strolling distance can be suggested by genial hosts Marv and Sharon Hampton; they want your holiday to be special in every way.

No pets; no children under twelve; smoking outside only; full country breakfast; parlor with pot-bellied stove; off-street parking; credit cards (V, MC). Unique old Miner's Cottage on property available at $100 ($15EP). Midweek rates. Brochure available.

ROOM	BED	BATH	ENTRANCE	FLOOR	DAILY RATES
					S - D (EP) +
A	1D	Pvt	Main	1	$85
B	1Q	Pvt	Main	1	$85
C	1Q	Pvt	Main	1	$90

51

Mountainside Bed & Breakfast   **(916) 626-0983**
P.O. Box 165, Kelsey, CA 95643
(Eight miles north of Placerville, off Highway 193)

At the top of the Georgetown Divide between the South and Middle
Forks of the American River is the rustic family home of Mary Ellen
and Paul Mello. These former educators take pleasure in sharing their
comfortable abode on eighty acres of wooded paradise with guests
who always leave as friends. There are decks galore and many
windows that take in a 180-degree view of the foothills and valley.
The Mellos have deep roots in the area and are most knowledgeable
about its wealth of outdoor recreation and mining history. Three
pleasant guest rooms on the main floor have private baths. A large,
pine-paneled attic space with its own bath and deck can sleep up to
eight people. Weddings, receptions, and group functions work well at
Mountainside Bed & Breakfast, as do romantic holidays and family
vacations. Outstanding hospitality and country living at its best await
you at this wonderful mountain retreat.

Two dogs in residence; no pets or young children; smoking outside
only; full breakfast; TV, fireplace, and piano in large parlor; hot tub.
$5 discount to Knighttime readers. Brochure available.

ROOM	BED	BATH	ENTRANCE	FLOOR	DAILY RATES	
					S - D	(EP) +
A	1Q	Pvt	Main	1	$70	
B	1Q	Pvt	Main	1	$70	
C	1Q	Pvt	Sep	1	$75	
D	1K, 1Q, 4T	Pvt	Main	2	$75	($15)

Carriage House Bed & Breakfast   (714) 336-1400
P.O. Box 982, Lake Arrowhead, CA 92352
(In San Bernardino Mountains; 472 Emerald Drive)

An old-fashioned carriage in the front yard says you've found it. Overlooking Lake Arrowhead through the pines, this New England-style home combines creature comforts, great views, and heartwarming hospitality. The interior is a treasure trove of charming country furnishings, handmade collectibles, and fine architectural details. Relax by the brick hearth in the parlor, catch a sunset from the sun room or deck, or take the woodland trail down to the lake. Dine in one of the superb local restaurants, then welcome a good night's sleep in mountain silence. Each of the three carriage rooms (Brougham, Surrey, and Victoria) features a European feather bed and down comforter, a ceiling fan, a rocking chair, and a view of the lake; one has a private balcony. Beyond that, each has its own unique blend of romantic accessories. Hosts Lee and Johan Karstens offer a memorable sojourn in a glorious setting.

Parrot in residence; no pets; children over twelve welcome; smoking outside only; full breakfast and afternoon hors d'oeuvres; TV in each room; VCR in Room A; year-round recreation, shopping, and dining nearby; off-street parking; Dutch and some German spoken. Brochure available.

ROOM	BED	BATH	ENTRANCE	FLOOR	DAILY RATES S - D (EP) +
A	1K	Pvt	Main	2	$115
B	1Q	Pvt	Main	2	$95
C	1Q	Pvt	Main	2	$85

Eagle's Landing   **(714) 336-2642**
Box 1510, Blue Jay, CA 92317
(In San Bernardino Mountains on west shore of lake)

This ingeniously designed home offers all the comfort and charm of a European mountain retreat, with many extra special touches. Finely crafted woodwork, plenty of view windows, and elements of Victorian styling make me think of a luxury tree house in a romantic Alpine setting. Each guest room is unique; all are private, quiet, and tastefully appointed with antiques, art, and handcrafted furnishings. Refreshments are served on a spacious deck or in the Hunt Room by a roaring fire, both with fantastic views of the lake. Breakfast at Eagle's Landing is a memorable event in the "Top of the Tower." Hosts Dorothy and Jack Stone provide unparalleled hospitality and attention to detail. In every respect, Eagle's Landing is a masterpiece.

No pets, children, or smoking; TV in Hunt Room; Room A has private deck; boutique shopping, ice skating, fine dining, and quaint towns of Blue Jay and Arrowhead Village nearby; off-street parking; credit cards (V, MC). Also available is a 900-square-foot suite with fireplace, queen bed, TV, stereo, king sofa bed, and expansive lake view at $165. Inquire about midweek discounts. Brochure available.

ROOM	BED	BATH	ENTRANCE	FLOOR	DAILY RATES S - D (EP) +
A	1Q	Pvt	Sep	3	$115
B	1K	Pvt	Main	3	$95
C	1K	Pvt	Main	2	$105

Salisbury House (213) 737-7817
2273 West 20th Street, Los Angeles, CA 90018 1(800) 373-1778
(Near Santa Monica Freeway and Western Avenue)

Experience a cozy kind of luxury at Salisbury House, located in
the historic West Adams district of Los Angeles. Here you'll find all
the amenities of a manor house in the country, yet you'll be only
minutes from downtown and major freeways. This turn-of-the-century
California Craftsman home is large and sturdy. An expert restoration
job has left its original integrity intact. Graciously proportioned
rooms are exquisitely furnished with antiques and collectibles. Colors, fabrics, and nostalgia pieces are imaginatively combined to give
each room a distinct personality. The total effect is enchanting. The
generous breakfasts served here are superb, the hospitality boundless.
Hosts Sue and Jay invite you to treat yourself to the many charms of
Salisbury House. I can't imagine a more relaxing or romantic intown
spot.

No pets; smoking on porch only; full breakfast; Room A has a
sink; D is the 600-square-foot Attic Suite; E is the Sun Room Suite;
ample street parking; credit cards (V, MC, AE). Inquire about weekly
and monthly rates. Brochure available.

ROOM	BED	BATH	ENTRANCE	FLOOR	DAILY RATES	
					S - D	(EP) +
A	1Q	Pvt	Main	2	$90	
B	1Q	Shd*	Main	2	$75	
C	1Q	Shd*	Main	2	$75	
D	1K & 1T	Pvt	Main	3	$100	($10)
E	1D & 2T	Pvt	Main	2	$90	($10)

Terrace Manor   **(213) 381-1478**
1353 Alvarado Terrace, Los Angeles, CA 90006
(Downtown L.A., near Convention Center)

It is the early 1900s on Alvarado Terrace where a crescent of stately, historic homes faces a small park. Terrace Manor is a three-story Tudor-style home restored to its former splendor by hosts Sandy and Shirley Spillman. Built in 1902 for the owner of a glass factory, the home retains its original leaded and stained-glass windows. Rich, polished woodwork and bold colors give the interior an elegant warmth. A gallery of artwork adorns the walls. Choosing among the guest rooms is difficult. Each has a theme carried out in meticulous detail by period furnishings and unique collectibles. Soak in a claw-foot tub, socialize in the library, or watch the world go by from the front porch swing; Terrace Manor takes you back to the genteel living of the prosperous, early Angelinos.

No pets or smoking; no children under ten; full breakfast; guest passes to Hollywood's Magic Castle; elegant dining next door at Salisbury Manor; secured parking; credit cards (V, MC, AE). Room D is Sun Room Suite. Brochure available.

ROOM	BED	BATH	ENTRANCE	FLOOR	DAILY RATES S - D (EP)
A	1D	Pvt	Main	2	$70
B	1D	Pvt	Main	2	$75
C	1Q	Pvt	Main	2	$85
D	2T & 1Q	Pvt	Main	2	$95
E	1K	Pvt	Main	2	$100

Marina Bed & Breakfast (310) 821-9862
P.O. Box 11828, Marina del Rey, CA 90295
(Across street from Marina del Rey Harbor)

Located in a quiet residential area near a commercial hub, Marina Bed & Breakfast is a neat, gray two-story home with a clean, new look inside and out. The spacious interior, done in white with accents in black, gray, and mauve, has a mild art deco flavor. Guest quarters are at the back of the second floor. The large room has two comfortable futon beds, a dining table for four, and a fully equipped kitchenette on one side. The split bathroom is attractively outfitted. Take a stairway to the rooftop deck for some sun or get out and explore the area by foot, bicycle, or even skates. "Muscle Beach" at Venice is a mile away, and Restaurant Row is even closer. The forty-mile bicycle path from Santa Monica to Long Beach is just across the street. There is handy bus transportation nearby, offering both city buses and motor coaches that tour major points of interest in greater Los Angeles.

Small dog in residence; children over twelve welcome; smoking outside only; expanded Continental breakfast; TV in room; bicycle and skate rental nearby; ample street parking.

ROOM	BED	BATH	ENTRANCE	FLOOR	DAILY RATES S - D (EP)
A	2D	Pvt	Sep	2	$50-$60 ($10)

Dick & Shirl's Bed & Breakfast   **(209) 966-2514**
4870 Triangle Road, Mariposa, CA 95338
(Five miles from Mariposa enroute to Yosemite)

Shirl Fiester is quite contented living on her fifteen forested acres. It's a quiet, secluded setting where you can slow down, unwind, and tune in to nature -- most people leave completely refreshed. The home itself is rustic, commodious, and very relaxing. On the main floor, there's an open living area with a large, stone fireplace and cathedral ceilings of warm, polished redwood. An open kitchen is adjacent, and just off the dining area is a guest suite (A) that can be closed off for complete privacy. A cabin (B) on the property provides additional accommodations. Large breakfasts and friendly conversation are part of the gracious hospitality to be found here. For country lodging on the way to Yosemite (forty miles away), Dick and Shirl's is a fine choice.

Dog and cat in residence; no pets; TV; off-street parking; credit cards (V, MC).

ROOM	BED	BATH	ENTRANCE	FLOOR	DAILY RATES	
					S - D	(EP) +
A	1Q	Pvt	Sep	1G	$60	
B	1Q & 1T	Pvt	Sep	1	$60	($10)

The Homestead Guest Ranch   **(209) 966-2820**
P.O. Box 13, Midpines, CA 95345
(Eight miles from Mariposa enroute to Yosemite)

The Homestead isn't the place for a quick stopover. You need some time just to take in the good fortune of having found it, and I promise that you won't want to leave when the time comes. This B&B, situated on twenty-three acres, has unusual character and privacy. It's a restored rustic ranch where you'll have an entire house to yourself. Downstairs there's a living room with a big stone fireplace, antiques, a well-stocked kitchen, and a large master bedroom and bath. Two smaller bedrooms and a half-bath are upstairs. Enjoy all this *plus* the superlative hospitality of hosts Blair and Helen Fowler, whose home is across a wide meadow from The Homestead. One could easily spend several blissful days in the woodland setting and utter peacefulness of this getaway abode.

Pets and children accepted conditionally; ducks in barnyard; horses graze nearby; barbecue; trails; some German and French spoken; airport pickup (Mariposa). Two-night minimum.

ROOM	BED	BATH	ENTRANCE	FLOOR	DAILY RATES
					S - D (EP) +
A	1Q	Pvt	Sep	1	$85 ($30)
B	3T	Pvt 1/2		2	

59

Meadow Creek Ranch Bed & Breakfast Inn   **(209) 966-3843**
2669 Triangle Road, Mariposa, CA 95338
(Twelve miles south of Mariposa; Highway 49 S at Triangle Road)

"A pleasant haven of rest" reads the description of this 1858 home in a book on the history of Mariposa. It was once a stop on the Mariposa-Oakhurst stagecoach run that provided overnight lodging for weary travelers. Though many improvements have been made for the sake of comfort, guests today feel the same welcoming spirit of the early days. Hosts Bob and Carol Shockley want you to feel completely at home here, whether you're relaxing in the cozy living room or strolling about the lovely grounds. Guests have a choice of three charming bedrooms in the main house, each decorated with a mixture of country and European antiques. To the rear of the property is the Country Cottage (D), an irresistible love nest with a private bath, a clawfoot tub for two, a sitting area, a canopy bed, and a fireplace. After a hard day of traveling, or of exploring the wonder that is Yosemite, you'll be glad to return to this pleasant haven of rest.

No pets; children twelve and older permitted; full breakfast; seasonal refreshments served on arrival; ample on-site parking; credit cards (V, MC, AE).

ROOM	BED	BATH	ENTRANCE	FLOOR	DAILY RATES S - D (EP) +
A	1Q	Shd*	Main	2	$75
B	1Q	Shd*	Main	2	$75
C	2T	Shd*	Main	2	$75
D	1Q	Pvt	Sep	1	$95

The Pelennor (209) 966-2832
3871 Highway 49 S, Mariposa, CA 95338 966-5353
(Five miles south of Mariposa at Bootjack)

Dick and Gwen Foster follow the Scottish tradition of offering simple, low-cost accommodations, which are in a newer building adjacent to their home. They can provide tips on enjoying the area, a bit of hospitality, and even some bagpipe tunes on request. Hosts are pipers in the Clan Campbell Pipe Band; Dick and Gwen occasionally get out the telescope for some stargazing. No other B&B that I know of specializes in "Stars and Pipes," but guests who have sampled this unique combination are not likely to forget it. Each morning the Fosters serve what they term "a solid breakfast." For informal lodgings just off the main route of the Mother Lode and a short hour's drive from Yosemite, The Pelennor makes a welcome stop for the passing traveler.

Hosts have dogs, cat, and cockatiels; other animals roam the property; smoking outside only; lap pool; spa; kitchen in guest building available on a "you use, you clean" basis; off-street parking. At most, two rooms share one bath. Two extra bedrooms in main house available as needed. Available for outdoor weddings. Rates to be $5 higher in 1993, with $10EP for adults. Brochure available.

ROOM	BED	BATH	ENTRANCE	FLOOR	DAILY RATES S - D (EP)
A	1Q	Shd*	Sep	2	$30-$40 ($7)
B	1Q	Shd*	Sep	2	$30-$40 ($7)
C	1D	Shd*	Sep	2	$30-$40 ($7)
D	2T	Shd*	Sep	2	$30-$40 ($7)

Winsor Farms Bed & Breakfast   **(209) 966-5592**
5636 Whitlock Road, Mariposa, CA 95338
(Three miles off Highway 140; seven miles from Mariposa)

Staying near Mariposa offers not only the advantage of good proximity to Yosemite National Park; it also enables one to explore many facets of gold rush history unique to this particular area. Hosts Donald and Janice Haag are well-versed on local attractions and provide all manner of information to enhance one's stay. Both park employees, their insights can be most valuable to those exploring the myriad wonders of Yosemite. At Winsor Farms, their quiet and comfortable ranch-style home is set on a hilltop surrounded by pine and oak trees. Savor country views from the patio while enjoying an afternoon glass of lemonade or a tasty Continental breakfast in the morning. The large living room, with a huge brick hearth and wood-burning stove, is a relaxing place in which to read or visit. Two guest rooms and a bath can be closed off from the rest of the house for extra privacy. The homey accommodations at Winsor Farms satisfy many year-round visitors to the intriguing Mariposa-Yosemite area.

Dog and cat in residence; smoking outside only; AC; rollaway bed available; TV; VCR; off-street parking; wheelchair access. Brochure available.

ROOM	BED	BATH	ENTRANCE	FLOOR	DAILY RATES S - D (EP)
A	1Q	Shd*	Main	1	$40-$50 ($15)
B	1D	Shd*	Main	1	$40-$50 ($15)

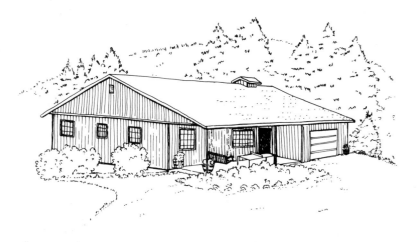

Mendocino Farmhouse   **(707) 937-0241**
P.O. Box 247, Mendocino, CA 95460
(One and one-half miles from Mendocino village)

If you're seeking the quintessential farmhouse in Mendocino for your north coast getaway, look no further. The home of Marge and Bud Kamb provides superb accommodations in the quietest possible setting, so near and yet so far from the busy village scene. Here, there's a permanent warm glow to the interior that feels authentic to the core -- not "decorated." Sloped ceilings, pretty fabrics and rugs, and country antiques give the bedrooms an ambient coziness. Two of the rooms are quite spacious; Room A has a fireplace; a slightly smaller one (C), with a wood-burning stove, is irresistibly romantic. Newer quarters have been added in the converted barn overlooking the garden. Each has a separate entrance and a charm all its own, as well as such inviting features as stone fireplaces, coffee makers, and small refrigerators. In the morning, savor a sumptuous farmhouse breakfast in the sun room of the main house while taking in the views of redwood forest, beautiful gardens, a pond, and a meadow. The aura of this lovely home makes an indelible impression on those fortunate enough to stay here.

Children or pets by arrangement; smoking outside only; full breakfast; off-street parking.

ROOM	BED	BATH	ENTRANCE	FLOOR	DAILY RATES	
					S - D	(EP) +
A	1K	Pvt	Main	2	$80-$85	($15)
B	1Q & 1T	Pvt	Main	2	$70-$75	($15)
C	1Q	Pvt	Main	2	$80-$85	($15)
D	1Q	Pvt	Sep	1	$90-$95	($15)
E	1Q	Pvt	Sep	1	$90-$95	($15)

63

The Goose & Turrets Bed & Breakfast (415) 728-5451
P.O. Box 370937, Montara, CA 94037-0937
(One-half mile from beach; twenty-five miles from San Francisco)

　　　Proximity to the Bay Area, a colorful history, and natural beauty that hasn't been overtaken by development make the coastal hamlet of Montara an ideal country escape. Raymond and Emily Hoche-Mong welcome guests to The Goose & Turrets -- built around 1908 in the Northern Italian villa style -- with "creature comforts, bonhomie, and solitude." The wonderful old building has been refurbished and decorated to reflect the hosts' myriad interests and world travels. Each of the five guest rooms has been fashioned with taste and imagination featuring German down comforters, English towel warmers, and bathrobes. Step out back to the old-fashioned gardens and "chat" with the resident mascot geese, hike down to beaches and rocky coves, or lounge about at The Goose & Turrets where you can lose yourself in a good book or practice the art of doing absolutely nothing.

　　　No pets; smoking outside only; four-course breakfast; afternoon tea; common room with woodstove, piano, game table, tape deck, and eclectic library; Room A has sitting area with woodstove; credit cards (V, MC, AE, D); French spoken; airport pickup by host/pilots (Half Moon Bay, San Carlos, Palo Alto) by prior arrangement; also, pickup for sailors at Pillar Point Harbor at Princeton; twenty minutes from San Francisco International Airport. Brochure available.

ROOM	BED	BATH	ENTRANCE	FLOOR	DAILY RATES S - D	(EP) +
A	1Q	Pvt	Main	1	$95	($10)
B	1D	Pvt	Main	1	$80	
C	1Q or 2T	Pvt	Main	1	$85	
D	1K	Pvt	Main	1	$85	
E	1D	Pvt	Main	1	$80	

Montara Bed & Breakfast (415) 728-3946
P.O. Box 493, Montara, CA 94037
(One-half mile from beach; twenty-five miles from San Francisco)

Bill and Peggy Bechtell have remodeled their inviting country home to include a private guest suite on two floors. The bedroom, attractively decorated in a seaside motif, opens onto a redwood deck where you might catch a bit of morning sun. Upstairs, a sitting room has a woodstove and a distant view of the ocean through the trees. A full breakfast is served in a solarium overlooking the garden. This rustic, cozy retreat is just moments away from beaches, seaside dining, historic Montara Lighthouse, Fitzgerald Marine Reserve, and miles of hiking trails at the largely undiscovered McNee Ranch State Park. Other Coastside towns to the south offer further pleasures. The Bechtells want you to enjoy your privacy while feeling very much at home during your stay at Montara Bed & Breakfast. No problem.

Dog, ducks, rabbit, and other critters on premises; no children or smoking; full breakfast; ample street parking; credit cards (V, MC); airport pickup (Half Moon Bay); twenty minutes from San Francisco International Aiport. Two-night minimum on weekends; seventh consecutive night free.

ROOM	BED	BATH	ENTRANCE	FLOOR	DAILY RATES S - D (EP)
A	2T or 1K	Pvt	Sep	1	$70-$80 ($20)

65

Frank & Virginia Hallman　　　　　　　**(510) 376-4318**
309 Constance Place, Moraga, CA 94556
(Five miles from Orinda BART station and Freeway 24)

At the Hallmans' Moraga home, you can have the best of both worlds while visiting the Bay Area. You can take off to "do" San Francisco in the ideal (car-less) fashion, then scoot back across the bay to the quiet luxury of this tastefully appointed home. The Hallmans will see that you have all the restorative comforts you need. There's a large pool and Jacuzzi spa in a private garden setting. Guest rooms are particularly pleasing. Moraga is usually sunny and is centrally located to many places of interest in the Bay Area. Hosts will help you find your way to the City, Berkeley, Napa Valley, Muir Woods, and elsewhere.

No pets or young children; no smoking preferred; full breakfast served at guests' convenience; robes provided; TV (B); swimming pool; spa; living room with fireplace for guests; five miles to JFK University, ten to UC Berkeley, twelve to Mills College; network of hiking trails through Moraga and Lafayette, as well as other East Bay regional parks, nearby; bus and BART service; airport connections from San Francisco and Oakland; street parking. Inquire about weekly and family rates.

ROOM	BED	BATH	ENTRANCE	FLOOR	DAILY RATES S - D (EP)	
A	1Q	Shd*	Main	1G	$50	($10)
B	1Q	Shd*	Main	1G	$50	($10)

Ward's "Big Foot" Ranch B & B   **(916) 926-5170**
P.O. Box 585, Mount Shasta, CA 96067
(1530 Hill Road; two miles northwest of downtown Mount Shasta)

After their careers as educators in Saratoga, Barbara and Phil Ward returned to Phil's native Mount Shasta. Now they can bask in the glory of the splendid mammoth mountain every day; their rural ranch-style home is situated for maximum views. A huge wrap-around deck is the scene of summer breakfasts. The beautifully maintained ranch has the feeling of a luxury resort with home-like warmth. There are two lovely guest rooms in the main house and a separate guest cottage (C) that sleeps up to six; it has a wood-burning stove, a deck overlooking a stream, and many other attractive features. The Wards are fond of entertaining and cooking for guests. (Phil's delicious *aebleskivers* have become a tradition.) On starry nights, gazing through a telescope from the deck is a sparkling experience. A restful atmosphere, generous hosts, and unprecedented views of Mount Shasta are yours at Ward's "Big Foot" Ranch.

Outdoor pets include dogs, cats, llamas, and a burro; no visiting pets, please; full breakfast; refreshments; TV; living room for guests; trout stream; walking trails; horseshoes; Ping-Pong and croquet in summer; off-street parking. **KNIGHTTIME PUBLICATIONS SPECIAL RATE: 10% discount with this book. *Open May-October.* Informative brochure available.

ROOM	BED	BATH	ENTRANCE	FLOOR	DAILY RATES	
					S - D	(EP) +
A	1K	Shd*	Main	1	$55-$60	
B	1Q	Shd*	Main	1	$45-$50	
C	1Q & 2T	Pvt	Sep	1	$75-$85	($20)

Dunbar House, 1880   **(209) 728-2897**
P.O. Box 1375, Murphys, CA 95247
(One block off Main Street at 271 Jones Street)

   The strong aura of authenticity is the thing I like best about Dunbar House, 1880. From inside you can hear the clip-clop of a horse-drawn buggy taking visitors around, and you are only a few steps from the main street of history-steeped Murphys, "Queen of the Sierra." It's a jewel of a gold rush town, one that's unusually well preserved and lots of fun to explore. Barbara and Bob Costa were drawn to Murphys as well as to the home they purchased in April 1987. The lovely Italianate structure with century-old gardens and wide porches echoes another era, and the Costas are keen on preserving the essence of that era at Dunbar House, 1880. As their guest, you can feel a part of it, too.

   Dog in residence; no pets; smoking outside only; full breakfast in dining room, in the gardens, or delivered to your room; afternoon refreshments; fridge in each room with complimentary bottle of local wine; sitting room with piano, games, books, and menus; caves, museums, wineries, shops and Bear Valley Ski Resort nearby; off-street parking; credit cards (V, MC); transfer from airport (San Andreas, Columbia) can be arranged. Brochure available.

ROOM	BED	BATH	ENTRANCE	FLOOR	DAILY RATES S - D (EP) +
A	1Q	Pvt	Main	1	$90-$95
B	1Q	Pvt	Main	1	$90-$95
C	1Q	Pvt	Main	2	$90-$95
D	1Q	Pvt	Main	2	$90-$95

Palley Place   **(916) 265-5427**
12766 Nevada City Highway, Nevada City, CA 95959
(Between Grass Valley and Nevada City)

If you're taking in the sights along the Highway 49 detour from I-80 between Lake Tahoe and Sacramento, you'll want to explore both Grass Valley and Nevada City -- and you'll find Palley Place a pleasant home base while you're at it. Weaver and fiber artist Meg Palley offers clean, comfortable rooms accented by her own work and that of other local artists. See her loom and spinning wheel in action on most any day. A healthful buffet breakfast is set out in the dining room, where the windows frame beautiful mountain tops in the distance. Meg has a keen interest in the environment, peace, and justice, and she particularly enjoys guests with similar inclinations.

No pets; smoking outside only (patio); FM radio in Room A; TV in Room B; fireplace in living room and on patio; host offers vast knowledge of extensive trails in surrounding areas; off-street parking. Child on cot, $15 extra. Discount to Knighttime readers for three or more nights in March. Brochure available.

ROOM	BED	BATH	ENTRANCE	FLOOR	DAILY RATES S - D (EP) +
A	2T	Shd*	Main	1	$30-$60
B	1Q	Shd*	Main	1	$30-$60

Anna's Bed & Breakfast   **(818) 980-6191**
10926 Hamlin Street, North Hollywood, CA 91606
(Two miles north of Hollywood Freeway)

Anyone desiring a quiet little spot convenient to some of L.A.'s main arteries (Ventura, Golden State, and Hollywood Freeways) will be pleased to discover Anna's Bed & Breakfast. It's a neat, Spanish-style bungalow offering one guest room attractively done in shades of blue. Anna's European background and love of travel are apparent in the decor. She enjoys serving breakfast in her delightful backyard garden on pretty days. From Anna's, it's a thirty-minute drive to downtown L.A. and just seven minutes to popular Universal Studios. Nearby Burbank offers a choice of new and noteworthy restaurants. For convenience, value, and homey accommodations, this B&B is a find.

Dog in residence; no children under twelve; no smoking; extra charge for full breakfast; fireplace, TV/VCR in living room; street or off-street parking; German spoken. Inquire about weekly rates.

ROOM	BED	BATH	ENTRANCE	FLOOR	DAILY RATES S - D (EP)
A	1D	Shd	Main	1	$32-$38

Faye & Robert Abbey   **(415) 892-5478**
55 Grande Vista, Novato, CA 94947
(Twenty-eight miles north of Golden Gate Bridge)

Novato is the northernmost city in Marin County and best known to some as the site of the annual Renaissance Pleasure Faire. Its location in the "Valley of Gentle Seasons" gives it a mild, healthful climate. Faye and Robert Abbey live in an older, well-groomed neighborhood. Their huge back yard is a beautiful landscape of flowers, ferns, and trees, with sitting areas for enjoying the park-like environment. Two bedrooms on the main floor and a suite on the upper floor comprise the B&B accommodations. A front room (A) is cheerfully decorated in red and white; the one across the hall (B) is done in peach with ivory lace and ruffles. The large master suite (C) offers complete privacy and a balcony with a view of the back yard. The Abbeys' home is an appealing place to stay, and its location poises the traveler for a foray into the Sonoma Wine Country, San Francisco, or Marin County's unique towns, parks, and coastline.

TV (in suite and family room); living room with fireplace available to guests; off-street parking.

ROOM	BED	BATH	ENTRANCE	FLOOR	DAILY RATES S - D (EP) +
A	2T	Pvt	Main	1	$40-$50
B	1Q	Pvt	Sep	1	$35-$45
C	1K	Pvt	Main	2	$60

71

Ople's Guest House   (209) 683-4317
41118 Highway 41, Oakhurst, CA 93644
(Fourteen miles from south entrance to Yosemite)

Ople Smith, long-time resident of Oakhurst, has been taking Yosemite-bound guests into her home for several years. Many make Ople's a regular stop because of the easygoing atmosphere, the clean and pleasant accommodations, and the affordable rates. Set on a hill and half-hidden by trees is the rambling, fifties-style house where families are welcome and guests may enjoy the whole house as their own. A fireplace and a TV in the living room are shared by all. Ople offers a friendly welcome and any help one needs, but independent travelers appreciate the fact that they are not restricted by rules or schedules in this convenient guest house.

Rollaway bed and cots available; off-street parking; wheelchair access.

ROOM	BED	BATH	ENTRANCE	FLOOR	DAILY RATES	
					S - D	(EP) +
A	2T	Shd*	Main	1	$40	($5)
B	1D	Shd*	Main	1	$40	($5)
C	1D	Shd*	Main	1	$40	($5)

Jessie & Pete Taylor   (510) 531-2345
59 Chelton Lane, Oakland, CA 94611
(Oakland Hills)

The Taylors love sharing their home, which is set on a quiet lane in the hills above Oakland and the San Francisco Bay. Here you'll be assured of a gracious welcome and a good night's rest -- but that's only the beginning. For these generous-spirited hosts, taking special care of guests is a top priority. Two lovely guest rooms and a bath on the lower level of the house can be closed off for an extra measure of privacy. You may have breakfast on the front deck enclosed by a soothing Japanese garden, or on the rear deck facing the bay. View jewel-like San Francisco by night from your bedroom, the living room, or the deck. Three islands (Yerba Buena, Alcatraz, and Angel) and two bridges (Bay and Golden Gate) are visible by day. Need I say more?

No RV parking; full breakfast; TV; decks. Two parties traveling together may share the bath or use an additional bath at the top of the stairs; inquire about street parking. Two-night minimum.

ROOM	BED	BATH	ENTRANCE	FLOOR	DAILY RATES S - D (EP)
A	2T	Pvt	Main	LL	$35-$45 ($10)
B	1D	Pvt	Main	LL	$35-$45 ($10)

Tudor Rose Bed & Breakfast   **(510) 655-3201**
316 Modoc Avenue, Oakland, CA 94618
(Oakland Hills, off Broadway Terrace)

Anglophiles, rejoice! Corinne Edmonson keeps her memories of things British alive in the decor of the private guest quarters in her home. A large space with its own entrance, fireplace, sitting area, bath, and mini-kitchen occupies the second level of this three-level home in upper Rockridge overlooking San Francisco Bay. A certain English coziness is created by forest green carpeting, Laura Ashley wallpaper, and treasures from the Mother land. To this comfortable haven add the convenience of being near shopping areas, numerous restaurants, major hospitals, and public transportation (bus, BART, and ferry), and you have an ideal home base in the Bay Area.

No pets; no smoking preferred; cable TV; mini-kitchen; guests welcome on lovely deck; ample street parking. Brochure available.

ROOM	BED	BATH	ENTRANCE	FLOOR	DAILY RATES S - D (EP)
A	1Q	Pvt	Sep	2	$55-$65

The Inn at Shallow Creek Farm   **(916) 865-4093**
Route 3, Box 3176, Orland, CA 95963
(North end of Sacramento River Valley; three miles west of I-5)

Who'd ever guess that just three miles away -- and worlds apart -- from I-5 you'd find a haven like The Inn at Shallow Creek Farm? The ivy-covered turn-of-the-century farmhouse is the centerpiece of this 3.5-acre citrus orchard where chickens, ducks, geese, and guinea fowl roam freely. It was revived in the early eighties by Kurt and Mary Glaeseman. The house and the hospitality have a genuine old-fashioned quality. Common rooms solely for guests' use include a large living room with a fireplace, a sitting room overlooking the orchard, and a cheery dining room. A large, airy suite on the first floor offers space and privacy; two nostalgic rooms on the second floor are perfect for two couples. A separate four-room cottage offers extra privacy. It has a wood-burning stove, a sun porch, and a full kitchen. In every season, The Inn at Shallow Creek Farm delights city-weary folks who relish its quiet rural atmosphere.

No pets; smoking outside only; full breakfast featuring farm fresh eggs and produce; excellent area for walking, cycling, exploring, birdwatching, stargazing, and photography; poultry, produce, and homemade jams and jellies available for purchase; off-street parking; French, German, and Spanish spoken; airport pickup (Orland). Brochure available.

ROOM	BED	BATH	ENTRANCE	FLOOR	DAILY RATES S - D	(EP) +
A	1Q	Pvt	Main	1	$60	
B	1Q	Shd*	Main	2	$45	
C	2T	Shd*	Main	2	$45	($15)
D	1Q	Pvt	Sep	1	$75	($15)

Jean's Riverside Bed & Breakfast　　　　**(916) 533-1413**
P.O. Box 2334, Oroville, CA 95965
(45 Cabana Drive, off Middlehoff Lane)

Jean Pratt's cedar home is set on the west bank of the Feather River. Sliding glass doors open to a deck and a lawn that slopes gently to the waterfront. Lucky visitors are treated to idyllic views of the river and peaceful countryside, as well as easy access to swimming, fishing, and panning for gold. Jean's acreage is so spacious and still that it's a haven for friendly wildlife. Your host, a seasoned traveler herself, knows an amazing variety of places in the area to explore. She recommends Feather Falls, Table Mountain, the Chinese Temple, the Pioneer Museum, historic cemeteries, and the Oroville Dam and Fish Hatchery (with up-to-date facilities, especially interesting during salmon run; personal tours arranged with advance notice). Oroville and the surrounding area are rich in culture, history, recreation, and scenery.

No pets (indoors); TVs, croquet, badminton, and horseshoes available; off-street parking; credit cards (V, MC); airport pickup (Oroville); host suggests day trips from Oroville to Sacramento, Grass Valley, Lake Tahoe, Mount Lassen, and Mount Shasta. Private suite available with 1K at $75 for two.

ROOM	BED	BATH	ENTRANCE	FLOOR	DAILY RATES S - D (EP) +
A	1D	Pvt	Sep	1G	$53
B	1Q	Pvt	Sep	1G	$53
C	1Q	Pvt	Sep	1G	$53
D	2T	Pvt	Sep	1G	$53
E	1K	Pvt	Sep	1G	$53

Sakura, Japanese Bed & Breakfast   **(619) 327-0705**
P.O. Box 9403, Palm Springs, CA 92263   **FAX:(619) 327-6847**
(Central Palm Springs, a short walk from Palm Canyon Drive)

If you're not able to make it to Japan, do the next best thing. Visit Fumiko and George Cebra's inn in Palm Springs and experience the serene graciousness of the Japanese lifestyle. Here you'll find a Japanese garden for guests, four bedrooms that open onto a beautiful patio with pool and spa, and a striking mountain background. Featured in the rooms are kimonos, futons, bedcovers and draperies designed and made by Fumiko. Refresh yourself in a hot Japanese bath, then don your kimono and slippers and relax as you listen to the delicate music that wafts through the inn. Enjoy a tour movie of Japan or a shiatsu massage and, if you choose, try an authentic Japanese breakfast. If you long for total immersion, join Fumiko (who was born in Hiroshima) and George (a professional musician) on an escorted bed and breakfast tour of Japan. Contact them for details about these moderately priced tours.

No pets or smoking; full Japanese or American breakfast; TV; VCR; AC; futon beds in each room; five rooms share three baths; additional Japanese-style bathing room; swimming pool; spa; shiatsu massage by appointment; off-street parking; major credit cards; airport pickup (Palm Springs). Double and EP rates $5 higher in 1993. Brochure available.

ROOM	BED	BATH	ENTRANCE	FLOOR	DAILY RATES S - D (EP) +
A	1D	Shd*	Main	1G	$55-$70
B	1Q & 1D	Shd*	Main	1G	$65-$80 ($10)
C	1D	Shd*	Main	1G	$55-$70
D	2T & 1D	Shd*	Main	1G	$65-$80 ($10)
E	1D	Shd*	Main	1G	$55-$70

Adella Villa   **(415) 321-5195**
P.O. Box 4528, Stanford, CA 94309   **FAX: (415) 325-5121**
(Thirty miles south of San Francisco between I-280 and U.S. 101)

Surround yourself with old-world luxury when you enter this private country estate. The spacious, pale pink Tyrolean home offers tranquility in a park-like setting of beautiful gardens with a fountain, a koi pond, and a solar-heated swimming pool. Inside, guests may enjoy a variety of common areas: the Fireside Room, with fireplace, large-screen TV/VCR and selected videos, and shiatsu massage lounge chair; the Dining Room, featuring an antique Louis XVI dining set; the Music Room, accented by a mahogany Steinway grand piano. Each tastefully appointed guest room is exceptional for its comfort and its singularity. The Grey Room has a large Jacuzzi tub; the French Room has a Japanese soaking tub; the Champagne Room has its own entrance overlooking the pool. To stay at Adella Villa is to Go First Class.

No pets; no children under twelve; smoking outside only; full breakfast; refreshments always available; radio, telephone, TV, and sherry in each room; laundry room, dry cleaning, copier, and FAX machine available; swimming pool; patio; off-street parking; most major credit cards. Brochure available.

ROOM	BED	BATH	ENTRANCE	FLOOR	DAILY RATES S - D (EP)
A	1Q	Pvt	Main	1	$95
B	1Q	Pvt	Main	1	$95
C	1Q	Pvt	Sep	LL	$95

Creekside Cabin (415) 879-0319
P.O. Box 478, Pescadero, CA 94060
(Adjacent to Butano State Park)

Make your way along a narrow country road as it winds its way into Butano Forest to a small community of homesites alongside Butano Creek. Steelhead spawn here, and you might catch a glimpse of a pair of wood ducks paddling upstream. A profusion of fuchsias, azaleas, and rhododendrons share space with native forest plants. Here, nestled in the ferns and redwoods near Bob and Jane Rynders' home, the cabin (A) offers respite from the hectic pace of the modern world. The mellowed redwood walls of the living room and bedroom add charm to the decor of soft colors, bamboo blinds, and comfortable furnishings. A pot-bellied woodstove on a brick hearth helps create an atmosphere conducive to relaxation, meditation, study, and/or sleep. Up to two extra people can be accommodated on the corner twin sofa in the living room. The kitchenette is equipped for preparing light meals. In a private wing of the main house, a bedroom (B) has a comfortable sleeper sofa. Picture windows offer pleasant forest and garden views.

No pets or RV parking; smoking on porch only; TV, VCR, AM/FM stereo, CD player, and cassette deck; sun deck; barbecue; hike to nearby waterfalls, parks, beaches; elephant seals and bird sanctuary in area; off-street parking. $10 extra charge for one-night stays; two-night minimum on holiday weekends; vacation rentals by prior arrangement.

ROOM	BED	BATH	ENTRANCE	FLOOR	DAILY RATES S - D (EP)
A	1Q & 2T	Pvt	Sep	1G	$70-$80 ($20)
B	1D	Pvt	Main	1G	$40-$45

Indian Creek Bed & Breakfast   **(209) 245-4648**
21950 Highway 49, Plymouth, CA 95669   **1(800) 24-CREEK**
(Fifteen miles north of Jackson)

In the golden foothills of Amador County, a fine old log home was built in 1932. Now Indian Creek Bed & Breakfast, it is most noteworthy for its beautifully crafted, tastefully restored interior. Upon entering, one is immediately struck by the warmth of polished tongue-in-groove log walls, cathedral ceilings, a huge quartz-stone fireplace, and shiny floors of Douglas fir -- a suitable milieu for wonderful paintings, Native American and Oriental accents, and a stunning antique piano. Off the upstairs balcony, guest rooms are decorated with equal panache. Imaginative painting techniques, color combinations, fabrics, and furnishings make each room as special as the lady who inspired it (wait and see...). Hosts Jay and Geof have hospitality down to a fine art, and their home is indeed a jewel.

Outdoor pets on property; smoking outside only (decks); full breakfast; swimming pool and spa; wide front porch; decks; fireplace in D; many walks, tiny towns, and wineries in area; off-street parking; credit cards (V, MC, D). Brochure available.

ROOM	BED	BATH	ENTRANCE	FLOOR	DAILY RATES
					S - D (EP) +
A	1Q	Shd*	Main	2	$60-$65
B	1Q	Shd*	Main	2	$50-$55
C	1Q	Pvt	Main	2	$80-$85
D	1Q	Pvt	Main	2	$90-$95

Carriage House   **(415) 663-8627**
P.O. Box 1239, Point Reyes Station, CA 94956
(325 Mesa Road; one-third mile from village)

Extensive renovations to this 1920s property have yielded accommodations consisting of two spacious suites full of comforts and modern conveniences. Interesting antiques and folk art lend charm and character. Add to these elements the overwhelming peacefulness of the natural surroundings, and you have an ideal retreat for two or a relaxing spot for a family vacation. Each unit has a full kitchen, a full bath, a bedroom, and a large living room that can be closed off for additional sleeping space. Guests may enjoy cooking in, warming themselves by the cast iron woodstove, or watching cable TV. Host Felicity Kirsch thoughtfully delivers a customized breakfast to the doorstep each morning and also provides plenty of information on the local area to help in planning activities. There is true quality in every aspect of Carriage House, along with many delightful surprises.

No pets; families welcome; smoking outside only; choice of full or Continental breakfast; $20 less without breakfast; additionally, queen sleeper sofa and single day bed in each unit. Inquire about massage, child care, cribs, corrals for horse boarding, and llama pack trips. Midweek and weekly rates.

ROOM	BED	BATH	ENTRANCE	FLOOR	DAILY RATES	
					S - D	(EP) +
A	1Q	Pvt	Sep	1	$120	($10)
B	1Q	Pvt	Sep	2	$120	($10)

The Country House (415) 663-1627
P.O. Box 98, Point Reyes Station, CA 94956
(On Mesa overlooking village of Point Reyes Station)

On an acre at the end of a quiet street where old-time houses share the landscape, The Country House stands surrounded by an apple orchard and English-style flower gardens. You'll get a wonderful view of Inverness Ridge from the property, as well as frequent glimpses of resident wildlife. The house itself exudes a casual, let-your-hair-down version of "Welcome home!" A hearth with a wood-burning Franklin stove is the focal point of the spacious living area that includes the dining area and kitchen. Cook pots hang from the open rafters, and an old Oriental rug covers the floor by the stove -- a heartwarming, comfortable scene. Two antique furnished bedroom suites have queen-sized beds and private baths. A third suite has its own sitting room with a fireplace, a queen-sized bed in a loft with a spectacular view, and a private bath. Hosts live in separate quarters, but they're on hand when you need them. In the morning you'll savor a huge country breakfast featuring specialties such as blue cornmeal pancakes and a variety of omelettes. You will be treated as a favored house guest in Ewell McIsaac's relaxing country retreat.

No pets; children welcome; smoking outside only; full breakfast; cable TV; Tomales Bay, villages of Point Reyes Station and Inverness, and many the many natural wonders of the Point Reyes National Seashore nearby; off-street parking. Excellent for families and reunions; midweek and extended stay rates. Brochure available.

ROOM	BED	BATH	ENTRANCE	FLOOR	DAILY RATES	
					S - D	(EP) +
A	1Q	Pvt	Main	1G	$80	($15)
B	1Q	Pvt	Main	1G	$75	($15)
C	1Q	Pvt	Sep	1G	$85	($15)

Thirty-nine Cypress   **(415) 663-1709**
P.O. Box 176, Point Reyes Station, CA 94956
(Near Point Reyes National Seashore)

Julia Bartlett feels a special connection to the Point Reyes area and, in particular, to the spot where she's made her home. One easily understands this after being a guest at Thirty-nine Cypress. The passive solar house is on 3.5 acres of land, set on a bluff overlooking a pastoral scene where cattle graze and all seems right with the world. Inside, there's a strong feeling of *home* -- a cozy fireplace, floors covered with aging Oriental rugs, warm quilts to sleep under. The house is natural and rustic, with an ambiance of warmth and comfort. Throughout the house, original works of art catch the eye. There are skylights in two of the rooms, and from your bed at night you may see stars and hear the hooting of owls. There is a state-of-the-art spa halfway down the bluff where you can relax after a day of hiking or beachcombing. Julia can provide a wealth of information for guests about the Point Reyes-Inverness area.

TV; patio; spa; off-street parking; credit cards (V, MC). Midweek rates, $5 less.

ROOM	BED	BATH	ENTRANCE	FLOOR	DAILY RATES S - D (EP) +
A	1K	Shd	Main	1G	$95-$110 ($20)
B	1D	Pvt 1/2	Main	1G	$90-$110 ($20)
C	1Q	Pvt 1/2	Main	1G	$85-$100 ($20)

Tradewinds Bed & Breakfast   **(415) 663-9326**
P.O. Box 1117, Point Reyes Station, CA 94956
(12088 Highway 1, one mile north of Point Reyes Station)

From the large, sunny deck at the front of John Walker's fine, handcrafted home, enjoy a vista of horse pastures and rolling hills. Step inside and you'll be in the art-filled living/dining area with cathedral ceilings, a woodstove, and inviting places to sit. Or, step into your spacious front bedroom, tailored for extraordinary comfort and sensual appeal. The ensuite bathroom is done all in pink marble, with a skylight, large walk-in shower, a double Jacuzzi tub, two shell-shaped sinks, and striking artwork. There are two other comfortable bedrooms, and all three have cable TV. John, who hails from England, offers his guests morning fare of tea and crumpets, along with jams, pastries, fruit, juice, and coffee. Tradewinds Bed & Breakfast provides gracious refuge amidst the blessedly untamed wilderness of the Point Reyes area.

Dog and horses on property; smoking outside only; horse boarding available; off-street parking; wheelchair access. Inquire about family rates. Brochure available.

ROOM	BED	BATH	ENTRANCE	FLOOR	DAILY RATES S - D (EP) +
A	1Q	Pvt	Main & Sep	1	$85-$95
B	1Q	Pvt	Main	1	$75-$85
C	1Q	Pvt	Main	1	$65-$75

Road's End at Poso Creek   **(805) 536-8668**
R.R.#1, Box 450, Posey, CA 93260
(Fifty-five miles northeast of Bakersfield)

Yes, it's Road's End -- literally and symbolically. When you finally arrive at this remote outpost nestled in the western slopes of the Sierra in Sequoia National Forest, you *have* to stop and relax. In a sunny, wooded spot at the very end of the road, Jane Baxter's home is surrounded by towering trees, gardens, and pathways, with a variety of places to sit, to dine, to contemplate, to do absolutely nothing. Leave the rest of the world behind, lulled by the sounds of sparkling clear Poso Creek as it rushes by. Cross the footbridge and enter the house; there's an open living/dining area with a stone fireplace, an open kitchen with a wood cookstove, and a loft. Choose a bedroom in the loft or one at the back of the main floor. Jane tailors her hospitality to one guest party at a time. She can set the stage for romance by offering indulgences like creekside candlelight dinners for two, morning coffee in the hot tub, and private time with the whole house to yourself. Road's End is a magical place, a place to celebrate simple pleasures.

Cat in residence; no pets; smoking outside only; special diets accommodated; creekside hammock and campfire area; miles of walking/hiking trails adjacent to property; off-street parking. Brochure available. *includes all meals and beverages

ROOM	BED	BATH	ENTRANCE	FLOOR	DAILY RATES S - D (EP)
A	1Q, 2T, or 1K	Pvt	Main	1 or 2	$190*

Buttons and Bows   **(916) 527-6405**
427 Washington Street, Red Bluff, CA 96080
(South downtown area)

In a lovely little town whose Victorian charms are legendary, the Johnsons' 1881 home is a splendid restoration on one of Red Bluff's graceful old tree-lined streets. Buttons and Bows has all the sweet nostalgia the name implies. Well-placed collections of various kinds, compelling works of art, assorted needlework, and beautiful antique furnishings please the eye at every turn. The blue and white dining room features a brick hearth and woodstove, a hand-crocheted table-cloth, and a boutique corner with home-crafted items for purchase. A Victorian organ highlights the guests' own parlor. Upstairs bedrooms -- even the closets -- are decorated with meticulous care, using appealing colors and cleverly combined wallcoverings. There are plenty of books to read. Hosts Marvin and Betty set out to create a welcoming environment full of the comforts of home. They have succeeded wonderfully.

No pets; smoking outside only; full breakfast; AC; large deck with hot tub; balcony (Room A); sink in Rooms B and C; off-street parking; airport pickup (Red Bluff). Brochure available.

ROOM	BED	BATH	ENTRANCE	FLOOR	DAILY RATES S - D (EP) +
A	1D	Shd*	Main	2	$63-$65
B	2T	Shd*	Main	2	$63-$65
C	1D	Shd*	Main	2	$63-$65

The Faulkner House **(916) 529-0520**
1029 Jefferson Street, Red Bluff, CA 96080
(North downtown area)

   Its setting beside the Sacramento River and the diverse styles of Victorian architecture to be found here make Red Bluff a unique community. It's also the home of the William Ide Adobe, where California's first and only president lived. A great place to stay while soaking up some local history is The Faulkner House, a gracious Queen Anne home on a quiet, shady street where you'll find four inviting guest rooms and a hospitable welcome from Mary and Harvey Klingler. The decor for each room is exactly fitting and the look uncontrived, like an elegant lady aging ever so gracefully. The Arbor Room has a European carved bedroom set, while the sunny Wicker Room has an iron bed and wicker accessories. The Tower Room is small but charming, and the spacious Rose Room features a brocade fainting couch. A satisfying and relaxing stop is certain to be yours at The Faulkner House.

   No pets or children; smoking outside only; AC; fireplace; ample street parking; credit cards (V, MC, AE) airport pickup (Red Bluff, Redding). Brochure available.

ROOM	BED	BATH	ENTRANCE	FLOOR	DAILY RATES S - D (EP) +
A	1D	Shd*	Main	2	$53-$55
B	1Q	Shd*	Main	2	$73-$75
C	1Q	Shd*	Main	2	$73-$75
D	1Q	Pvt	Main	2	$78-$80

Palisades Paradise   **(916) 223-5305**
1200 Palisades Avenue, Redding, CA 96003
(Central Redding, at edge of Sacramento River)

The name Palisades Paradise isn't an exaggeration. What else would you call a beautiful, newly decorated contemporary home of exceptional comfort with a panoramic view of city lights and river bluff? From the Sunset Suite (B), glass doors open onto a patio with a garden spa where you can watch day turn to evening and soak your cares away. Both the suite and the Cozy Retreat (A) are restful indeed, with soft, muted colors and comfortable beds. The work of some local artists adds to the pleasant decor. Gail Goetz welcomes business and pleasure travelers, making them feel totally at home in the relaxed atmosphere of her Palisades Paradise.

Small dog in residence; children welcome when reserving both rooms; no smoking in bedrooms; living room with fireplace, wide-screen TV and VCR; AC; spa; off-street parking; credit cards (V, MC, AE). Brochure available.

ROOM	BED	BATH	ENTRANCE	FLOOR	DAILY RATES S - D (EP) +
A	1D	Shd*	Main	1G	$55
B	1Q	Shd*	Main	1G	$65

Ruth Simon & Hy Rosner   **(510) 237-1711**
2723 Esmond Avenue, Richmond, CA 94804-1311
(Off San Pablo Avenue)

In this quiet Richmond neighborhood, a new contemporary home that fits in agreeably with the older homes around it was recently built. The lot is small, but the house was cleverly designed to seem spacious inside. The owners are Ruth Simon, a writer and seismologist, and Hy Rosner, who's retired. Their home is filled with books, art, and music, making the ambiance one of civility and comfort. The large upstairs guest room is light and airy, with a crewel-embroidered bedspread, a sofa bed, and a private half-bath. While you're in Richmond, explore picturesque Point Richmond Historical District. All the bridges across San Francisco Bay are visible from the waterfront, and you'll find some beautifully restored buildings and good restaurants there as well.

No pets or smoking; TV; VCR; crib and single rollaway bed available; shared full bath; garden hot tub; swimming at nearby municipal indoor pool; good public transportation; ample street parking; airport pickup (Buchanan, Oakland, San Francisco).

ROOM	BED	BATH	ENTRANCE	FLOOR	DAILY RATES S - D (EP)
A	1D	Pvt 1/2	Main	2	$30-$35 ($5)

Spring Oaks Bed & Breakfast Inn   **(714) 867-9636**
P.O. Box 2918, Running Springs, CA 92382
(In San Bernardino Mountains in vicinity of Lake Arrowhead)

Located appropriately near Rim of the World Drive, this romantic country retreat is perched at what *feels* like the rim of the world. On the occasional clear day, there's a panorama that even takes in Santa Catalina Island! At other times, look out over a fluffy blanket of clouds or a dramatic sunset -- all the while enjoying the homey colonial ambiance of pine, antiques, and a huge stone fireplace. The well-separated guest rooms include one on the first floor with a prize view and one on either side of the second-floor loft. Each was decorated with a warm, delicate touch by Laura Florian. She and her husband, William -- a singer/songwriter known as "Florian" -- enjoy hosting intimate "Concerts on the Mountain." Their inn is an irresistible setting for listening to a broad range of live music by different artists. Ask how you can add this treat to your romantic stay at Spring Oaks Bed & Breakfast Inn.

Dog and cat in residence; no pets; children over twelve welcome; smoking outside only; full breakfast; large deck with view; lakes, skiing, hiking, shops, and restaurants nearby; off-street parking. Brochure available.

ROOM	BED	BATH	ENTRANCE	FLOOR	DAILY RATES S - D (EP) +
A	1Q	Pvt	Main	1	$120-$130
B	1Q	Shd*	Main	2	$85-$95
C	1Q	Shd*	Main	2	$85-$95

Hilltop House Bed & Breakfast   **(707) 944-0880**
P.O. Box 726, St. Helena, CA 94574
(9550 St. Helena Road)

Poised at the very top of the ridge that separates the famous wine regions of Napa and Sonoma is a country retreat with all the comforts of home and a view of pristine mountain wilderness that you must see to believe. Annette and Bill Gevarter built their contemporary home with this panorama in mind, and the vast deck allows you to enjoy it at your leisure with a glass of wine in the afternoon, with breakfast in the morning, or with a long soak in the hot tub. From this vantage point, sunrises and sunsets are simply amazing. Enter your lovely room through sliding glass doors from the deck and be assured that everything you need to make your stay a pleasure is there. After a restful night's sleep, look to a day of exploring either the Napa Valley (fifteen minutes to the east) or the Sonoma Valley (twenty minutes to the west). At Hilltop House, you'll cherish the natural setting, the caring hospitality, and the prize location.

Dog in residence; no pets or smoking; no children under twelve; queen sofa bed extra in Room C; hot tub; hiking trails nearby; full complement of amenities; off-street parking; credit cards (V, MC, AE). Midweek rate for Room A, $95; B and C, $105. Two-night minimum on weekends. Brochure and photos available.

ROOM	BED	BATH	ENTRANCE	FLOOR	DAILY RATES	
					S - D	(EP) +
A	1Q	Pvt	Main	1G	$105	
B	1Q & 1T	Pvt	Main	1G	$125	($15)
C	1Q	Pvt	Main	1G	$125	($15)

Judy's Bed & Breakfast   **(707) 963-3081**
2036 Madrona Avenue, St. Helena, CA 94574
(One-half mile west of Main Street, or Highway 29)

You'll get a warm, wine-country welcome at Judy's. Bob and Judy Sculatti have enjoyed their vineyard setting for many years. They've converted a spacious, private room at one end of their home to a B&B accommodation of great charm and comfort. The large space is furnished with lovely antiques, Oriental rugs, and a romantic brass bed. There is also a wood-burning stove with a glass door. Complimentary beverage and cheese are offered upon your arrival. Breakfast is served in your room or outside by the pool. Judy's is a gracious place to return to after a day of touring and tasting. To round out your perfect day, dine at one of the Napa Valley's superb restaurants.

No pets or RV parking; no smoking preferred; TV; AC; off-street parking; Italian spoken. ****KNIGHTTIME PUBLICATIONS SPECIAL RATE: 10% discount with this book. Brochure available.

ROOM	BED	BATH	ENTRANCE	FLOOR	DAILY RATES S - D (EP) +
A	1Q	Pvt	Sep	1G	$85

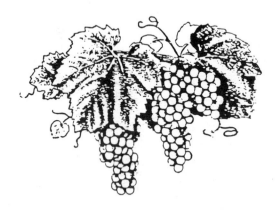

Judy's Ranch House   **(707) 963-3081**
701 Rossi Road, St. Helena, CA 94574
(Just west of Silverado Trail in Conn Valley)

The Sculatti family operates an additional B&B home on the opposite side of the Napa Valley but just as accessible to it. The spacious, comfortable ranch-style home is built around an interior courtyard. Everywhere you look, there are idyllic views of the Conn Valley countryside. Guests have use of an inviting living room with fireplace, a large country kitchen, and a Jacuzzi spa -- a marvelous place to unwind while watching cattle, deer, and quail feed in neighboring pastures and vineyards. Relax on the front patio, which looks out upon century-old oak trees lining a seasonal creek. Each bedroom has a ceiling fan, private bath, and hillside view. Your hosts can help you with plans for enjoying the Napa Valley's many attractions.

Some farm animals on property; no pets; smoking outside only; round-the-clock hot beverages available; Jacuzzi spa; off-street parking. **KNIGHTTIME PUBLICATIONS SPECIAL RATE: 10% discount with this book. Brochure available.

ROOM	BED	BATH	ENTRANCE	FLOOR	DAILY RATES S - D (EP) +
A	2T or 1K	Pvt	Main	1G	$85
B	1Q	Pvt	Main	1G	$95

Mario & Suellen Lamorte   **(415) 456-0528**
45 Entrata Drive, San Anselmo, CA 94960
(Walking distance from central San Anselmo)

To stay at the Lamortes' three-story brown-shingled house is to savor the taste of old Marin. It's on a quiet, tree-lined lane that was cut into a hillside long ago; from here, the views of the hilly terrain are a visual feast. The lower floor of the house is a private guest suite that can accommodate up to four people. Natural wood paneling and floors, Oriental rugs, unique paned windows, and a curved redwood sleeping alcove give the interior a warm rustic charm. French doors lead to a private deck where sunlight filters through a canopy of fruit and oak trees. The home is within walking distance of fine restaurants, shops, hiking trails, and lakes. San Anselmo is less than an hour from the wine country and Point Reyes National Seashore, yet only fourteen miles from the Golden Gate Bridge. Whether you plan to do the town or explore the country, the Lamortes' is a good place to start.

Children welcome ($10 extra for one or two); no smoking; full breakfast; kitchen; TV; phone; rollaway bed available; off-street parking; Italian spoken.

ROOM	BED	BATH	ENTRANCE	FLOOR	DAILY RATES S - D (EP)	
A	1D & 1T	Pvt	Sep	LL	$70	($10)

Bed & Breakfast in Mission Valley　　　　**(619) 283-5146**
Box 100, 4102 - 30th Street, San Diego, CA 92104
(Above Hotel Circle)

You couldn't ask for a more central location than this Mission Valley home -- the main attractions of San Diego are only minutes away. Lee Grace has the fine points of gracious hospitality down; her guests always leave with high praise for the cuisine, the amenities, and the comfortable lodgings. She and her husband, Ziggy, can be the most genial of company as well. The lower level of their home (a bedroom, bath, and sitting room) can accommodate up to four people and affords extra privacy. Add to all this an outstanding view of Mission Bay from the main floor, and you have an unbeatable combination. It's a great value all the way around.

No pets or RV parking; children over eight welcome; afternoon refreshments; TV; laundry privileges; sitting room has queen-sized sofa bed; charge is $60 if both beds are used; $65 for four people; inquire about parking.

ROOM	BED	BATH	ENTRANCE	FLOOR	DAILY RATES	
					S - D	(EP) +
A	1Q	Pvt	Main	LL	$35-$45	($10)

Carole's Bed & Breakfast (619) 280-5258
3227 Grim Avenue, San Diego, CA 92104
(Near northeast edge of Balboa Park)

Host Carole Dugdale is just as keen on preserving her home's history as she is her own. A designated historical site, the 1904 home captures the flavor of the days when San Diego was a "frontier port." Enhanced by a lovely rose garden, the Vernacular Craftsman-style home typically features a gabled dormer roof; leaded glass in some windows; interior wood paneling, ceiling beams, and built-in cabinetry. But it is Carole's appreciation of the past -- her home, interesting antiques, and family mementoes -- that inspired her to create an environment of old-fashioned warmth, comfort, and friendliness. The bedrooms are furnished with queen-sized beds, handmade quilts, and some antiques. Feel free to take a dip in the large swimming pool, play a tune on the piano, or enjoy TV or a movie in the spacious living room. From such a convenient location, you'll explore San Diego with ease.

No pets; no children under sixteen; two and one-half baths; ceiling fans; Jacuzzi; near city buses; walking distance to Balboa Park, zoo, and museums; off-street and street parking; Spanish spoken.

ROOM	BED	BATH	ENTRANCE	FLOOR	DAILY RATES S - D (EP) +
A	1Q	Shd	Sep	2	$55
B	1Q	Shd	Sep	1	$55
C	1Q	Shd	Main	2	$55
D	1Q	Shd	Main	2	$55

The Cottage   **(619) 299-1564**
3829 Albatross Street, San Diego, CA 92103
(Hillcrest area, near Balboa Park)

The Hillcrest area is characterized by old homes and canyons, offering an unhurried, isolated atmosphere. Conveniently located on a quiet cul-de-sac, this private cottage (A) recreates the feeling of a Victorian country home. It is furnished with beautiful antiques, including such pieces as an oak pump organ and an old-time coffee grinder that still works. The accommodation includes a living room with a wood-burning stove, a bedroom, a bath, and a fully equipped kitchen; each is uncommonly charming. The Garden Room (B) is a bedroom in the main house with its own entrance and bath. Your hosts, Bob and Carol Emerick, have thought of everything a traveler might need while in residence, and their vast collection of information about the area is yours to peruse (history, architecture, menus, maps, directions, etc.). If ever a place could inspire affection, The Cottage does just that. You may find yourself returning soøner than you think.

TV; public transportation; inquire about parking; major credit cards. Brochure available.

ROOM	BED	BATH	ENTRANCE	FLOOR	DAILY RATES	
					S - D	(EP) +
A	1K & 1T	Pvt	Sep	1	$65	($10)
B	1K	Pvt	Sep	1	$49	

Monet's Garden   **(619) 464-8296**
6343 El Cajon Boulevard, #139, San Diego, CA 91945
(Off Highway 94, eight miles east of downtown)

Peace and harmony mark the ambiance of Monet's Garden, where art is definitely the focus. The Picasso Suite includes a full kitchen and dining area, a living room, a bath, and two bedrooms -- the Van Gogh and the Picasso. A walkway leads through the botanical gardens where a striking sculpture is the centerpiece and many rare and exotic plants thrive. Overlooking this scene is a guest house with a soothing environment and some special works of art. On one side, the Georgia O'Keefe Room shares a bath with the Hamada Room; on the other, The Toulouse Lautrec Suite has an ensuite bath with a sunken tub. In between, there is a living room with a fireplace as well as a nicely tiled full kitchen. Breakfast is served at a table set in much the same way that Monet did for his guests. Surely he'd approve.

No pets; smoking outside only; full breakfast; TV/VCR in Picasso Suite and guest house; robes provided; picnic baskets available; excellent public transportation by San Diego Trolley and Dial-A-Ride; off-street parking. Brochure available.

ROOM	BED	BATH	ENTRANCE	FLOOR	DAILY RATES S - D (EP) +
A	2T	Shd*	Sep	1	$45
B	1Q	Shd*	Sep	1	$45
C	1Q	Shd*	Sep	1	$45
D	1D	Shd*	Sep	1	$40
E	1Q	Pvt	Sep	1	$65

Casa Arguello   **(415) 752-9482**
225 Arguello Boulevard, San Francisco, CA 94118
(Presidio Heights, between California and Lake)

Mrs. Emma Baires makes her B&B guests feel right at home in Casa Arguello, a large, two-floor flat located in a safe residential area; it's within easy walking distance of shops and restaurants on Sacramento Street, Clement Street, and in Laurel Village. Spacious, immaculate rooms feature brass or iron beds with comfortable mattresses. The view from each room is a constant reminder that you couldn't be anywhere *but* San Francisco. Casa Arguello celebrates its fourteenth year as a B&B home in 1992, and, not surprisingly, it has more return visitors than ever. People appreciate the cheerful, home-like accommodations that Mrs. Baires so graciously provides.

No pets or smoking; expanded Continental breakfast; TV in each room; large living room for guests; inquire about street parking; Spanish spoken; good public transportation and airport connections. D is a two-room master suite; $99 for four people; $5 extra charge for one-night stays; two-night minimum preferred.

ROOM	BED	BATH	ENTRANCE	FLOOR	DAILY RATES	
					S - D	(EP) +
A	1D	Shd*	Main	3	$50	
B	1K	Shd*	Main	3	$50	
C	1K	Pvt	Main	3	$65	
D	1K & 2T	Pvt	Main	2	$75	
E	1K	Pvt	Main	3	$67	

The Clyde House   (415) 929-1623
2034 Golden Gate Avenue, San Francisco, CA 94115
(Near University of San Francisco, between Central and Lyon)

Tall, dark, and handsome describes this Victorian gem with gingerbread trim. The richly detailed interior is one of high ceilings, polished wood floors, wainscoting, and beautifully wrought mouldings. Hosts Jeanne and Quentin serve breakfast in the formal dining room and welcome guests to enjoy the delights of the rear garden on mild days. Two light, airy accommodations comprise the whole second floor and allow for great flexibility. The spacious Fireplace Room at the front of the house is done in mauve and has an attached dressing room/closet and bathroom. This may be expanded to a two-bedroom suite (queen bed in second bedroom) with hallway access to the bath. The peach-colored Garden Room at the back of the house has a crystal chandelier, a large bay window, and a split bath off the hallway. A second bedroom with a double bed augments the Garden Room when needed. At The Clyde House, there's plenty of space and privacy for each set of guests, a warm and hospitable atmosphere, and a most convenient location.

Children welcome; no pets or smoking; full breakfast; public transportation; street parking. Rate for second bedroom with Room A or B is $35; weekly rates; two-night minimum.

ROOM	BED	BATH	ENTRANCE	FLOOR	DAILY RATES S - D (EP)
A	1Q	Pvt	Main	2	$85
B	1Q	Pvt	Main	2	$75

Dorothy Franzblau   **(415) 564-7686**
2207 Twelfth Avenue, San Francisco, CA 94116
(South of Golden Gate Park and U.C. Medical Center)

Dorothy Franzblau's home is nestled in Golden Gate Heights, one of San Francisco's many interesting neighborhoods. Some of its assets include exhilarating views, good places for walking and running, and proximity to the lively shops and restaurants near Ninth and Irving. Guests in Dorothy's home are treated with care. Breakfast is a potpourri of her special creations, served in the dining room with a vast Pacific panorama as a backdrop. The guest room, decorated in blue and white, is a calm haven to return to after a busy day. And a peaceful night's sleep is assured in this quiet, safe neighborhood.

No pets or smoking; full breakfast; TV; good public transportation; ample parking.

ROOM	BED	BATH	ENTRANCE	FLOOR	DAILY RATES S - D (EP) +
A	2T	Shd	Main	2	$50-$60

The Garden Studio   (415) 753-3574
1387 Sixth Avenue, San Francisco, CA 94122
(Two blocks from Golden Gate Park and U.C. Medical Center)

John and Alice Micklewright are the second owners of this 1910 Edwardian-style home. It is quite handsome in appearance, from the unusual sloped roof to the extensive interior woodwork. The house feels rich, solid, and handcrafted. The Garden Studio was recently completed on the garden level. It has a separate entrance from the street and a fully carpeted interior. The peach and green color scheme accents the fully equipped kitchen with slate floor and marble counters, and is carried throughout the bath and dressing rooms. The queen-sized iron bed has a down comforter and a cover with a Marimeko green and white motif. The light and airy apartment opens onto a compact city garden with lawn, flowering border, and a private, serene feeling. Well-traveled guests appreciate the attention to detail hosts have shown in providing many conveniences to enhance their stay in the City.

No pets or smoking; TV; iron and ironing board; private telephone (with deposit); rollaway bed; information and maps for neighborhood and City attractions provided; public transportation and airport connections; inquire about parking; French spoken. Brochure available.

ROOM	BED	BATH	ENTRANCE	FLOOR	DAILY RATES
					S - D (EP) +
A	1Q	Pvt	Sep	1G	$65-$70 ($15)

Moffatt House   **(415) 661-6210**
431 Hugo Street, San Francisco, CA 94122   **FAX:(415) 564-2480**
(Between Fifth and Sixth Avenues near Golden Gate Park)

This pale blue Edwardian home is in close proximity to the popular neighborhood haunts of Ninth and Irving, Golden Gate Park, and U.C. Medical Center. Ruth Moffatt knows the area well and offers assistance with just about anything her guests might need. The four guest rooms are neat and cheerful, with artistic touches in the decor and, typically San Franciscan, shared split baths. The quiet, safe location of Moffatt House makes walking a pleasure -- neighborhood shops, cafes, bakeries, and markets invite browsing. A "Cafe Walk" through the nearby Haight-Ashbury district can be arranged, an experience that's both fun and memorable. The new exercise discount really pays off in a form most everyone can enjoy. Moffatt House pays a quarter a mile for any running or walking guests do in Golden Gate Park. Yes, Ruth puts the cash right in your hand! Moffatt House puts San Francisco at your feet -- the possibilities are endless....

Cat in residence; kitchen privileges; crib available; one-night stays and late arrivals OK; Spanish, Italian, and French spoken; good public transportation and airport connections; inquire about parking; credit cards (V, MC).

ROOM	BED	BATH	ENTRANCE	FLOOR	DAILY RATES S - D (EP) +
A	2T	Shd*	Main	2	$39-$46
B	1D	Shd*	Main	2	$39
C	1Q & 1T	Shd*	Main	2	$49-$56 ($7)
D	1Q	Shd*	Main	2	$49-$56

North View Bed & Breakfast   **(415) 775-9236**
5 North View Court, San Francisco, CA 94109
(Behind Ghirardelli Square)

When many people think of San Francisco, they picture the Golden Gate Bridge, Fisherman's Wharf, the lively street scene, shopping, and dining at Ghirardelli Square and the Cannery, and the cafes and clubs of North Beach. From North View Bed & Breakfast, all these are practically at your doorstep. You'll feel like a native with a key to your own ground-floor apartment in the lovely home of long-time residents Daniel and Emily Warner. The well-maintained unit includes two narrow bedrooms, each with a single bed, a small kitchen stocked with breakfast supplies to consume at your leisure, a bathroom with a stall shower, and a good-sized closet. The arrangement is ideal for a variety of travelers' needs, and the convenience of being able to walk to so many places adds to the strong overall appeal of North View Bed & Breakfast.

No pets, children, or smoking; good public transportation. Private parking for guests at the apartment door, but no room for RVs or very large vehicles. Two-night minimum.

ROOM	BED	BATH	ENTRANCE	FLOOR	DAILY RATES S - D (EP)
A	2T	Pvt	Sep	1G	$65-$70

Ed & Monica Widburg   (415) 564-1751
2007 Fifteenth Avenue, San Francisco, CA 94116
(South of Golden Gate Park and U.C. Medical Center)

The Widburgs' home has an individual charm of its own, both
inside and out. Their wide, quiet street is elevated to allow striking
views of the ocean and the Golden Gate. The rose-beige stucco home
and landscaped yard have a look of understated elegance. European
and Indonesian art objects, antiques, maps, and family heirlooms fit
well into an interior graced with exquisite finishing details. At the
front of the main floor, a bed/sitting room (A) and adjacent bath are
available to guests. Another bed/sitting room (B) is just off the
hallway and is used only for extra guests traveling in the same party.
Hosts sleep downstairs, so there's an extra degree of privacy. Large
view windows across the back of the house make the dining and living
rooms unusually pleasant. The Widburgs' European background con-
tributes to their unfailing graciousness: they are not only well traveled
but accustomed to hosting visitors from other countries. Bed and
breakfast is a way of life to them, and sharing their special city by the
sea is second nature.

No pets, children, or smoking; TV in Room A; European languages spoken; good public transportation and airport connections;
ample street parking.

ROOM	BED	BATH	ENTRANCE	FLOOR	DAILY RATES S - D (EP)
A	1Q	Pvt	Main	2	$55-$65
B	1Q				$50-$55

Rancho San Gregorio   **(415) 747-0810**
P.O. Box 21, San Gregorio, CA 94074
(Five miles east of Highway 1 on Highway 84)

As you wend your way from the coast highway through the idyllic valley of San Gregorio, it's easy to feel that you're back in the time of the Spanish land grants. Then you arrive at Bud and Lee Raynor's fifteen-acre rancho, where peace and quiet abound. Every arched window of the Spanish Mission-style house frames a scenic view of hills, gnarled oak trees, and wide open sky. The interior offers a comfortable blend of natural colors and materials, country antiques, and Indian artifacts. Rooms in the guest wing are named for creeks in the area, and historical pictures provide rare glimpses of the valley's past. Numerous Coastside excursions from the rancho are possible, or you may choose to do nothing more than walk, picnic under old apple trees, plop down by a rambling creek, or sun yourself on a patio. The Raynors invite you to an utterly relaxing retreat at Rancho San Gregorio.

No pets; children by special arrangement; smoking outside only; full ranch breakfast; coffee, tea, other beverages, snacks, and refrigerator in guest wing; extra double bed in Room A; decks, patios, and gazebo; off-street parking. Room D is a suite with woodstove, refrigerator, VCR, and balcony. Inquire about midweek rates and extended stay discount. Brochure available.

ROOM	BED	BATH	ENTRANCE	FLOOR	DAILY RATES S - D (EP)	
A	2T or 1K	Pvt	Main	2	$80	($15)
B	1Q	Pvt	Main	2	$80	($15)
C	1Q	Pvt	Main	2	$90	($15)
D	1K & 2T	Pvt	Main	2	$125	($15)

The Palm House   **(415) 573-7256**
1216 Palm Avenue, San Mateo, CA 94402
(A block east of El Camino Real, between 12th and 13th Avenues)

Alan and Marian Brooks have enjoyed creating The Palm House, and they're justifiably proud of it. Built in 1907, it's a picture-book, Craftsman-style home in a quiet residential area of San Mateo. The interior has a warm, European ambiance created by multi-paned windows and dark wooden panels and beams. Some of the stunning works of art on the walls were done by Alan, an accomplished and successful painter. B&B guests are treated to gracious breakfast service and sun-dried, 100% cotton sheets and towels. The Palm House is located within walking distance of shops and restaurants; San Francisco International Airport is a short ride away by bus or taxi. You can get to San Francisco, Stanford University, or the Pacific Ocean in less than thirty minutes, and all can be reached by public transportation. Alan and Marian wish to convey the spirit of British bed and breakfast to their guests -- and you'll see a surprising bit of evidence to prove it.

Children welcome; ample street parking.

ROOM	BED	BATH	ENTRANCE	FLOOR	DAILY RATES S - D (EP)
A	1Q	Pvt	Main	2	$55-$60 ($10)
B	1D	Shd	Main	2	$50-$55
C	1T	Shd	Main	2	$50

Casa Soldavini   **(415) 454-3140**
531 C Street, San Rafael, CA 94901
(Central San Rafael)

A gem of a little guest house in an old Italian neighborhood in "with it" Marin County? Naturalmente! Casa Soldavini dates from 1932 when winemaker Joseph Soldavini settled here. He and his neighbors took pride in their gardens and their traditions, following the old-country ways for decades. His granddaughter Linda and her husband, Dan, have been careful to save the Casa's best aspects for all to enjoy, including the gardens that still thrive. Original antiques, woodwork, family photos, and delightful bathroom tiles have been preserved; redecoration has added new freshness and comfort. Choose among three individually charming guest rooms and settle in for a memorable stay. In no time the house will fit like a favorite pair of slippers. B&Bs just don't get any homier than Casa Soldavini.

Smoking outside only; large sitting room with TV, VCR, and piano, plus garden patio with BBQ for guests; massage by appointment; candlelight dinners; parks, restaurants, Mission San Rafael, buses, and ferry nearby; airporter from SFO; street and off-street parking; senior discounts. Brochure available.

ROOM	BED	BATH	ENTRANCE	FLOOR	DAILY RATES S - D (EP)
A	1Q	Shd*	Main	1	$60-$65
B	1Q	Shd*	Main	1	$60-$65
C	2T & 1Q	Pvt	Main	1	$70-$75

Bed & Breakfast at Valli's View   **(805) 969-1272**
340 North Sierra Vista, Montecito, CA 93108
(Foothills of Montecito)

Valerie Stevens has fashioned the house of her dreams in a gorgeous spot. She has reason to be proud: Valli's View is a beauty inside and out. Its ambiance of tranquility and comfort will soothe even the most frazzled nerves. There's a variety of places to relax outdoors -- a spacious patio with lounge chairs, a porch swing, or a deck with a view of the mountains. In the evening, it's a pleasure to sit in the living room around the grand piano and fireplace. Guest quarters are at the far ends of the house, affording added privacy. Soft-colored fabrics and rich carpeting enhance the charming decor. A choice of tempting breakfasts (using seasonal fruits and vegetables from the garden) may be served to you in bed, on the patio, or by the fireplace. As a guest of Valerie and her husband, Larry, you'll feel that your every need has been anticipated -- a satisfying experience indeed.

No indoor pets or smoking; full breakfast; TV; off-street parking; train or airport pickup (Santa Barbara). Seventh consecutive night free.

ROOM	BED	BATH	ENTRANCE	FLOOR	DAILY RATES	
					S - D	(EP)
A	1D	Pvt	Main	1G	$55	($10)
B	1Q	Pvt	Main	1G	$65	($10)

Ocean View House　　　　　　　　　　**(805) 966-6659**
P.O. Box 20065, Santa Barbara, CA 93102
(Three blocks from the ocean)

　　Bill and Carolyn Canfield offer guests an attractive private suite in their home. It has a bedroom, a bath, and an adjoining paneled den with a sofa bed. Interesting books and collections may be perused at your leisure. A generous Continental breakfast featuring fruit from backyard trees is served on the patio, a good vantage point for viewing sailboats and the Channel Islands with a background of vivid blue. Close by are beaches and lovely Shoreline Drive, a popular place for joggers, skaters, cyclists, and sightseers. The harbor and downtown Santa Barbara are within three miles. The playhouse in the back yard is a big favorite with children. If you need a relaxing spot that the whole family can appreciate, Ocean View House has all the necessary ingredients.

　　Dog and cat in residence; smoking on patio preferred; two TVs; refrigerator; ample street parking. Two-night minimum.

ROOM	BED	BATH	ENTRANCE	FLOOR	DAILY RATES S - D (EP)
A	1Q	Pvt	Sep	1G	$45-$50 ($10)

Madison Street Bed & Breakfast   **(408) 249-5541**
1390 Madison Street, Santa Clara, CA 95050
(Near Santa Clara University and San Jose Municipal Airport)

One doesn't necessarily associate the Santa Clara Valley with historic homes and genteel living, but that is exactly what you'll find at Theresa and Ralph Wigginton's completely restored Victorian on Madison Street. The result of their painstaking work is a unique lodging establishment with turn-of-the-century style and personal service. The high-ceilinged rooms are appointed with wallcoverings of authentic Victorian design, Oriental rugs, antique furnishings, brass beds, and one romantic four-poster. Deluxe breakfasts are served in a dining room that overlooks landscaped grounds with a pool, spa, and barbecue area. Hosts will try to accommodate your business or personal needs; they can arrange for such things as private meetings and intimate, home-cooked dinners. A most pleasant atmosphere for work or relaxation is yours at Madison Street Bed & Breakfast.

No smoking; full breakfast; TV and movies available; sink in Rooms C and D; robes provided; telephones in rooms; dry cleaning services; tantalizing dinners for four to sixteen guests by arrangement; Winchester Mystery House and Great America Amusement Park ten minutes away; ample street parking; credit cards (V, MC, D, AE).

ROOM	BED	BATH	ENTRANCE	FLOOR	DAILY RATES S - D (EP) +
A	1Q	Pvt	Main	1	$85
B	1D	Pvt	Main	1	$75
C	1D	Shd*	Main	1	$60
D	1D	Shd*	Main	1	$60
E	1D	Pvt	Sep	LL	$85

Bruce C. Bangert   **(408) 476-1906**
2501 Paul Minnie Avenue, Santa Cruz, CA 95062
(One quarter-mile from Highway 1, Soquel Avenue Exit)

Bruce's inviting old farmhouse seems to welcome you as you draw
near, and once inside, the feeling is complete. Restored with loving
care over the years, the home stands ready to delight any traveler
lucky enough to discover it. The decor centers around the many
works of art collected and the dazzling array of ceramic pieces
selected by Bruce, former head of The Aesthetic Studies - Ceramics at
U.C. Santa Cruz. Artists-in-residence, including painters, work on
the premises, and there's a new clay studio behind the house where
guests are welcome. A warm patio and a relaxing deck are shared and
enjoyed by all. The two gable-roofed bedrooms with an adjoining
half-bath are available to B&B guests. The truly welcoming atmosphere, along with some nice surprises, have turned many guests into
friends.

TV; refrigerator and barbecue available; shared full bath on first
floor; off-street parking; bus transportation.

ROOM	BED	BATH	ENTRANCE	FLOOR	DAILY RATES S - D	(EP)
A	1D	Shd	Main	2	$50	($10)
B	1D	Shd	Main	2	$50	($10)

Valley View (415) 321-5195
P.O. Box 66593, Santa Cruz, CA 95066 (Reservations)
(Santa Cruz Mountains, off State Highway 17)

Total privacy and seclusion, a fabulous view, all the comforts of home, and only two minutes to Highway 17 and another twelve to the beaches of Santa Cruz? Indeed. This un-hosted B&B can make your fantasy getaway a reality. The home was designed with many elements of Frank Lloyd Wright's style by his protege, John Taggart. Walls of glass on the back side of the house bring in the beauty of the more than 20,000 acres of redwood forest that the home overlooks. A large deck has the same view, a Jacuzzi, and comfortable places to relax. The sound of trickling water from the circulating pond on the property adds to the feeling of serenity. The interior features a unique kitchen-in-the-round, mirrored walls, luxurious carpeting throughout, and a large stone fireplace. Imaginatively shaped rooms offer wide vistas of the valley of redwoods. Unwind in country splendor, take a hike along redwood-lined paths, or head for Santa Cruz and the beach. It's all here to be savored by a fortunate few.

No children or pets; smoking outside only; no RV parking; stocked refrigerator, including provisions for a generous Continental breakfast; small barbeque; cable TV; stereo and tapes; piano; off-street parking; German spoken; most major credit cards. House used for one party at a time; Room A filled first. Midweek discount; two-night minimum.

ROOM	BED	BATH	ENTRANCE	FLOOR	DAILY RATES S - D (EP)
A	1K	Pvt	Sep	1G	$125
B	1Q	Pvt		1G	$75

Pygmalion House   **(707) 526-3407**
331 Orange Street, Santa Rosa, CA 95407
(Convenient to downtown and historic Railroad Square)

How fittingly named is Pygmalion House, a rare Santa Rosa survivor of the 1906 earthquake. Once a fading Queen Anne Victorian, it underwent a painstaking transformation to its present beauty. Everything about the home speaks a heartfelt welcome, from the (seasonal) glow of the parlor fire to the presentation of afternoon refreshments to the multi-course breakfast. Most of all, it is Lola Wright who makes her home feel like your home. She is ever ready to help guests in any way and has many who return again and again. Each of five guest rooms, mostly on the ground floor with its own entrance, is an individual creation. Selected antiques and an abundance of handwork -- needlepoint, quilting, embroidery, and lace -- lend warmth and personality to the decor. Pygmalion House, notable for its history and hospitality, is a treasure.

No pets; smoking outside only; full breakfast; AC; showers and clawfoot tubs available; off-street parking; credit cards (V, MC, AE). Brochure available.

ROOM	BED	BATH	ENTRANCE	FLOOR	DAILY RATES S - D (EP)+
A	1Q & 2T	Pvt	Sep	1G	$65-$70 ($15)
B	1K	Pvt	Main	1	$65-$70
C	1Q	Pvt	Sep	1G	$55-$60
D	1Q	Pvt	Sep	1G	$55-$60
E	1Q	Pvt	Sep	1G	$55-$60

Sunrise Bed & Breakfast　　　　　　　　　**(707) 542-5781**
1500 Olivet Road, Santa Rosa, CA 95401
(West of Santa Rosa in the Russian River Valley)

　　Imagine a home in the Sonoma wine country, surrounded by orchard and vineyard, where you can taste award-winning wines made on the premises, view the vineyard from a hot-air balloon, and be served a different delicious breakfast each morning. Denyse and Bob Linde provide these experiences for their guests to take with them as beautiful memories. Bob is a winemaker, hot-air balloon pilot, and building contractor, among other things -- a very talented chap. Denyse is the creator of the gracious, serene atmosphere that makes Sunrise Bed & Breakfast an ideal place to unwind and remember what living is all about. Two lovely bedrooms share a bath off the hallway; the luxurious master suite has an oversized private bath and exquisite decorator touches. You'll find fresh flowers and fruit, American oak antiques, and a place to relax, undisturbed, until you feel like moving again.

　　No pets, children, or smoking; full breakfast; TV; VCR; bicycles for rent; balloon rides by reservation; many wineries nearby; off-street parking; airport pickup (Sonoma County). Brochure available.

ROOM	BED	BATH	ENTRANCE	FLOOR	DAILY RATES S - D　(EP) +
A	1Q	Shd*	Main	1G	$75
B	1Q	Shd*	Main	1G	$75
C	1Q	Pvt	Main	1G	$95

La Casa Inglesa   **(209) 532-5822**
18047 Lime Kiln Road, Sonora, CA 95370
(Two and one-half miles from downtown)

Wooded hills and splendid flower gardens surround the fine English Tudor home of Mary and John Monser, set in the countryside where the Kincaid gold mine once flourished. The baronial elegance of La Casa Inglesa is apparent in its architecture and in the many finishing details throughout the interior. Handsome oak panels, mouldings, and cabinetry create a regal setting in the formal dining room where breakfasts fit for nobility may be served; guests are also drawn to the marvelous country kitchen. Quiet places to relax include a delightful patio and a spacious living room with a fireplace. The entire upper floor is for guests, and the accent is on romance. At one end is a huge suite with a bath featuring beautiful tile work, a whirlpool tub, and a separate shower. Exquisitely decorated rooms are especially light and private (no rooms adjoin). Wall and bed coverings, original paintings, and lovely iron beds are just a few of the special touches. A large deck with a hot tub and plenty of sun is made to order for basking in glorious country stillness.

No pets, children, or smoking; full breakfast; TV in suite; AC; off-street parking; Spanish spoken; credit cards (V, MC, D). Two-night minimum on holiday weekends. Brochure available.

ROOM	BED	BATH	ENTRANCE	FLOOR	DAILY RATES S - D (EP)
A	1Q	Pvt	Main	2	$75
B	1Q	Pvt	Main	2	$75
C	1Q	Pvt	Main	2	$75
D	1Q	Pvt	Main	2	$75
E	1Q	Pvt	Main	2	$100

Lavender Hill Bed & Breakfast   **(209) 532-9024**
683 South Barretta Street, Sonora, CA 95370
(Central Sonora)

Set on a hill overlooking town and countryside, Lavender Hill Bed & Breakfast is a turn-of-the-century Victorian with period furnishings and plenty of old-fashioned comfort. Alice Byrnes presides with good humor and an easy manner that make for a relaxing stay. On the main floor there are spacious common areas where guests are welcome, as well as a formal dining room where three-course breakfasts are graciously served. Bedrooms on the second floor vary in size and combine the charm of sloped ceilings, papered walls, quilts, and floral themes. To visit Lavender Hill Bed & Breakfast is to enjoy the unhurried pace and abundant hospitality that make staying here an unqualified pleasure.

No pets or smoking; full breakfast; TV, stereo, books and games available; porch swing; lawn furniture under shade trees; walk to shops and restaurants; off-street parking.

ROOM	BED	BATH	ENTRANCE	FLOOR	DAILY RATES S - D (EP)
A	1Q	Pvt	Main	2	$75
B	1Q	Shd*	Main	2	$65
C	1Q	Shd*	Main	2	$65
D	1Q	Pvt	Main	2	$75

117

Lulu Belle's, A Bed & Breakfast   **(209) 533-3455**
85 Gold Street, Sonora, CA 95370
(Central Sonora)

This vintage home captures the many faces of the gold rush days as few places do. Lulu Belle's, circa 1886, is chock-full of character, offering rooms to satisfy a diversity of tastes. In the main house, The Parlor Suite (B) with its theme of red velvet and crystal has the sizzle of a fancy bordello. In the adjacent carriage house, The Calico Room (C) has a cozy, rustic appeal, while the rose-toned Suite Lorraine (E) features four-poster, canopied beds. Full country breakfasts may be served in your private quarters, in the dining room, or outdoors in the garden. Guests find the living area of the main house a warm and welcoming place to gather. Hosts Janet and Chris Miller have taken care to preserve the colorful slice of history that is Lulu Belle's.

No pets; smoking outside only; full breakfast; TV, fireplace in living area; music room with many instruments; AC; walk to shops and restaurants; street parking; some German and Spanish spoken; credit cards (V, MC, D, AE); theater packages and ski discounts.

ROOM	BED	BATH	ENTRANCE	FLOOR	DAILY RATES S - D (EP)
A	1Q	Pvt	Sep	1	$65-$80 ($15)
B	1Q	Pvt	Sep	1	$75-$90 ($15)
C	1Q	Pvt	Sep	1	$65-$80 ($15)
D	1K	Pvt	Sep	2	$65-$80 ($15)
E	2D	Pvt	Sep	2	$75-$90 ($15)

The Ryan House (209) 533-3445
153 South Shepherd Street, Sonora, CA 95370
(Central Sonora)

Nancy and Guy Hoffman have guests enter through the side door of their home, and the impact is surprising. At once, you know this is a home with a heart. The grandmotherly kitchen has blue ruffled curtains at the windows, sets of lovely dishes on display, a collection of salt-glazed pottery, shiny red apples in a blue spatter-ware bowl, a pitcher collection, a marble slab for making scones, and an iced-tea dispenser. Since moving into this Victorian home, the Hoffmans have done nothing but enhance its sweet simplicity. A different pastel shade is used in each room, and twelve-foot ceilings heighten its appeal. Furnishings are perfect in both style and placement; each piece seems absolutely to *belong* where it is. Natural gathering spots include a handsome front parlor, a library with a wood-burning stove, and a side yard studded with roses and flowering Hawthorne. Old-time pleasures abound at The Ryan House.

Pets in residence; no pets; smoking outside only; full breakfast; no RV parking; off-street parking; major credit cards.

ROOM	BED	BATH	ENTRANCE	FLOOR	DAILY RATES S - D (EP) +
A	1Q	Pvt	Main	1	$70-$80
B	1Q	Pvt	Main	1	$70-$80
C	1Q	Pvt	Main	1	$70-$80

Serenity -- A Bed & Breakfast Inn   **(209) 533-1441**
15305 Bear Cub Drive, Sonora, CA 95370   **1(800) 426-1441**
(Off Phoenix Lake Road, east of Sonora)

The tranquil beauty of the wooded countryside prevails on the approach down a long, winding driveway to the Hoovers' pristine white two-story home. Every detail of its construction and interior design is perfection, and it possesses all of the soothing relaxation that the name suggests. Choose a favorite flower -- lilac, violet, rose, or daffodil -- and you've chosen your room, each theme expressed through color, wallpaper, art, and quilts. Countless small touches abound, such as lace-trimmed, freshly ironed sheets. Most furnishings in the common rooms are fine reproductions of English antiques, especially handsome against walls of pale peachy-pink. Linger by the stone hearth in the parlor, nose through the second-floor library, or stroll lovely grounds teeming with stately trees and wildflowers. Charlotte and Fred Hoover's exquisite home and caring hospitality assure a memorable sojourn in the country.

No pets; not appropriate for children; smoking on veranda only; full breakfast; major credit cards.

ROOM	BED	BATH	ENTRANCE	FLOOR	DAILY RATES S - D (EP)
A	1Q	Pvt	Main	2	$80
B	1Q	Pvt	Main	2	$80
C	1Q	Pvt	Main	1	$80
D	2T or 1K	Pvt	Main	1	$65-$80

Via Serena Ranch   **(209) 532-5307**
18007 Via Serena, Sonora, CA 95370
(Between Sonora and Jamestown)

   Set on beautiful rolling acreage that only *seems* miles from anywhere, Via Serena Ranch is ideally located for sampling the old west
flavor of the historic mining towns of Jamestown and Columbia.
Sonora, a hub of activity, is just moments away. While you're exploring this rich and varied area, Beverly Ballash will make you feel truly
welcome in her elegant ranch-style home. Here you'll find comfortable, immaculate accommodations and a breakfast to remember. Each
guest room is a work of art. It's difficult choosing among them, but I
found the one with an English hunting theme particularly striking. A
large living room and a deck are yours for reading, socializing, or just
relaxing. In every way possible, the climate is always perfect at Via
Serena Ranch.
   No pets, children, or smoking; TV; AC; robes provided; off-street
parking; airport pickup (Columbia). Brochure available.

ROOM	BED	BATH	ENTRANCE	FLOOR	DAILY RATES S - D (EP)
A	2T	Shd*	Main	1G	$60
B	1Q	Shd*	Main	1G	$60
C	1Q	Shd*	Main	1G	$60

The Blue Spruce Inn　　　　　　　　**(408) 464-1137**
2815 Main Street, Soquel, CA 95073
(Edge of Soquel Village, mid-Santa Cruz County)

Located within easy walking distance of antique shops and restaurants of historic Soquel Village, The Blue Spruce Inn is comprised of two fully refurbished neighboring houses. Five individually decorated rooms emphasize Lancaster County quilts, specially commissioned local artwork, and a host of luxurious appointments. Most rooms have their own entrances, and some have private spas and/or gas fireplaces. Enjoy the inn's lovely sitting room with a bay window and a wood-burning fireplace or the private patio garden with a grape arbor and a hot tub -- that is, when you're not out exploring the Monterey Bay Area that stretches from Santa Cruz to Monterey. It's all here: beaches, wineries, shops, hiking trails, quaint coastal towns, and the first-rate hospitality of innkeepers Pat and Tom O'Brien.

No pets; smoking outside only; full breakfast; Spanish spoken; off-street parking; major credit cards. Senior and corporate discounts. Brochure available.

ROOM	BED	BATH	ENTRANCE	FLOOR	DAILY RATES
					S - D (EP) +
A	1T & 1Q	Pvt	Sep	1	$110-$115($15)
B	1Q	Pvt	Sep	1	$85-$90
C	1Q	Pvt	Main	2	$75-$80
D	1Q	Pvt	Sep	1	$110-$115
E	1Q	Pvt	Sep	1	$95-$100

Annie's Bed & Breakfast   **(209) 539-3827**
33024 Globe Drive, Springville, CA 93265
(In Sierra foothills off Highway 190)

Annie Bozanich and her husband, John, offer B&B guests something delightfully unusual in lodging. Oh, all the comforts are here in abundance, but then...well...about the hosts...John is a horse trainer and saddlemaker who can hitch up an antique carriage and take you for a country ride. Annie, who takes dancing lessons, happens to love pigs; her pet, Blossom, who lives in a pen in the side yard, weighs in at around 800 pounds and loves to be fed and have her picture taken. When John and Annie had their swimming pool built, they equipped it with spouting fountains all around, inside jets, and a place to install a volleyball net.   Staying at Annie's is just plain fun -- and each individually decorated room is just plain gorgeous.   Full country breakfasts are beautifully served, and fine dinner cuisine may be catered in by advance arrangement. Here *everything* is a special treat.

No pets, children, or smoking; full breakfast and afternoon refreshments; golf, fishing, boating, tennis, hiking, and swimming nearby; off-street parking; credit cards (V, MC). Brochure available.

ROOM	BED	BATH	ENTRANCE	FLOOR	DAILY RATES S - D (EP)
A	1D	Pvt	Sep	1	$85-$95
B	2T	Pvt	Sep	1	$75-$85
C	1D	Pvt	Sep	1	$75-$85

Mountain Top Bed & Breakfast (209) 542-2639
607 Ponderosa Star Route 2, Springville, CA 93265
(An hour east of Springville in Sequoia National Forest)

When you reach the 7200-foot level of elevation, just off Highway 190, you're in the area known as Ponderosa. Here Claudia and Richard's home resembles a small rustic mountain lodge with just the kind of feeling you'd wish for in such a setting. It has cathedral ceilings, a large stone fireplace that goes all the way to the roofbeams with the requisite deer trophy in place, and pine walls throughout. Two cozy bedrooms with brass and iron beds and TV/VCRs make ideal retreats after a day of hiking, mountain climbing, snowmobiling, or cross country skiing (roads are well plowed in winter). A few steps away, Ponderosa Lodge offers fine, hearty meals. For me, the main lure of this wonderful spot is an environment enhanced by plenty of crisp, clean air; fresh, clear water; and sparkling stars in the night sky.

Dog and cats in residence; no pets; large video library; off-street parking. Self-catering apartment with space for up to seven people available at $75 double occupancy; slight charge for additional guests; weekly rates available. Brochure available.

ROOM	BED	BATH	ENTRANCE	FLOOR	DAILY RATES S - D (EP)
A	2T & 1Q	Shd*	Main	1	$60 ($10)
B	1K	Shd*	Main	1	$60

Cedar Tree
(916) 583-5421

P.O. Box 7106, Tahoe City, CA 95730
(Between Highway 89 and Lake Tahoe)

Walt and Doris Genest make it easy for their guests to enjoy Lake Tahoe in a variety of ways. Cedar Tree, an aptly named mountain retreat, is just a short distance from a private beach and pier on the lake. You can try your luck at fishing, or at other games of chance in the North Shore casinos. Golfing, boating, cycling on trails, hiking, rafting, skiing, and fine dining are all possible in the vicinity of Cedar Tree. In addition to two of the bedrooms, there's a loft with cable TV on the second floor. Doris takes pride in serving nourishing home-made treats for breakfast. If you're looking for a vacation spot with the comforts of home *and* lots of things to do close by, Cedar Tree hits the jackpot.

Bird in residence; smoking outside only; children, kitchen privileges, and fishing by special advance arrangement; sinks in Rooms A and B; barbecue; deck; hot tub; bicycles available; off-street parking. Two-night minimum on weekends.

ROOM	BED	BATH	ENTRANCE	FLOOR	DAILY RATES S - D (EP)
A	1Q	Shd*	Main	2	$50
B	2T	Shd*	Main	2	$50
C	1Q	Pvt	Main	1	$50

Chaney House   **(916) 525-7333**
P.O. Box 7852, Tahoe City, CA 95730
(Overlooking west shore of Lake Tahoe)

    Few homes around Lake Tahoe possess the unique sense of history that Chaney House has. Some of the Italian stonemasons who built Vikingsholm at nearby Emerald Bay in the twenties also worked on this impressive home. Eighteen-inch-thick stone walls, elaborately carved woodwork, Gothic arches, and a massive stone fireplace reaching to the top of the cathedral ceiling give the interior an old-world European flavor. Stone arches and walls outline the paths around the three patios; on one of these, superb breakfasts are served on mild days. Across the road, enjoy the private pier that juts out into the crystal clear water or take a bike ride on the path alongside the lake; in winter, choose from the many ski areas close at hand. Hosts Gary and Lori Chaney love the territory around them and they are well-versed on its wealth of outdoor and indoor activities for year-round pleasure. Let the warmth of their hospitality enhance your next visit to spectacular Lake Tahoe.

    Dog and cat in residence; no pets; children over twelve welcome; smoking outside only; full breakfast; sofa bed extra in Room C; TV/VCR; barbecue; ski boat by advance arrangement; off-street parking. Additional lodging in quaint, European-style honeymoon hideaway (D) with kitchen and extra futon; weekly rate, $600. Two-night minimum on weekends.

ROOM	BED	BATH	ENTRANCE	FLOOR	DAILY RATES S - D	(EP) +
A	1D	Pvt	Main	1	$75	
B	1Q	Shd*	Main	2	$75	
C	1K	Shd*	Main	2	$85	($15)
D	1D	Pvt	Sep	2	$100	($15)

Chalet A-Capella (916) 577-6841
P.O. Box 11334, Tahoe Paradise, CA 95708
(Near intersection of Highways 89 and 50)

Richard and Suzanne Capella's chalet-style home blends well with the Alpine scenery that surrounds it. You can go cross-country skiing from the doorstep, drive to a number of ski touring trails or downhill slopes in about thirty minutes, or fish right across the street in the Upper Truckee River. South Shore casinos are a short distance away. The interior woodwork and sloped ceilings of the upstairs guest quarters create a snug, rustic feeling. A bedroom and a private bath are just right for a couple. Summer or winter, Chalet A-Capella is a picture-perfect vacation spot.

No pets; no smoking preferred; TV; deck; off-street parking; Italian spoken. $5 extra for one-night stays; two-night minimum preferred.

ROOM	BED	BATH	ENTRANCE	FLOOR	DAILY RATES S - D (EP)
A	1Q	Pvt	Sep	2	$45

Cort Cottage **(209) 561-4671**
P.O. Box 245, Three Rivers, CA 93271   **561-4036**
(East of Visalia, near entrance to Sequoia National Park)

    The setting for this B&B is breathtaking. The private cottage with a panoramic view of mountain and sky was built by architect/owner Gary Cort to fit snugly into a hillside near the Corts' home. At sunrise and sunset, colors play off the rocks in a constantly changing show. In the spring, wildflowers bloom in profusion along the path you'll probably want to take down to seasonal Salt Creek. A private outdoor hot tub is located, as Cathy Cort says, "directly under the Milky Way." The cottage is a splendid home base for exploring Sequoia, where you can witness trees that are the largest living things on earth. You'll feel dwarfed by their size and awed by their beauty -- and love every minute of it. Those with an interest in art will want to visit the hosts' Cort Gallery in Three Rivers; it is "dedicated to the ideal that art is a part of every moment."

    No pets; smoking outside only (deck); no RV parking; sunken bathtub; kitchen; sofa bed in living room; hot tub; off-street parking. Two-night minimum except for last-minute availability.

ROOM	BED	BATH	ENTRANCE	FLOOR	DAILY RATES S - D (EP)
A	1Q	Pvt	Sep	1	$70-$75 ($10)

The Garden Room   **(209)561-4853**
43745 Kaweah River Drive, Three Rivers, CA 93271
(East of Visalia, near entrance to Sequoia National Park)

Set among large oak trees at the end of a private road near the Kaweah River, The Garden Room is a self-contained guest accommodation that was architecturally designed to blend with the vintage home of Mike and Celeste Riley. Connected by a breezeway to their home, the unit was built partially around a large boulder that was integrated into the design and serves as a base for a free-standing fireplace. Cascading plants thrive among rocks that extend from the boulder. The total effect is ingeniously organic, with built-in furnishings and everything perfectly coordinated, from the forest green floral chintz fabric right down to the dishes. Mike's artistic touches highlight the decor: lovely oil paintings of rural scenes on the walls and stenciled designs on the wooden doors, dining table, and headboard. Above the bed, there's a large skylight, and beyond the sliding glass doors, a rock-enclosed garden patio. The Garden Room was custom-crafted for comfort; it's a place to bask in country seclusion surrounded by art and nature.

No pets; smoking outside only; full breakfast; TV; patio with chairs; coffee/tea-making area with small fridge; extra sleeping space on built-in seating; off-street parking; excellent hiking nearby; summer recreation at Lake Kaweah.

ROOM	BED	BATH	ENTRANCE	FLOOR	DAILY RATES	
					S - D	(EP)
A	1Q	Pvt	Sep	1G	$75	($10)

MICHAEL E. RILEY

129

Oak Hill Ranch   **(209) 928-4717**
P.O. Box 307, Tuolumne, CA 95379
(Ten miles southeast of Sonora, off Highway 108)

Even though I knew this Victorian ranch home was built in 1980, I had to keep reminding myself that it wasn't here at the turn of the century. Sanford and Jane Grover conceived of the home some thirty-five years ago and began collecting authentic Victorian building materials. Two years of restoring the pieces preceded construction of the home, which was the Grovers' son's senior architectural project in college. Today it stands on fifty-six of the most beautiful acres imaginable. The silence is broken only by the sounds of local fauna, and each room of the home exudes a quietly elegant personality. Oak Hill Ranch is tailored "for a perfect sojourn into the past," to quote an early guest. The superb hospitality offered by the Grovers takes many forms (including a breakfast fit for a gourmet) -- I suggest you relax and enjoy the total experience.

No pets; young people over fourteen welcome; smoking outside only; full breakfast; fireplaces; porches, balcony, and gazebo; bicycles available; hiking trails on and off property; tennis courts and swimming pool nearby; one and one-half hours to Yosemite; off-street parking; airport pickup (Columbia). Victorian honeymoon cottage with fireplace, $105. EP rate with rollaway bed, $18. Brochure available.

ROOM	BED	BATH	ENTRANCE	FLOOR	DAILY RATES
					S - D (EP) +
A	1D	Shd*	Main	2	$68
B	1Q	Shd*	Main	2	$73
C	1Q	Pvt	Main	2	$80
D	1Q	Pvt	Main	1	$80

Oak Knoll Bed & Breakfast **(707) 468-5646**
P.O. Box 412, Ukiah, CA 95482
(Seven miles south of Ukiah)

Surrounded by classic wine country scenery of rolling hills and
vineyards, Oak Knoll is a contemporary home of generous proportions
and sweeping views. Shirley Wadley, a former college music teacher,
keeps an immaculate house that's both elegant and comfortable.
Guests are invited to enjoy the piano in the living room, a fire in the
fireplace and perhaps a movie on the 40-inch screen in the family
room, and games, reading, or television in the study/sitting room
adjacent to the bedrooms. Snacks and breakfast are often served on
the spectacular 3,000 square-foot deck. It is beautifully landscaped
and features an enormous solar spa that is ever so enticing to the
weary traveler. Oak Knoll's location is central to many attractions:
the coast, the redwoods, Lake Mendocino, and wineries of Mendocino
County. It's an altogether satisfying bed and breakfast stop.

No pets or children; smoking outside only; TV; VCR; AC; study;
deck; spa; off-street parking; airport pickup (Ukiah). Brochure available.

ROOM	BED	BATH	ENTRANCE	FLOOR	DAILY RATES S - D (EP) +
A	1Q	Shd*	Main	2	$60-$65
B	1Q	Shd*	Main	2	$60-$65

Dunmovin   **(408) 728-4154**
1006 Hecker Pass Road, Watsonville, CA 95076
(Between Watsonville and Gilroy)

    Located at the top of Hecker Pass, Ruth and Don Wakefield's rambling gray Tudor home is set on twenty-two acres with a giant redwood grove, Christmas trees, and free-roaming wildlife. The view from the many-windowed home is unsurpassed (a delight during breakfast in the family room). Dunmovin is situated partway between Santa Cruz and Monterey at such an elevation that you can see both towns plus the entire Monterey Bay. There is a separate wing for guests. Room A can be closed off and entered by its own door. Room B can be added to the accommodations and share the bath, ideal for couples traveling together. Room C is great for families; it's removed from the main part of the house and is entered separately. It has long, built-in twin beds and a queen-sized sofa bed. If you stay at Dunmovin, you can partake of the U-Pick fruits and vegetables of Watsonville; go wine-tasting at the small, family-run Hecker Pass wineries; and discover the many thrills of the Monterey Bay Area.

    Llama, dog, cat, and four peacocks on premises; no pets in house; full breakfast; TV; tennis court; hot tub; near Mount Madonna Park with restaurant and golf course; off-street parking; airport pickup (Watsonville). If bath is shared by Rooms A and B, rate is $70 per room. $5 extra for one-night stays; two-night minimum preferred.

ROOM	BED	BATH	ENTRANCE	FLOOR	DAILY RATES	
					S - D	(EP) +
A	1Q	Pvt	Sep	1	$75	
B	1D	Shd*		1	$70	
C	1Q & 2T	Pvt	Sep	1	$65	($20)

Knighttime Bed & Breakfast (408) 684-0528
890 Calabasas Road, Watsonville, CA 95076
(Upper Monterey Bay Area)

Our well constructed custom home is set in a clearing on twenty-six acres of eucalyptus, redwood, and manzanita just a few minutes from the beaches between Santa Cruz and Monterey. Built with conventional wood siding in the style of a New England log home, it has a pitched roof and wide porches. The bright interior is filled with art, pine and walnut cabinetry, and creature comforts. Eclectic furnishings include some antiques as well as reproductions, wicker, and new pieces tucked into inviting nooks and crannies. The main floor has a country French flavor, and the decor of the upper floor -- the guests' private area -- is strongly influenced by shells and the sea. Luscious shades of pink and peach prevail in the sitting room, large bath, commodious bedroom, and second bedroom that can sleep two additional persons in the same party. My husband, Ray, and I enjoy guests from all walks of life.

No smoking; pets by arrangement; off-street parking.

ROOM	BED	BATH	ENTRANCE	FLOOR	DAILY RATES S - D (EP) +
A	1T, 1D, 1Q	Pvt	Main	2	$50-$60 ($20)

Howard Creek Ranch   **(707) 964-6725**
P.O. Box 121, Westport, CA 95488
(Three miles north of Westport on Highway 1)

Sally and Sonny invite you to retreat to the romance of yesteryear at Howard Creek Ranch. Their ranch house was built in 1872 by Alfred Howard, newly arrived from the coast of Maine. At one time a stagecoach stop, it is now a quaint and cozy home filled with collectibles and antiques. The guest suites allow privacy, and the old fireplace inspires conversation and fun. The house is set in a wide, secluded valley at the mouth of Howard Creek. It faces the ocean and a wide, sandy beach where you can walk for miles at low tide. Several uniquely constructed, private guest units on the property offer additional accommodations. At this bed and breakfast resort, you can find your own pace and tune in to the natural beauty all around you.

Various animals on property; full ranch breakfast; kitchen privileges by arrangement; barbecue; swimming pool; hot tub; sauna; massage by reservation; off-street parking; credit cards (V, MC). All guest units have sinks; most have skylights; A has a balcony. Unit D is a boathouse; E and F are cabins; both have woodstoves and electricity. Off-season and midweek rates. Brochure available.

ROOM	BED	BATH	ENTRANCE	FLOOR	DAILY RATES	
					S - D	(EP) +
A	1Q	Pvt	Main	2	$75	
B	1K & 1T	Shd	Sep	1	$69	($10)
C	1Q & 1T	Shd	Main	2	$59	($10)
D	1D	Pvt	Sep	1	$85	
E	1D	Shd	Sep	1	$50	
F	1Q & 1D	Pvt	Sep	1	$100	($10)

Coleen's California Casa
(310) 699-8427

P.O. Box 9302, Whittier, CA 90608

(Five minutes from I-605; thirty minutes east of downtown L.A.)

Staying at Coleen Davis's contemporary hillside home is one pleasant surprise after another. Park in front, then make your way through the lush foliage to the back where you'll find a delightful patio/garden and the entrance to the private guest quarters. After settling in, join Coleen on the patio for wine and hors d'oeuvres. After dark you can view the lights of Whittier, and maybe the fireworks of Disneyland, from the large front deck (pictured) where ample breakfast specialties are served. If you're inclined to watch TV, write, or read in bed, the adjustable king-sized bed in Room A will please you. The Casa is a quiet retreat where families can share a private space and get all the help they need to plan a day's adventure in the booming L.A. area. You may even wind up with a little memento from Coleen to remind you of your wonderful visit; she's great with surprises.

No pets; full breakfast; TV, robes in each room; use of fridge and microwave; off-street parking; wheelchair access. Rooms A and B as a suite, $85. C is a room off front deck with king bed and sitting room with sofa bed; as a suite, $85. Two-night minimum; one night only, $10 extra. Host operates a B&B reservation service: Co-Host, America's Bed & Breakfast, with listings throughout California.

ROOM	BED	BATH	ENTRANCE	FLOOR	DAILY RATES S - D (EP)
A	1K	Pvt	Sep	1G	$55 ($15)
B	2T	Pvt	Sep	1G	$55
C	1K	Pvt	Sep	1G	$55

Redwood House   **(707) 895-3526**
21340 Highway 128, Yorkville, CA 95494
(Twenty miles from Cloverdale and U.S. 101)

I call Redwood House a buried treasure. It's tucked into the woods in a part of the wine country which is currently being discovered -- a real "find." The Hanelts have a private guest cottage that's all redwood and glass. It has a living room with a woodstove, a small kitchen, a bath, a spiral staircase leading to a sleeping loft, and a screened-in porch. There are views from the cottage of trees, sky, and a creek you can swim or row in during the summer. There are wooded paths to explore, a small children's beach, a dock, and two decks overlooking the creek. The Hanelts take pleasure in sharing this heavenly spot with their guests, whose options include wine-tasting at fine Anderson Valley wineries, side-tripping to the Mendocino coast (thirty-five miles away), or simply settling into the freedom and joy of country living.

Children welcome; no smoking; double futon and crib available; fridge, stove, microwave, and dishes in kitchen; sauna; off-street parking. Rate is $65 without breakfast; EP rate is for adults; two-night minimum.

ROOM	BED	BATH	ENTRANCE	FLOOR	DAILY RATES S - D (EP)
A	1D & 1T	Pvt	Sep	2	$70 ($10)

Sheep Dung Estates   **(707) 895-2774**
P.O. Box 49, Yorkville, CA 95494 **or (707) 462-8745, unit 5285**
(Three miles north of Yorkville, two miles off Highway 128)

    "With a name like Sheep Dung Estates..." Yes, and it is not just good, but great! Perched on the side of a hill in the company of old oak trees, this new and compact private cottage offers vistas across the coastal range of mountains that surround the Anderson Valley. Here you may bask in sweet isolation from the rest of the world, hike to your heart's content on hosts Anne and Aaron's forty acres, or even traverse the old country roads through 4,000 acres of the original sheep ranch. There are wineries, restaurants, and other attractions of the Anderson Valley to explore -- and Mendocino is about forty miles away. But the cottage is so enticing for its functional comfort, serene ambiance, quality craftsmanship, and close proximity to nature that staying put may be the biggest temptation of all. There's a nifty little kitchenette stocked with provisions, a modern bathroom, a wood-burning stove with a tiled hearth, and heavenly views from the bed, sitting area, and deck. Alternative energy sources are used. Sheep Dung Estates offers a unique experience in lodging, to say the least.
    Dogs welcome; no smoking; provisions for full breakfast provided. Two-night minimum; weekly rate, $375. Brochure available.

ROOM	BED	BATH	ENTRANCE	FLOOR	DAILY RATES	
					S - D	(EP)
A	1Q	Pvt	Sep	1	$75	

Waldschloss Bed & Breakfast   **(209) 372-4958**
7486 Henness Circle, Yosemite West, Y. N. P., CA 95389
(Midway between Wawona and Yosemite Valley)

Many who visit John and Betty Clark envy their unique location. Surrounded on three sides by the national park, their property is in a private development at 6400 feet, well away from the congestion of the valley yet ideally poised for exploring a variety of wonders. Waldschloss is a beautifully appointed mountain home with two distinctive accommodations. A spacious room done in ivory and lace features a collection of fine old quilts; it has a large bath with oak cabinetry. A detached two-floor suite has a sitting room with a free-standing circular stairway leading to the sleeping quarters: a twin-bedded room with oak and brass furnishings, a ceiling fan, lace curtains, and fluffy bedspreads in ivory, pink, and blue. A full bath completes the suite. Country silence, starry night skies, home cooking, freshly ironed cotton sheets, cozy comforters, a brick fireplace, and old toys tucked discreetly about enhance Waldschloss -- a real Yosemite experience.

No pets; children by arrangement; smoking on deck only; full breakfast; TV/VCR; off-street parking; some German spoken. Brochure available.

ROOM	BED	BATH	ENTRANCE	FLOOR	DAILY RATES S - D (EP) +	
A	1Q	Pvt	Main	1	$68	($15)
B	2T	Pvt	Sep	1 & 2	$78	($15)

Please read "About Dining Highlights" on page *vii*.

ALAMEDA
Le Bouc Restaurant Francais, 2424 Lincoln Avenue; (510) 522-1300

AMADOR CITY
Ballads, 14220 Highway 49; (209) 267-5403; California

Imperial Hotel, Highway 49; (209) 267-9172; Continental

ANGELS CAMP
Utica Mansion Inn, 1090 Utica Lane; (209) 736-4209; changing eclectic menu

APTOS
Cafe Sparrow, 8042 Soquel Drive; (408) 688-6238; French style home cooking

Chez Renee, 9051 Soquel Drive; (408) 688-5566; French/Continental

Manuel's, 261 Center Street; (408) 688-4848; casual Mexican

The Veranda, 8041 Soquel Drive; (408) 685-1881; American/California

Palapas, 21 Seascape Village, Seascape Boulevard and Sumner Avenue; (408) 662-9000; upscale Mexican

ARCATA
Folie Douce, 1551 G Street; (707) 822-1042; French/innovative pizzas

ARROW BEAR
Czech Made, 33329 Highway 18; (714) 867-2700; Czechoslovakian

BERKELEY
Cafe at Chez Panisse, 1517 Shattuck Avenue; (510) 548-5525; California

Cafe Fanny, 1603 San Pablo Avenue; (510) 524-5447; fresh, simple breakfasts/lunches

Cafe Fanny de Noche; 1603 San Pablo Avenue; (510) 524-5451; Mexican food Thursday/Friday/Saturday nights

Caffe Venezia, 1903 University Avenue; (510) 849-4681; Italian

Enoteca Mastro, 933 San Pablo Avenue; (510) 524-4822; northern Italian/ nouvelle northern California

Gertie's Chesapeake and Bay Cafe, 1919 Addison Street; (510) 841-2722; Maryland and Louisiana seafood dishes

Kirala Japanese Restaurant, 2100 Ward Street; (510) 549-3486

Lalime's, 1329 Gilman Street; (510) 527-9838; Mediterranean French

New Delhi Junction, 2556 Telegraph Avenue; (510) 486-0477; Indian

Plearn Thai Cuisine, 2050 University Avenue; (510) 841-2148

Rick & Ann's, 2922 Domingo Street; (510) 649-8538; American

Ristorante Venezia, 1902 University Avenue; (510) 644-3093; Italian

Trudy's, 1585 University Avenue; (510) 649-1230; ethnic American

Yujean's Modern Cuisine of China, 843 San Pablo Avenue; (510) 525-8557

BEVERLY HILLS
Matsuhisa, 129 North La Cienega Boulevard; (213) 659-9639; Japanese

BIG SUR
Deetjen's Big Sur Inn, Highway 1; (408) 667-2377; vegetarian/fish/meat

Glen Oaks Restaurant, Highway 1; (408) 667-2623; seafood/Continental

Nepenthe, Highway 1; (408) 667-2345; American

BLUE JAY

The Royal Oak, 7187 Highway 189; (714) 337-6018; Continental

BOLINAS

Blue Heron Inne, 11 Wharf Road; (415) 868-1102; eclectic menu

Bolinas Bay Bakery & Cafe, 20 Wharf Road; (415) 868-0211; eclectic menu

BOONVILLE

The Boonville Hotel, Highway 128; (707) 895-2210; California

CALISTOGA

All Seasons Cafe & Wine, 1400 Lincoln Avenue; (707) 942-9111; bistro/wine

Calistoga Inn, 1250 Lincoln Avenue; (707) 942-4101; fresh seafood/American

CAMBRIA

Creekside Gardens Cafe, 2114 Main Street; (805) 927-8646; California country

The Hamlet at Moonstone Gardens, Highway 1; (805) 927-3535; American/Continental

Linn's Main Bin, 2277 Main Street; (805) 927-0371; fresh, wholesome foods in bright, casual atmosphere served all day and in evening

Robin's, 4095 Burton Drive; (805) 927-5007; breakfast/lunch/dinner from huge variety of ethnic and vegetarian dishes

The Sea Chest, 6216 Moonstone Drive; (805) 927-4514; shellfish

The Sow's Ear, 2248 Main Street; (805) 927-4865; ribs/chicken/fish

CAPITOLA

Balzac Bistro, 112 Capitola Avenue; (408) 476-5035; informal Continental

Caffe Lido Bar & Ristorante, 110 Monterey Avenue, Capitola Village at the beach; (408) 475-6544; casual Italian dining

Country Court Tearoom, 911 B Capitola Avenue; (408) 462-2498; breakfast/lunch/afternoon tea/ brunch served in quaint English/Southern style

Fiorella's, 911 Capitola Avenue; (408) 479-9826; fine authentic Italian

Masayuki's, 427 Capitola Avenue; (408) 476-7284; sushi/Japanese

Shadowbrook Restaurant, 1750 Wharf Road; (408) 475-1511; Continental

CARMEL

Capriccio, Mission and Fifth Streets; (408) 626-0440; Italian

Casanova Restaurant, Fifth Street between San Carlos and Mission; (408) 625-0501; country style French/Italian

La Boheme Restaurant, Dolores Street near Seventh; (408) 624-7500; country European

L'Escargot, Mission Street at Fourth; (408) 624-4914; French

Rio Grill, 101 Crossroads Boulevard; (408) 625-5436; creative American food

CATHEYS VALLEY

The Chibchas, 2747 Highway 140; (209) 966-2940; Colombian/American

CLAYTON

La Cocotte, 6115 Main Street; (510) 672-1333; Continental

COLUMBIA

City Hotel Restaurant, Main Street; (209) 532-1479; nouvelle California

CONCORD

Yvonne Thi's, 2118 Mount Diablo Street; (510) 680-1656; Vietnamese

CORTE MADERA

Il Fornaio, 233 Corte Madera Town Center; (415) 927-4400; Italian

Savannah Grill, 55 Tamal Vista Boulevard; (415) 924-6774; American

COULTERVILLE

Jeffery Hotel & Restaurant, 1 Main Street; (209) 878-3471; American

CRESTLINE

San Moritz Restaurant in Lake Gregory, 24640 San Moritz Drive; (714) 338-7791; fine European dining

DANVILLE

Blackhawk Grille, 3540 Blackhawk Plaza Circle; (510) 736-4295; contemporary Mediterranean

Bridges Restaurant and Bar, 44 Church Street; (510) 820-7200; California with Asian influence

Faz, 400 South Hartz Avenue; (510) 838-1320; Mediterranean/Greek/Italian

Florentine Restaurant and Pasta Market, 3485 Blackhawk Plaza Circle; (510) 736-6060; Italian

DAVENPORT

New Davenport Cash Store Restaurant, Highway 1; (408) 426-4122; fresh home cooking, California style

EMERYVILLE

Bucci's, 6121 Hollis Street; (510) 547-4725; Italian

Townhouse Bar & Grill, 5862 Doyle Street; (510) 655-5929; American

ESCONDIDO

Acapulco Mexican Restaurant, 1514 East Valley Parkway; (619) 741-9922

Bamboo House, 320 North Midway Drive; (619) 480-9550; Chinese

EUREKA

Bay City Grill, 508 Henderson Street; (707) 444-9069; light, imaginative meals/casual atmosphere

Bristol Rose Cafe, Eureka Inn, Seventh and G Streets; (707) 442-6441; upscale European cafe

Michael's Steak House, 909 Fifth Street; (707) 443-0877; steaks/prime rib

The Landing, foot of C Street; (707) 443-2707; fresh fish

The Rib Room, Eureka Inn, Seventh and G Streets; (707) 442-6441; Continental

The Sea Grill, 316 E Street, Old Town; (707) 443-7187; seafood/steaks

Tomo Japanese Restaurant, 2120 Fourth Street; (707) 444-3318

FISH CAMP

The Narrow Gauge Inn, Highway 41; (209) 683-6446; Continental

FORESTVILLE

Chez Marie, 6675 Front Street; (707) 887-7503; country French

DINING HIGHLIGHTS: CALIFORNIA

FORT BRAGG

Egghead Omelettes of Oz, 326 North Main Street; (707) 964-5005

GROVELAND

Charlotte Hotel & Restaurant, Highway 120; (209) 962-7872; American

Pine Mountain Lake Country Club Restaurant, Mueller Drive; (209) 962-7866; Continental

HALF MOON BAY

San Benito House, 356 Main Street; (415) 726-3425; French/northern Italian

Pasta Moon, 315 Main Street; (415) 726-5125; homemade pasta and sauces

HEALDSBURG

Tre Scalini, 241 Healdsburg Avenue; (707) 433-1772; fine Italian cuisine

IDYLLWILD

Bread Basket, 54710 North Circle Drive; (714) 659-3506; European specialties in converted old house with friendly ambiance

Hidden Village, 25840 Cedar Street; (714) 659-2712; Mandarin Chinese

INVERNESS

Drake's Beach Cafe, Kenneth C. Patrick Visitor Center, Drake's Beach; (415) 669-1297; grilled fish/oysters/snacks/chowders

Inverness Inn Restaurant, 2 Inverness Way; (415) 669-1109; local seafood +

Manka's, Argyle at Callender Way; (415) 669-1034; Continental/game

JACKSON

Buscaglia's, 1218 Jackson Gate Road; (209) 223-9992; Italian/American

Cafe Tazza, 214 North Main Street; (209) 223-3547; lunches/weekend dinners

Michael's Restaurant, 2 Water Street, National Hotel; (209) 223-3448

Teresa's, 1235 Jackson Gate Road; (209) 223-1786; Italian/American

KELSEYVILLE

Lakewood Restaurant & Bar, 6330 Soda Bay Road; (707) 279-9450; French/American

LAFAYETTE

Spruzzo! Ristorante, 210 Lafayette Circle; (510) 284-9709; Italian

Duck Club, Lafayette Park Hotel; (510) 283-3700; regional American

Miraku, 3740 Mount Diablo Boulevard; (510) 284-5700; Japanese

Wistaria, 3547 Wilkinson Lane; (510) 283-6322; regional American

LAKE ARROWHEAD

Candlewood Restaruant and Bar, Lake Arrowhead Village; (714) 336-4300; Continental

LAKEPORT

Park Place Cafe, 50 Third Street; (707) 263-0444; homemade pasta

Rainbow Restaurant & Bar, 2599 Lakeshore Boulevard; (707) 263-6237; dinners

LARKSPUR

Lark Creek Inn, 234 Magnolia Avenue; (415) 924-7766; American

LITTLE RIVER
Little River Restaurant, 7750 Highway 1; (707) 937-4945; seafood/meat/poultry

LOS ANGELES
Angeli Caffe, 7274 Melrose Avenue; (213) 936-9086; Italian

Campanile, 624 South La Brea Avenue; (213) 938-1447; Italian

El Cholo, 1121 South Western Avenue; (213) 734-2773; Mexican

Engine Company Number 28, 644 South Figueroa Street; (213) 624-6996; American

Gill's Cuisine of India, Stillwell Hotel, 838 South Grand Avenue; (213) 623-1050

Ho Ban Restaurant, 1040 South Western Avenue; (213) 737-9051; Korean

House of Chandara, 310 North Larchmont; (213) 467-1052; Thai

L.A. Nicola, 4326 Sunset Boulevard; (213) 660-7217; American regional

Mon Kee, 679 North Spring Street; (213) 628-6717; Chinese seafood

Pazzaria, 755 North La Cienega Boulevard; (213) 657-9271; Italian

Salisbury Manor, 1345 Alvarado Terrace; (213) 382-1345; California influenced home cooking in elegant mansion

Trattoria Angeli, 11651 Santa Monica Boulevard; (213) 478-1191; Italian

Tuttobene, 945 North Fairfax Avenue, West Hollywood; (213) 655-7051; Italian

LOS GATOS
Valeriano's Ristorante, 160 West Main Street; (408) 354-8108; Italian

MANHATTAN BEACH
Pancho's, 3615 Highland Avenue; (310) 545-6670; Mexican

MARINA DEL REY
Angeli Mare, 13455 Maxella Avenue; (310) 822-1984; Italian

East Wind Cafe, 2928 Washington Boulevard; (310) 305-8779; Thai

Killer Shrimp, 523 Washington Boulevard; (310) 578-2293

The Red Onion, 4215 Admiralty Way; (310) 821-2291; Mexican

MARIPOSA
Bon Ton Cafe, 7307 Highway 49 North; (209) 377-8229; Guatemalan/American

Charles Street Dinner House, Highway 140 and Seventh Street; (209) 966-2366; Continental

China Station, Highway 140 at Highway 49 South; (209) 966-3889; Chinese

Old Sawmill Restaurant, 5111 Coakley Drive; (209) 742-6101; down-home cooking

MC CLOUD
McCloud Guest House, 606 West Colombero Drive; (916) 964-3160; Continental

MENDOCINO
Bay View Cafe, Main Street; (707) 937-4197; breakfast/lunch/dinner/ocean view

Chocolate Mousse Cafe, 390 Kasten Street; (707) 937-4323; eclectic menu

MacCallum House Restaurant and the Grey Whale Bar & Cafe, 45020 Albion Street; (707) 937-5763; Continental/fresh local ingredients; bistro menu

DINING HIGHLIGHTS: CALIFORNIA

MENLO PARK

The Acorn, 1906 El Camino Real; (415) 322-6201; Mediterranean

Fontana's Italian Restaurant, 1850 El Camino Real; (415) 328-0676

Pete's Place, 1246 El Camino Real; (415) 328-0676; informal American

MILLBRAE

Hong Kong Flower Lounge, 51 Millbrae Avenue; (415) 878-8108 - and - 1671 El Camino Real; (415) 873-3838; Chinese

MILL VALLEY

The Avenue Grill, 44 East Blithedale Avenue; (415) 388-6003; American

Buckeye Roadhouse, 15 Shoreline Highway; (415) 321-2600; American

Calasia, 639 East Blithedale Avenue; (415) 389-8989; California/Asian

MONTARA

The Foglifter Restaurant, Corner of Eighth Street and Highway 1; (415) 728-7905; eclectic menu

MORAGA

Chez Maurice, 360 Park Street; (510) 376-1655; French/Continental

MT. SHASTA

Bellissimo, 204-A West Lake Street; (916) 926-4461; eclectic menu

MURPHYS

Murphys Hotel, Main Street; (209) 728-3444; Continental

NEVADA CITY

The Apple Fare, 307 Broad Street; (916) 265-5458; American breakfast/lunch

Country Rose, 300 Commercial Street; (916) 265-6252; country French

Rainbow Mountain Inn, 238 Commercial Street; (916) 265-5757; Japanese dinners

Selaya's, 320 Broad Street; (916) 265-5697; California

NICASIO

Rancho Nicasio, in Nicasio, off Sir Francis Drake Boulevard; (415) 662-2219; meat specialties in western atmosphere

OAKHURST

Erna's Elderberry House, Victoria Lane off Highway 41; (209) 683-6800; fine European dining

OAKLAND

Bay Wolf Restaurant, 3853 Piedmont Avenue; (510) 655-6004; California/Mediterranean

Creme de la Creme, 5362 College Avenue; (510) 420-8822; California/country French

Jade Villa, 800 Broadway; (510) 839-1688; Chinese/dim sum

La Brasserie, 542 Grand Avenue; (510) 893-6206; traditional French

Little Shin Shin, 4258 Piedmont Avenue; (510) 658-9799; Chinese

Nan Yang, 301 Eighth Street; (510) 465-6924; Indian/Chinese/Burmese home cooking

New Sunshine Ristorante, 3891 Piedmont Avenue; (510) 428-2500; pizza/Italian

Olivetto, 5655 College Avenue; (510) 547-5356; Mediterranean

Sorabal, 372 Grand Avenue; (510) 839-2288; Korean

Ti Bachio Ristorante, 5301 College Avenue; (510) 428-1703; Italian

OLEMA

Olema Inn Restaurant, 10000 Sir Francis Drake Boulevard at Highway 1; (415) 663-9559; Continental

OROVILLE

The Depot, Oliver and High Streets; (916) 534-9101; steaks/seafood/prime rib

Ivar's, 2066 Bird; (916) 534-8277; vegetarian/meat/chicken/seafood

PACIFIC GROVE

Fish & Basil, American Tin Cannery Outlet Center; (408) 649-0707; fresh fish with an Oriental touch

PALM SPRINGS

Alfredo's, 292 East Palm Canyon Drive; (619) 320-1020; Italian

Cedar Creek Inn, 1555 South Palm Canyon Drive; (619) 325-7300; American

Las Casuelas Terraza, 222 South Palm Canyon Drive; (619) 325-2794; Mexican

Original Thai Cuisine Siamese Gourmet, 4711 East Palm Canyon Drive at Gene Autry Trail; (619) 328-0057

Otani, A Garden Restaurant, 266 Avenida Caballeros; (619) 327-6700; Japanese

PALO ALTO

Fresco, 3398 El Camino Real; (415) 493-3470; California

Gordon Biersch Brewing Company, 640 Emerson Street; (415) 323-7723; brewpub/ California

PESCADERO

Duarte's Tavern, 202 Stage Road; (415) 879-0464; seafood/local specialties

PHILO

The Flood Gate Store & Grill, 1810 Highway 128; (707) 895-3000; regional dishes/grilled items

POINT REYES STATION

Chez Madeleine, 10905 Highway 1; (415) 663-9177; French

RED BLUFF

The Green Barn, 5 Chestnut Avenue; (916) 527-3161; prime rib/fish/salads

REDDING

Jack's Grill, 1743 California Street; (916) 241-9705; steakhouse

Nello's Place, 3055 Bechelli Lane; (916) 223-1636; Italian

River City Bar & Grill, 2151 Market Street; (916) 243-9003; Cajun/Creole/ Continental/American

REDWOOD CITY

Barbarossa European Restaurant, 3003 El Camino Real; (415) 369-2626

RICHMOND

Hawthorne's, 1900 Esplanade Drive, on the marina, Point Richmond; (510) 620-0400; imaginative American

Hidden City Cafe, 109 Park Place, Point Richmond; (510) 232-9738; California

RUNNING SPRINGS

The Chateau Pines, 31575 Hill Top Boulevard; (714) 867-7355; American

Toto's, 31927 Hill Top Boulevard; (714) 867-2469; Mexican

SACRAMENTO

Biba,2801 Capitol Avenue; (916) 455-2422; northern Italian/Bolognese

ST. HELENA

Rissa, 1420 Main Street; (707) 963-7566; varied Oriental dishes

Terra, 1345 Railroad Avenue; (707) 963-8931; California

Tra Vigne, 1050 Charter Oak; (707) 963-4444; rustic Italian

Trilogy, 1234 Main Street; (707) 963-5507; American

SAN ANSELMO

Comforts, 337 San Anselmo Avenue; (415) 454-6790; eclectic menu

SAN DIEGO

Busalacchi's Ristorante, 3683 Fifth Avenue; (619) 298-0119; Sicilian

California Cafe Bar & Grill, Horton Plaza; (619) 238-5440; California

Calliope's Greek Cafe, 3958 Fifth Avenue; (619) 291-5588

Canes California Bistro, 1270 Cleveland Avenue; (619) 299-3551

Celadon, a Thai Restaurant, 3628 Fifth Avenue; (619) 295-8800

Cilantros, 3702 Via de la Valle; (619) 259-8777; Mexican/Southwest

City Delicatessen, 535 University Avenue; (619) 295-2747; Jewish/American

Five Fifteen Fifth Avenue, 515 Fifth Avenue; (619) 232-3352

The French Side of the West, 2202 Fourth Avenue; (619) 234-5540; French

La Gran Tapa, 611 B Street; (619) 234-8272; Spanish

SAN FRANCISCO

Bay One Cafe, Ghirardelli Square; (415) 775-1173; seafood/meat dishes

Brasserie Savoy, 580 Geary Street; (415) 474-8686; French/seafood

Buca Giovanni, 800 Greenwich Street; (415) 776-7766; Italian

Cafe For All Seasons, 350 West Portal Avenue; (415) 665-0900; American

Cafe Kati, 1963 Sutter Street; (415) 775-7313; international

Citrus North African Grill, 2373 Chestnut Street; (415) 563-7720; Moroccan

Cleopatra Restaurant, 1755 Noriega Street; (415) 753-5005; Middle Eastern

Compass Rose, Westin St. Francis Hotel, Union Square; (415) 774-0167; lunch/ high tea/cocktails in splendid surroundings

Des Alpes, 732 Broadway; (415) 391-4249; Basque

Etrusca, 121 Spear Street (2 Rincon Center); (415) 777-0330; upscale Italian

Fog City Diner, 1300 Battery Street; (415) 982-2000; contemporary American

The Flying Saucer, 1000 Guerrero Street; (415) 641-9955; neighborhood French

Harry Denton's, 161 Steuart Street; (415) 882-1333; American

The Helmand, 430 Broadway; (415) 362-0641; Afghanistani

Hong Kong Flower Lounge, 5322 Geary Boulevard; (415) 668-8998; Chinese

Hyde Street Bistro, 1521 Hyde Street; (415) 441-7778; California

Jackson Pavilion, 640 Jackson Street; (415) 982-2409; inexpensive prime rib/daily specials

Julie's Supper Club, 1123 Folsom Street; (415) 861-0707; American

Kabuto, 5116 Geary Boulevard; (415) 752-5652; sushi/Japanese

Kuleto's, 221 Powell Street (adjacent to Villa Florence Hotel); (415) 397-7720; Italian

La Bergerie, 4221 Geary Boulevard; (415) 387-3573; neighborhood French

La Creme, 2305 Irving Street; (415) 664-0669; neighborhood French

La Folie, 2316 Polk Street; (415) 776-5577; upscale French

L'Avenue, 3854 Geary Boulevard; (415) 386-1555; Mediterranean/provencale/ traditional American

Le Central, 453 Bush Street; (415) 391-2233; French bistro/brasserie

L'Olivier, 465 Davis Street; (415) 981-7824; lighter classic French

Manora's Thai Restaurant, 1600 Folsom Street; (415) 861-6224

McCormick & Kuleto's, Ghirardelli Square; (415) 929-1730; upscale seafood/ California

Noe's Cook, 3782 Twenty-fourth Street; (415) 826-3811; neighborhood German

Michelangelo Cafe, 579 Columbus Avenue; (415) 986-4058; hearty Italian

Miss Pearl's Jam House, 601 Eddy Street; (415) 775-5267; Caribbean

Palio D'Asti, 640 Sacramento Street; (415) 395-9800; regional Italian

Rosemarino, 3665 Sacramento Street; (415) 931-7710; neighborhood Mediterranean

Roosevelt Tamale Parlor, 2817 Twenty-fourth Street; (415) 550-9213; no-frills Mexican

Royal Thai, 610 Third Street; (415) 485-1074

Square One, 190 Pacific Street; (415) 788-1110; multi-ethnic cuisine

Stars Cafe, 555 Golden Gate Avenue; (415) 861-7827; light food/fish & chips

The Stinking Rose, 325 Columbus Avenue; (415) 781-7673; garlic specialties

Suppers, 1800 Fillmore Street; (415) 474-3773; homestyle American

Suzie Kate's, 2330 Taylor Street; (415) 776-5283; Southern home cooking

Ton Kiang, 3148 Geary Boulevard; (415) 752-4440 - and - 5827 Geary Boulevard; (415) 386-8530; northern Chinese

Tung Fong, 808 Pacific Avenue; (415) 362-7115; dim sum

Wu Kong Restaurant, 101 Spear Street (1 Rincon Center); (415) 957-9300; Shanghai Chinese

Yoshida-Ya, 2909 Webster Street; (415) 348-3431; Japanese

Zola's, 395 Hayes Street; (415) 775-3311; upscale French/Mediterranean

Zuni Cafe, 1658 Market Street; (415) 552-2522; Mediterranean

SAN JOSE

Eulipia Restaurant & Bar, 374 South First Street; (408) 280-6161; California

Gordon Biersch Brewing Company, 33 East San Fernando Street; (408) 294-4052; brewpub/California

SAN LUIS OBISPO

Cafe Roma, 1819 Osos Street; (805) 541-6800; cucina rustica Italiana

DINING HIGHLIGHTS: CALIFORNIA

SAN MARCOS
Fish House Vera Cruz, 1020-124 W. San Marcos Boulevard; (619) 744-8000
SAN MATEO
Eposto's Four Day Cafe, 1119 South B Street; (415) 345-6443; Italian
SAN RAFAEL
Cafe 901, 901 Lincoln; (415) 457-0450; Southwest

La Bergerie, 1130 Fourth Street; (415) 457-2411; classic French

Milly's, 1613 Fourth Street; (415) 459-1601; vegetarian

Rice Table, 1617 Fourth Street; (415) 456-1808; Indonesian
SANTA BARBARA
Cold Spring Tavern, 5995 Stagecoach Road; (805) 967-0066; American/game

La Super-Rica, 622 North Milpas Street; (805) 963-4940; tacos/Mexican

Mousse Odile, 18 East Cota; (805) 962-5393; French

Paradise Cafe, 702 Anacapa; (805) 962-4416; seafood/California
SANTA CLARA
Birk's, 3955 Freedom Circle; (408) 980-6400; classic American grill
SANTA CRUZ
Casablanca Restaurant, overlooking beach at 101 Main Street; (408) 426-9063; Continental cuisine/elegant atmosphere

Crow's Nest, by beach at Santa Cruz Yacht Harbor; (408) 476-4560; seafood/steaks/oyster bar

Hollins House, 20 Clubhouse Road; (408) 425-1244; Continental

India Joze, 1001 Center Street; (408) 427-3554; Asian/Middle Eastern

O'mei Restaurant, 2361 Mission Street; (408) 425-8458; Chinese

Rojo, 2-1490 East Cliff Drive; (408) 476-0972; California

The Swan/Heavenly Goose, 1003 Cedar Street; (408) 425-8988; Szechwan Chinese
SANTA ROSA
Italian Affair, 1612 Terrace Way; (707) 528-3336

John Ash & Co., 4330 Barnes Road at U.S. 101 and River Road; (707) 527-7687; wine country cuisine

La Gare, 208 Wilson Street; (707) 528-4355; Swiss/French

La Province, Stony Point Lake; (707) 526-6233; French/Continental

Mixx, 135 Fourth Street; (707) 573-1344; Continental

Restaurant Matisse, 620 Fifth Street; (707) 527-9797; new French/new American

Ristorante Siena, 1229 North Dutton Avenue; (707) 578-4511; Italian
SAUSALITO
Arawan, 47 Caledonia Street; (415) 332-0882; Thai

Casa Madrona Restaurant, 801 Bridgeway; (415) 331-5888; California

North Sea Village, 300 Turney; (415) 331-3300; Chinese

SCOTTS VALLEY

Zanotto's Pasta & More, 5600 Scotts Valley Drive; (408) 438-0503; pasta/ Italian dishes

SEBASTOPOL

Chez Peyo, 2295 Gravenstein Highway (116); (707) 823-1262; country French

SONORA

Banny's California Cafe, 14751 Mono Way; (209) 533-4709; bistro/seasonal

Good Heavens, a Food Concern, 49 North Washington; (209) 532-3663; lunch/ Sunday brunch in tearoom atmosphere/historic setting/creative menu

La Torre Restaurant, 39 North Washington; (209) 533-9181; pasta/veal/steaks/ nightly specials/charming historic atmopshere

SOQUEL

Ranjeet's, 3051 Porter Street; (408) 475-6407; California

The Salmon Poacher Restaurant, 3035 Main Street; (408) 476-1556; seafood

Star of Siam, 3005 Porter Street; (408) 479-0366; Thai cuisine/sushi bar

Theo's, 3101 Main Street; (408) 462-3657; French

Tortilla Flats, 4580 Soquel Drive; (408) 476-1754; Mexican

STINSON BEACH

Sand Dollar, 3458 Shoreline Highway; (415) 868-0434; simple seaside food

SUTTER CREEK

Pelargonium, #1 Hanford Street (Highway 49 N); (209) 267-5008; California

TAHOE CITY

La Playa, 7046 North Lake Boulevard; (916) 546-5903; creative fresh seafood

River Ranch, Highway 89 at Alpine Meadows Road; (916) 583-4264; Continental/seafood

Rosie's Cafe, 571 North Lake Boulevard; (916) 583-8504; breakfast/lunch/ dinner/varied menu/nightly specials

Swiss Lakewood, 5055 West Lake Boulevard; (916) 525-5211; Continental

THREE RIVERS

The Gateway, 45978 Sierra Drive/Highway 198; (209) 561-4133; steaks/sea-food/riverside setting

Staff of Life, 41651 Sierra Drive; (209) 561-4937; lunches/homemade soups/ salads/sandwiches with vegetarian accent

White Horse Inn, 42975 Sierra Drive; (209) 561-4185; American

TIBURON

The Caprice, 2000 Paradise Drive; (415) 435-3400; Continental

Guaymas, 5 Main Street; (415) 435-6300; upscale Mexican

UKIAH

Sunset Grill, 228 East Perkins Street; (707) 463-0740; eclectic menu for breakfast/lunch/dinner/brunch

VENICE

North Beach Bar & Grill, 111 Rose Avenue at Main Street; (310) 399-3900; old-fashioed steakhouse/contemporary California

West Beach Cafe, 60 North Venice Boulevard; (310) 823-5396; upscale California

VISALIA

The Vintage Press Restaurante, 216 North Willis Street; (209) 733-3033; California

WALNUT CREEK

Calda! Calda!, 1646 North California Boulevard; (510) 939-5555; unusual individual pizzas

The Cantina, 1470 North Broadway; (510) 934-3663; Mexican

Mai Thai, 1414 North Main Street; (510) 937-7887

Max's Opera Cafe, 1676 North California Boulevard; (510) 932-3434; American/New York-style deli

Montecatini, 1528 Civic Drive; (510) 943-6608; Italian

Prima Cafe, 1522 North Main Street; (510) 935-7780; California

Ristornate Toscano, 1520 Palos Verdes Mall; (510) 934-3737; Italian

Spiedini, 101 Ygnacio Valley Road; (510) 939-2100; Italian

Takao, 1690 Locust Street; (510) 944-0244; Japanese

Taos Grill, 1345 Treat Boulevard, Embassy Suites Hotel; (510) 934-3850; Southwest

Wan Fu, 1375 North Broadway; (510) 938-2288; elegant Szechwan/Mandarin

WATSONVILLE

Cilantros, 1934 Main Street in Watsonville Square; (408) 761-2161; Mexican

Jalisco, 618 Main Street, downtown Watsonville; (408) 728-9080; Mexican

WOODSIDE

Bella Vista, 13451 Skyline Boulevard; (415) 851-1229; Continental

YOUNTVILLE

The Diner, 6476 Washington Street; (707) 944-2626; American by day, Mexican by night

Mama Nina's, 6772 Washington Street; (707) 944-2112; northern Italian

Mustards Grill, 7399 St. Helena Highway; (707) 944-2424; American grill

OREGON

Oregon

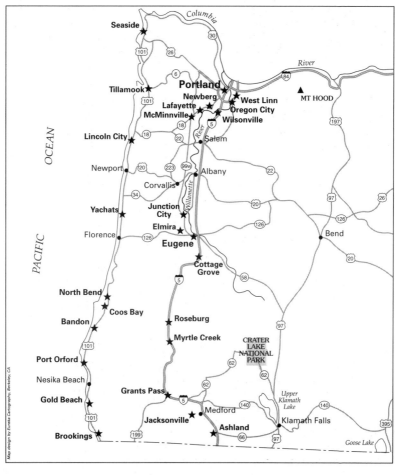

Ashland's Victory House   (503) 488-4428
271 Beach Street, Ashland, OR 97520
(Between theater district and Southern Oregon State College)

A ten-minute walk north along historic Siskiyou Boulevard from Ashland's Victory House takes you downtown, to the theaters, and to enchanting Lithia Park. Devoted to the momentous events and figures of the 1940s, the simple Tudor-style home is full of reminders of that critical era: an old jukebox with forties' tunes in FDR's Den, a Victory Garden outside the window, a collection of appropriate movies, an eclectic mix of furnishings, and WW II warship and airplane pictures along the stairwell leading up to the guest rooms -- Ike's, Harry's, and Winston's. There is even a hot tub called Warm Springs on the deck. It's obvious that host Dale Swire had fun carrying out the theme that so influenced his early years. Rarely is nostalgia quite so entertaining for guests as well.

No pets; no children under twelve; smoking outside only; full breakfast; VCR; AC; fireplace; many non-theater activities (skiing, rafting, fishing, and more) nearby; off-street parking; wheelchair access to Ike's Room. Brochure available.

*Note: Seasonal rates from $59 to $75. RESERVE *WELL* IN ADVANCE DURING SHAKESPEARE FESTIVAL MONTHS, ESPECIALLY MAY-SEPTEMBER!

ROOM	BED	BATH	ENTRANCE	FLOOR	DAILY RATES S - D (EP) +
A	1Q	Pvt	Main	1	
B	2T or 1K	Pvt	Main	2	*See
C	2T or 1K	Pvt	Main	2	note.

Cowslip's Belle   (503) 488-2901
159 North Main Street, Ashland, OR 97520
(Three blocks from Shakespearean theaters)

When visiting Ashland it's a plus to stay in the heart of town and walk everywhere; when staying at Cowslip's Belle, that's just the icing on the cake. This 1913 Craftsman-era home is filled with features that charm its year-round guests: handsome woodwork, Oriental rugs, beveled glass, wainscoting, an extensive book collection, a fireplace, and vintage furnishings. Each of four guest rooms and the house itself were named for old flowers of Shakespeare's day. Antique quilts, brass and iron beds, a willow canopy bed, and garden views enhance the bedrooms, two of which are located in a beautifully renovated carriage house. At Cowslip's Belle, be assured of some of the finest lodging Ashland has to offer.

Dog and cat on premises; no pets; children by prior arrangement; smoking outside only; AC; patio; off-street parking; credit cards (V, MC). Brochure available.

*Note: Rates vary from $50 to $95 depending on season and day. RESERVE *WELL* IN ADVANCE DURING SHAKESPEARE FESTIVAL MONTHS, ESPECIALLY MAY-SEPTEMBER!

ROOM	BED	BATH	ENTRANCE	FLOOR	DAILY RATES S - D (EP) +
A	1Q	Pvt	Main	1	
B	1Q & 1T	Pvt	Sep	1	*See
C	1Q & 1T	Pvt	Sep	1	note.
D	1Q & 1T	Pvt	Sep	1	

Lighthouse Bed & Breakfast   **(503) 347-9316**
P.O. Box 24, Bandon, OR 97411
(650 Jetty Road)

The contemporary wood home of Linda and Bruce Sisson overlooks Bandon's historic lighthouse and the point where the Coquille River meets the Pacific Ocean. Plant-bedecked rooms are spacious, bright, and comfortable. One (A) offers spectacular sunset views; another (B) has a unique greenhouse bath with a whirlpool tub for two and a fireplace in front of the bed. Park your car for a while and explore the Old Town shopping area on foot. Walk to the beach and join the folks out fishing, crabbing, or clamming; take an easy stroll to one of the fine seafood restaurants close by. The Sissons will be happy to enjoy your company, offer suggestions for making the most of your time in Bandon, or provide you with all the relaxing privacy you need. Your contentment is their aspiration.

Toy poodle in residence; no pets; children over ten welcome; no smoking; Continental plus breakfast; off-street parking; credit cards (V, MC); airport pickup (Bandon). Off-season rates November-May. Brochure available.

ROOM	BED	BATH	ENTRANCE	FLOOR	DAILY RATES
					S - D (EP) +
A	1Q	Pvt	Main	2	$75-$85
B	1K	Pvt	Main	2	$90-$100($15)
C	1Q	Pvt	Main	2	$75-$85 ($15)
D	1Q	Pvt	Main	2	$70-$80

The Chetco River Inn **(503) 469-8128**
21202 High Prairie Road, Brookings, OR 97415
(Sixteen miles up North Bank Road)

Here's a destination spot that's as out-of-the-ordinary as it is
out-of-the-way. Worldly concerns seem to melt away as you drive
through pristine countryside following the Chetco River -- sparklingly
clear and inviting. In a remote setting on the river bank, Sandra
Brugger welcomes guests to her new lodge-type inn. It has modern
lines, a spacious interior, and a rustic, old-world flavor. Shiny marble
floors, Oriental rugs, and fine traditional furnishings grace the large,
open living area. On one end, a wood-burning stove is backed by a
wall of native stone; on the other end, there's an open kitchen and
dining area where country breakfasts and memorable dinners are
served. Two of the guest bedrooms have enchanting river views, crisp
white walls, elegant brass beds, and delightful memorabilia such as
old decoys and photography equipment. Whether you're contemplat-
ing the river from a secluded park bench, taking a hike or a swim,
angling for steelhead, or just curling up with a good book, an uncommonly relaxing escape awaits you at The Chetco River Inn.

Dog and cat in residence; no pets; older children welcome; smoking outside only (porch); full breakfast; robes provided; dinner with
advance notice; picnic lunches available; satellite TV and movies;
library; games; fishing and hunting packages available; off-street
parking; credit cards (V, MC). Reservations also through Pelican Bay
Travel: 1-800-327-2688. Brochure available.

ROOM	BED	BATH	ENTRANCE	FLOOR	DAILY RATES S - D (EP)
A	2T or 1K	Pvt	Main	2	$75-$85
B	1Q	Pvt	Main	2	$85
C	1K	Pvt	Main	2	$85

Holmes Sea Cove Bed & Breakfast   **(503) 469-3025**
17350 Holmes Drive, Brookings, OR 97415
(North side of Brookings overlooking Pacific)

Many a guest has been reluctant to leave Holmes Sea Cove Bed &
Breakfast. Who would willingly give up the comfort of a private
paradise with a heavenly view of the rugged Oregon coast? Each of
three guest accommodations has its own entrance, bath, refrigerator,
and color TV. One is a large room with a sitting area, another a large
suite, and the third a separate cottage. All have excellent views, but
the one from the cottage is panoramic. Hosts Jack and Lorene Holmes
know how to make you feel welcome and then leave you alone to savor
a total escape. They deliver breakfast to your doorstep in the morning
and invite you to make full use of the gazebo overlooking the ocean,
the benches and picnic tables, and the pathway leading to the beach.
Landscaped grounds and gardens round out a truly perfect setting for
making memories with that special someone.

No pets; children limited; smoking outside only; no RV parking;
sofa bed in each room; off-street parking; airport pickup (Sierra
Pacific); credit cards (V, MC). Brochure available.

ROOM	BED	BATH	ENTRANCE	FLOOR	DAILY RATES	
					S - D	(EP) +
A	1Q	Pvt	Sep	LL	$80	($15)
B	1Q	Pvt	Sep	LL	$85	($15)
C	1Q	Pvt	Sep	1	$95	($15)

This Olde House   **(503) 267-5224**
202 Alder Avenue, Coos Bay, OR 97420
(Just off U.S. 101 at North Second Street)

   This stately house on the hill is every inch a lady. She is pale blue trimmed in white, with all her grandeur still intact. Ed and Jean Mosieur moved from Monterey to Coos Bay, trading one coastal location for another. Things are calmer in Coos Bay, slower paced. Renovations and furnishings have made the Mosieurs' new old home a gracious, inviting place for guests to enjoy a special brand of hospitality. There are four generously proportioned guest rooms, three with a bay view and one with a canopied bed. A short drive takes you to one of my favorite parts of the Oregon coast, the fishing village of Charleston (great for buying fresh and smoked fish) and three adjacent state parks that are worth a special trip: Sunset Bay, Shore Acres, and Cape Arago. Ed, Jean, and Brice are sure to make your stop in Coos Bay a memorable one.

   No pets or smoking; no children under forty-three (a bit of Jean's humor); ample street parking.

ROOM	BED	BATH	ENTRANCE	FLOOR	DAILY RATES S - D	(EP) +
A	1K	Pvt	Main	2	$60	($15)
B	1K	Shd*	Main	2	$55	($15)
C	1D	Shd*	Main	2	$55	($15)
D	1Q	Shd*	Main	2	$55	($15)

Upper Room Chalet   **(503) 269-5385**
306 North Eighth Street, Coos Bay, OR 97420
(Central Coos Bay near Mingus Park)

On a quiet little street near downtown, surrounded by evergreen and rhododendron, is the warm family home of Carl and Barbara Solomon. A piano in the foyer, a living room with cushy places to sit, a fireplace, and country Victorian decor combine to create the essence of hospitality. Family antiques, mementoes, and photos fill the house. Flanking the stairwell to the second floor is Barbara's collection of dolls. Three upstairs bedrooms have different focal points: a colorful patchwork quilt, two iron day beds done up in ivory eyelet and mauve, and a king-sized antique brass bed.   On the main floor is a cheery bedroom suitable for one. The Solomons' big country kitchen is the heart of the house, a magnet for people who appreciate its old-time ambiance and camaraderie -- not to mention the comfort foods, such as biscuits and gravy, berries and dumplings, or homemade pies, that are served here.

No pets; no alcohol; no children under sixteen; smoking outside only; full country breakfast; tennis courts across street; off-street and street parking. Brochure available.

ROOM	BED	BATH	ENTRANCE	FLOOR	DAILY RATES S - D (EP) +
A	1D	Shd*	Main	2	$50-$55
B	2T	Shd*	Main	2	$50-$55
C	1K	Pvt 1/2	Main	2	$55-$60
D	1T	Shd*	Main	1	$35

Hillcrest Dairy Bed & Breakfast   **(503) 942-0205**
79385 Sears Road, Cottage Grove, OR 97424
(Northeast Cottage Grove, Exit 176 from I-5)

Here's an opportunity to experience Dutch hospitality on a working dairy farm. Mike and Grace Eisenga bring a bit of the old country to their style of bed and breakfast. Accommodations are immaculate, the breakfasts large and nourishing. The comfortable ranch-style home has common rooms where guests may feel free to play games, read, or use the pool table. There are large and small bicycles available for exploring the beautiful area surrounding the farm. They're great for viewing wildlife such as deer, elk, and birds. If the workings of a dairy farm interest you, witness them firsthand as Mike goes about his daily routine. A visit to Hillcrest Dairy will add a pleasant change of pace to your trip.

No pets; infants and children over six welcome; smoking outside only; full breakfast; TV; single cot extra in Room C; off-street parking; bicycles available.

ROOM	BED	BATH	ENTRANCE	FLOOR	DAILY RATES S - D (EP)
A	1Q	Shd*	Main	1	$30-$45 ($10)
B	1D	Shd*	Main	1	$30-$40
C	2T	Shd*	Main	1	$30-$40 ($10)

McGillivrays' Log Home Bed & Breakfast   (503) 935-3564
88680 Evers Road, Elmira, OR 97437
(Off Highway 126, west of Eugene enroute to the coast)

The McGillivrays' unique, built-from-scratch log home is well-suited to its environment: five acres mostly covered with pine and fir trees. Much care and hard work went into the construction of the home, which combines the best of the past with the comforts of today. Throughout the interior, there is handcrafted woodwork displaying a variety of different woods. One guest room (A) with private bath is on the ground floor. An impressive stairway of half-logs leads to a balcony which overlooks the living and dining areas. Doors lead from the balcony to a spacious bedroom (B) with a bath and an outside deck. Old-fashioned breakfasts are usually prepared on the antique, wood-burning cookstove in the dining room, a good place to linger over coffee and plan your day. Many people are understandably quite taken with the McGillivrays' log home, but I think a child guest summed it up best when he asked them, "You mean you get to live here *all* the time?"

No pets; families welcome; smoking on covered porches only; TV; AC; extra beds; crib; winery touring and tasting nearby (Forgeron Vineyards); outdoor recreation at Fern Ridge Reservoir; off-street parking; wheelchair access; credit cards (V, MC); airport pickup (Mahlon Sweet).

ROOM	BED	BATH	ENTRANCE	FLOOR	DAILY RATES
					S - D (EP) +
A	1K	Pvt	Main	1G	$45-$55
B	1K	Pvt	Main	2	$55-$65

Aristea's Guest House   **(503) 683-2062**
1546 Charnelton Street, Eugene, OR 97401
(Downtown area)

As a newcomer to Eugene in 1990, Arie Hupp took to its "little Berkeley" atmosphere right away. She has happily made her home here in the wonderfully restored 1928 bungalow that had in recent years been operated as Shelley's Guest House. She carries on the tradition of hospitality whose hallmarks of elegance and personal service continue to bring many repeat visitors. The gardens have been expanded and new breakfast specialties developed. Gleaming woodwork and floors, traditional wallcoverings, brass accents, and selected antiques grace the interior. There's comfortable seating around the living room fireplace and an extensive library to peruse. The upstairs is exclusively for guests. A cozy sitting room with cable television and a phone connects the Master Bedroom and the Guest Room, both full of charming details. The spacious bathroom has a tub and a separate tile shower. The delightful character of Aristea's Guest House is matched only by that of Arie herself.

Dog and cat in residence; no pets; smoking outside only; full breakfast; ample street parking. Brochure available.

ROOM	BED	BATH	ENTRANCE	FLOOR	DAILY RATES S - D (EP) +
A	1Q & 1T	Shd*	Main	2	$55-$60 ($15)
B	1D	Shd*	Main	2	$45-$50

Atherton Place (formerly Gile's Guest Haus)   **(503) 683-2674**
690 West Broadway, Eugene, OR 97402
(Downtown area)

Atherton Place is an inviting Dutch Colonial dating from the twenties that occupies a corner lot on a lovely, tree-lined street near downtown Eugene. The fresh, light-bathed interior has a welcoming quality combining wicker, antiques, and comfortable places to relax. Oak floors, shiny brass and crystal doorknobs, and a stunning stained glass window, "The Crane," are some of the original features that enhance the home's beauty. Delicate spring colors and floral motifs highlight the decor in each attractive bedroom. Host Marne Krozek addresses a variety of needs her guests may have. There are phone jacks in the rooms, a library with a work space, a small sitting room on the second floor with cable TV, daily newspapers provided, and light refreshments served, as well as full homemade breakfasts emphasizing local products. Thoughtful hospitality abounds in the easygoing atmosphere of Atherton Place.

Dog in residence; children over seven welcome; no smoking; full breakfast; bicycles available; off-street parking. Brochure available.

ROOM	BED	BATH	ENTRANCE	FLOOR	DAILY RATES S - D (EP) +
A	1Q	Pvt	Main	2	$55-$65
B	1T & 1Q	Shd*	Main	2	$45-$55 ($15)

B&G's Bed & Breakfast   **(503) 343-5739**
711 West Eleventh Avenue, Eugene, OR 97402
(Downtown area)

   To stay at the home of Barbara Koser and her son Gerritt is to feel
like a resident of their convenient, tree-shaded neighborhood. Both
guest quarters offer a space that is completely one's own. The top
floor is a large private apartment with Scandinavian accents. Lots of
interesting angles, greenery, natural wood and bricks, and works by
local artists add to its appeal. There is a full kitchen and dining room,
plus seating and sleeping spaces for up to six people. The ambiance
of the private guest cottage overlooking the garden is like a breath of
fresh air. A skylight, vaulted windows, crisp white walls, and colorful artwork give the small space an open, spring-like feeling. Full
breakfasts are served in the Kosers' sunny, plant-filled dining area.
Here, with the help of knowledgeable hosts, you can plan your day to
best take advantage of Eugene's rich diversity.
   Families welcome; smoking outside only; TV/VCR; extensive
book collection; bicycles; laundry facilities; walking distance to
shops, restaurants, galleries, Rose Garden, and Ridgeline Trail; off-
street and street parking; airport pickup (Mahlon Sweet). Guests
invited to join Barbara for daily walks/hikes. Brochure available.

ROOM	BED	BATH	ENTRANCE	FLOOR	DAILY RATES	
					S - D	(EP) +
A	2Q, 1D & 1T	Pvt	Sep	2	$59	($10)
B	1Q	Pvt	Sep	1	$49	

Duckworth Bed & Breakfast Inn   **(503) 686-2451**
987 East Nineteenth Avenue, Eugene, OR 97403
(South campus area)

When Fred and Peggy Ward first saw this English Tudor home, they could see its potential as a charm-filled haven for guests. With this vision and much loving care, they truly outdid themselves in capturing its heartwarming essence. A duck decoy on the mantelpiece sets the color scheme of evergreen and ivory. The main floor is a study in nostalgia, a comforting blend of English and American antiques, family photos and mementoes, fine old clocks and lamps, a player piano, wallpaper and wainscoting, lace curtains, an intimate hearth, and inviting sofas and chairs. Bouquets of fresh flowers decorate the entire house. Upstairs guest rooms are marked by sloped ceilings, English floral print fabrics, and a variety of homey touches. The endless pampering at Duckworth B&B takes many forms, making a stay here endlessly delightful.

Dog in residence; no pets; children over eleven welcome; shared bath off hallway; full breakfast; round-the-clock coffee, tea, and cookies; TV/VCR in each room; 600-video library; gardens with stone pathways; bicycles; off-street parking. Brochure available.

ROOM	BED	BATH	ENTRANCE	FLOOR	DAILY RATES S - D (EP) +
A	1Q	Shd*	Main	2	$65
B	1Q & 1T	Shd*	Main	2	$65
C	1Q	Pvt	Main	2	$75

Getty's Emerald Garden Bed & Breakfast   **(503) 688-6344**
640 Audel, Eugene, OR 97404
(North Eugene area)

The setting is one of extraordinary beauty: landscaped grounds that seem to go on and on with a remarkable variety of vegetation. Huge beds of flowers and vegetables, an orchard, thick shrubbery, mature trees, and lawns surround the contemporary home of long-time residents Bob and Jackie Getty. (Jackie is a Master Gardener.) Vaulted ceilings and tall windows endow the interior with natural light and garden views. Guests like to gather before the fireplace in the comfortable open living area and around the dining room table where exceptional, fresh-from-the-garden breakfast creations are served. At one end of the house, a guest suite that accommodates up to five people makes a neat and spacious retreat for one party at a time. The south-facing patio in back is the perfect place to relax while enjoying the peaceful, country-like atmosphere of Getty's Emerald Garden Bed & Breakfast.

Small dog in residence; no pets; children welcome; smoking outside only; full breakfast; TV/VCR; crib available; family room for guests; great area for walking; park less than a block away offering pool, sauna, Jacuzzi, playgrounds, picnic tables; bicycles; good bus service; off-street parking; can accommodate wheelchair users. Brochure available. *plus bunk bed

ROOM	BED	BATH	ENTRANCE	FLOOR	DAILY RATES S - D (EP) +
A	1Q & 2T*	Pvt	Main	1G	$55 ($15)

The House in the Woods   **(503) 343-3234**
814 Lorane Highway, Eugene, OR 97405
(Southwest Eugene, South Hills area)

The Lorane Highway is a thoroughfare for joggers and cyclists and a convenient route to downtown Eugene, three miles away. The House in the Woods is set back from the road, with a periphery of fir and oak trees, an abundance of azaleas and rhododendrons, and some formally landscaped open areas. Friendly wildlife still abounds on the two acres. Long-time residents Eunice and George Kjaer have restored their 1910 home to its original quiet elegance. There are hardwood floors with Oriental carpets, high ceilings, lots of windows, and three covered porches (one with a swing). A large, comfortable parlor is most pleasant for visiting, listening to music, or reading by the fireplace. Guest rooms are spacious and tastefully decorated. Parks, cultural events, outdoor recreation, and good restaurants can be pointed out by your versatile hosts, but the house and grounds are so peaceful and relaxing that you may be compelled to stay put.

No pets; children over twelve welcome; smoking on outside covered areas; full breakfast (Continental style for late risers); TV; piano; music library; off-street parking; airport pickup (Mahlon Sweet). Additional bedroom with twin bed and shared bath at $38 is available as an alternate choice; winter rates. Brochure available.

ROOM	BED	BATH	ENTRANCE	FLOOR	DAILY RATES S - D (EP) +
A	1Q	Pvt	Main	1	$40-$65
B	1D	Shd	Main	2	$38-$55

The Lyon & The Lambe   **(503) 683-3160**
988 Lawrence Street at Tenth, Eugene, OR 97401
(Downtown area)

Henri and Barbara Brod built their inn on a corner lot to blend into the quiet older neighborhood. Much to their guests' advantage, they planned every detail to maximize comfort, convenience, and enjoyment. The two-story gray inn is trimmed in violet and has a wide wrap-around porch. The interior is immaculate, light, and artistically appointed. Contemporary furnishings, accented with antiques and other interesting pieces, are supremely comfortable. Each guest room is a relaxing haven where it seems one's every need has been anticipated. Sumptuous breakfasts are described on daily menus; they sound too tantalizing to be true but match the overall high standards of The Lyon & The Lambe. The Brods appreciate the finer things in life and assume that their guests do, too.

Dog in residence; children over twelve welcome; full breakfast; fondue dinners by arrangement; TV/VCR; AC; library; private Tub Room with whirlpool bath; phone jack and work space in each room; iron/ironing board available; off-street parking; European languages spoken; credit cards (V, MC). Brochure available.

ROOM	BED	BATH	ENTRANCE	FLOOR	DAILY RATES
					S - D (EP) +
A	1Q	Pvt	Main	2	$70-$75 ($10)
B	1Q	Pvt	Main	2	$65-$70 ($10)
C	1Q	Pvt	Main	2	$60-$65
D	2T	Pvt	Main	2	$55-$60

Inn at Nesika Beach   **(503) 247-6434**
33026 Nesika Road, Gold Beach, OR 97444
(North of Gold Beach)

The setting alone won me over: a new Victorian-style home built
on a bluff overlooking the Pacific. Inn at Nesika Beach offers deluxe
accommodations and the comfort-oriented hospitality of innkeepers
Ann and Ken Arsenault. All four guest rooms are done in Victorian
themes and have down comforters, private baths with whirlpool tubs,
and ocean views. Three rooms have feather beds, double bathtubs,
and fireplaces; two have seaside private balconies. There is a large
recreation room for guests to lounge with TV, fireplace, and a music
and card area. From the covered porch, sit and contemplate the
mysteries of the Pacific, or use the nearby access to the beach and take
a closer look. Inn at Nesika Beach is a place to nourish the senses and
kindle some romantic notions.

No pets or children; smoking outside only; full breakfast; bird and
animal sanctuaries, salmon and steelhead fishing, golfing, Rogue
River jet boat rides, crabbing and clamming nearby; off-street parking; credit cards (V, MC); midweek rates. Brochure available.

ROOM	BED	BATH	ENTRANCE	FLOOR	DAILY RATES
					S - D (EP) +
A	1Q	Pvt	Main	1	$75
B	2T	Pvt	Main	1	$85
C	1K	Pvt	Main	1	$85
D	1K	Pvt	Main	2	$85

The Tale Spinner Bed & Breakfast   **(503) 247-4115**
33134 Nesika Road, Gold Beach, OR 97444
(North of Gold Beach)

When native New Englanders Don and Suzanne Pilgrim spotted several white frame buildings with red roofs on four prime acres overlooking Nesika Beach, they knew this could be home. They live in the largest house, sharing it with B&B guests. Two fresh, light guest rooms are decorated with country simplicity and feature beautiful handmade quilts. The homey living/dining area faces the sea. Some of the furniture was made by Don, a fine craftsman in wood who is also known as a spinner of tales. Suzanne's country breakfasts are as irresistible as the view. A spectacular beach awaits you at the end of a private boardwalk, and the Captain's deck is a great vantage point from which to watch whales, sunsets, and crashing surf. As the Pilgrims declare, The Tale Spinner is a place "where you can relax and have fun." They also offer accommodations in a cottage on the property (C) for those desiring more privacy.

Two dogs on premises; no pets; smoking outside only; full breakfast; Rogue River jet boat rides, crabbing, fishing, agate hunting, kite-flying, and summer theater nearby; off-street parking. Brochure available.

ROOM	BED	BATH	ENTRANCE	FLOOR	DAILY RATES S - D (EP)	
A	1Q	Shd	Main	1	$55-$65	
B	1Q	Shd	Main	1	$55-$65	
C	2Q	Pvt	Sep	1	$85	($10)

Clemens House   **(503) 476-5564**
612 NW Third Street, Grants Pass, OR 97526
(Central Grants Pass)

The huge corner lot where Clemens House stands is a botanical wonderland, a proper setting for a home of its stature. The 1905 three-story Craftsman was a joyous discovery for owners Gerry and Maureen Clark. All its original charm is intact, and the addition of modern amenities has enhanced its comfort. The interior has considerable aesthetic appeal: lots of gorgeous woodwork, including coffered ceilings and polished floors, combined with soft colors; pretty fabrics, rugs, and wallcoverings; antiques and family heirlooms; lace curtains; and handmade quilts. Upstairs bedrooms are simply beautiful, down to the last elegant detail. Share the joy of the Clarks' discovery as you relax in the warmth of their gracious hospitality.

No pets; smoking outside only; full breakfast; AC; desk and space to set up computer available for business travelers; Rogue River activities five minutes away; off-street parking; credit cards (V, MC). Room B is a large suite including a sitting room with a fireplace and an adjoining bedroom with extra-long twin beds. Inquire about off-season rates. Brochure available.

ROOM	BED	BATH	ENTRANCE	FLOOR	DAILY RATES S - D (EP) +
A	1Q	Pvt	Main	2	$60
B	1Q & 2T	Pvt	Main	2	$70 ($12)
C	1Q	Pvt	Main	3	$70

Riverbanks Inn   **(503) 479-1118**
8401 Riverbanks Road, Grants Pass, OR 97527
(Northwest of town on bank of Rogue River)

Riverbanks Inn, situated on twelve acres along the scenic Rogue, is as multifaceted as its owner, Myrtle Franklin. The secluded retreat is a rich tapestry woven from the strands of her life. The completely refurbished main house is endowed with view windows, natural materials, and comfortable seating. Two rooms on the lower level evoke two distinct moods: The Casablanca (A), exotic romance; The Jean Harlow (B), a sort of Floridian art deco glamor. The three-room Caribbean Dream Suite (C) features a Jacuzzi, a rain forest shower, and a plantation bed with Mombasa netting to add to the mood of a tropical paradise. Two nearby cabins include The Log Cabin (D), with antiques, pine floors, and a covered front porch; and The Zen House (E), a traditional Japanese tea house, with a double futon and a black marble shower. Riverbanks Inn offers a range of options few places can match. Come share in its wealth.

No pets; children welcome; smoking outside only; full country breakfast; TVs; VCRs; fireplace; refrigerators; robes provided; extra long beds; outdoor hot tub; steam room; massage; pond; playhouse; nearby lodge and cottage for families, fishing groups; retreats welcome; rafting and birding; off-street parking; credit cards (V, MC). Brochure available.

ROOM	BED	BATH	ENTRANCE	FLOOR	DAILY RATES S - D (EP)
A	1Q	Pvt	Sep	LL	$110
B	2T or 1K	Pvt	Sep	LL	$95
C	1Q	Pvt	Sep	1	$150
D	2T & 1D	Pvt	Sep	1	$95 ($20)
E	1D	Pvt	Sep	1	$65

Birch Leaf Farm Bed & Breakfast   (503) 742-2990
R.R.#1, Box 91, Halfway, OR 97834
(Foot of Wallowa Mountains in far eastern Oregon)

Fascination with the Hells Canyon and Eagle Cap Wilderness region is fast spreading beyond a few privileged adventurers. Here in beautiful Pine Valley is the forty-two acre working farm where Dave and Maryellen Olson have refurbished their handsome turn-of-the-century farmhouse with maximum respect for original features such as the wainscoting, the stairway bannister, and the upstairs pine floors. This respect extends to the carefully preserved vintage orchards and the still-used gravity irrigation system. The vividly colored bedrooms feature pretty rugs and stocked bookshelves. The main living area is the picture of civilized comfort: an entire wall of books, a baby grand piano, a cozy woodstove, and inviting places to sit. Genuine country spirit is built into every facet of Birch Leaf Farm.

No pets indoors; farm animals on grounds; smoking outside only; full breakfast; wrap-around veranda; fishing, hiking, birding, llama trekking, horse pack trips, skiing and panoramic viewing in area; credit cards (V, MC); airport pickup (Baker City, Halfway). Brochure available.

ROOM	BED	BATH	ENTRANCE	FLOOR	DAILY RATES S - D (EP)
A	1K	Shd*	Sep	2	$65 ($20)
B	2T	Shd*	Main	2	$50 ($20)
C	1D & 1T	Shd*	Main	2	$55 ($20)
D	1D & 1T	Pvt	Main	1	$65 ($20)

Reames House 1868   **(503) 899-1868**
P.O. Box 128, Jacksonville, OR 97530
(540 East California Street)

    Reames House 1868 is just four blocks from the center of Jacksonville, a well-preserved gold rush town on the National Register of Historic Places. Encircled by a white picket fence, spacious lawns, and perennial flower gardens, the Queen Anne beauty is also on the Register. It has a fine array of exterior woodwork and an interior enhanced by handsome antiques. Accommodations on the second floor share a lovely sitting room which has a telephone for guests. Exquisite wall stenciling sets the tone for the decor, and period details combined with flair give each bedroom a charm all its own. Reames House 1868 offers superb hospitality to attendees of the celebrated Britt Music Festivals as well as year-round visitors who just want to steep themselves in the history of colorful Jacksonville.

    No pets; children by arrangement; smoking outside only; full breakfast; AC; use of bicycles, tennis rackets, and gold pans; Ashland, fifteen miles away; day trips to Crater Lake National Park, Oregon Caves National Monument, and Rogue River rafting; off-street parking. Brochure available.

ROOM	BED	BATH	ENTRANCE	FLOOR	DAILY RATES S - D (EP)
A	1D	Pvt	Main	2	$90
B	2T	Pvt	Main	2	$90
C	1Q	Shd*	Main	2	$80
D	1Q	Shd*	Main	2	$75

Black Bart Bed & Breakfast   **(503) 998-1904**
94125 Love Lake Road, Junction City, OR 97448
(Fifteen minutes north of Eugene)

    The heartland of the Willamette Valley is green, flat, and expansive with hills to the east and west. Here the thoroughly renovated 1880s farmhouse of Irma and Don Mode is situated on thirteen acres. The home's namesake is a National Grand Champion mammoth donkey who resides on the property, along with mules Nip and Tuck -- all may be booked in advance for rides in an antique carriage or a farm wagon. Guest rooms, like the rest of the home, have personality plus. The Rose Petal features ruffled priscilla curtains, an ornate brass bed, and Early American furnishings. The Canopy Room is done in ivory and blue, with floral carpeting and a fancy maplewood canopy bed. A handcrafted donkey and mule quilt adorns one wall of the twin-bedded Quilt Room. A spirit of whimsy, an appreciation of interesting antiques and collectibles, and a dedication to old-fashioned country comfort abound at Black Bart's.

    Dog and cats on property; no pets; no children under twelve; full farm breakfast; TV/VCR; AC; antique shops, fresh fruit stands, and good places to walk, jog, or cycle close by; off-street parking; airport pickup (Mahlon Sweet). Brochure available.

ROOM	BED	BATH	ENTRANCE	FLOOR	DAILY RATES
					S - D (EP) +
A	1K	Pvt	Main	2	$60
B	1K	Pvt	Main	2	$60
C	2T	Pvt 1/2	Main	2	$50

Kelty Estate   **(503) 864-3740**
P.O. Box 817, Lafayette, OR 97127
(675 Highway 99 W; central Yamhill County wine region)

Lafayette was an early farming settlement where the James Keltys first built their rural Gothic farmhouse in 1872. In 1934, son Paul Kelty -- then prominent editor of *The Oregonian* in Portland -- bought back his boyhood home, refurbished it in the colonial style, and used it as a summer home. Most recently, Ronald and JoAnn Ross's painstaking restorations have left the interior with a new feeling, while graceful architectural details and selected antiques recall another era. The proud white house with green trim is surrounded by lush lawns, gardens, and trees. Choose one of two lovely corner bedrooms where soft pastels create a soothing ambiance. Guests enjoy gathering around the living room fireplace, on the front porch, or in the beautiful back yard. Kelty Estate is a gracious way station for travelers who appreciate a warm welcome and immaculate accommodations.

No children, pets, or smoking; full breakfast; popular Lafayette Antique Mall diagonally across from B&B; off-street parking.

ROOM	BED	BATH	ENTRANCE	FLOOR	DAILY RATES S - D (EP)
A	1Q	Pvt	Main	2	$55
B	1Q	Pvt	Main	2	$55

The Brey House Ocean View Bed & Breakfast   **(503) 994-7123**
3725 NW Keel, Lincoln City, OR 97367
(North of town center, across street from ocean)

Seeking a casual, relaxing place by the ocean to unwind? A homey respite right across the street from a walk-forever beach is The Brey House, where Milt and Shirley Brey's guests appreciate the do-as-you-please atmosphere, the walking-distance proximity to shops and restaurants, and the unobstructed ocean view from most every room. A nautical theme prevails throughout the house. A new dining room with glass on three sides is the perfect place to enjoy the extravagant breakfasts Milt whips up. The ground-floor accommodation may be used by a family or group; it has two bedrooms, a family room with a pool table, comfy places to sit, a fireplace, and a TV/VCR, as well as a full kitchen. Guests are welcome to use the barbecue grill, picnic tables, and hot tub. Guest rooms on the second and third floors have unforgettable ocean views.

No pets; no children under fifteen; smoking restricted; full breakfast; fishing, golf, hiking, antique shopping and more nearby; off-street parking; credit cards (V, MC, D). Midweek rates. Brochure available.

ROOM	BED	BATH	ENTRANCE	FLOOR	DAILY RATES	
					S - D	(EP) +
A	1Q	Shd*	Sep	1	$55-$65	($10)
B	1Q	Shd*	Sep	1	$45-$55	($10)
C	1Q	Pvt	Main	2	$55-$65	($10)
D	1Q	Shd	Main	3	$55-$65	($10)

Rustic Inn   (503) 994-5111
2313 NE Holmes Road, Lincoln City, OR 97367
(North of town center, east of U.S. 101)

In a setting of trees and gardens, Rustic Inn is possessed of a warm, country ambiance inside and out. Many relish the surroundings while relaxing on the front porch or the pleasant deck, but it's just a half-mile walk to a glorious stretch of beach. Setting the mood of the inn are the open, wood-paneled living/dining area, a cathedral ceiling with exposed beams, a loft library/study, a rustic hearth, and the true character of a loving home. The main-floor guest room, Touch of Lace, has a crocheted bedspread, lace curtains, lovely framed pictures, a loft, and a private bath off the hallway. Two rooms on the lower level are entered separately: Romance of Roses, done in rose tones and white, with a Jacuzzi tub for two in the private bath; and Country, a smaller room with its own sitting room and bath. Hosts Lloyd and Evelyn Bloomberg keep the genial glow of their hospitality going all year round.

No pets; no children under twelve; smoking outside only; full breakfast; TV in each room; off-street parking; credit cards (V, MC). Midweek rates. Brochure available.

ROOM	BED	BATH	ENTRANCE	FLOOR	DAILY RATES	
					S - D	(EP) +
A	1Q	Pvt	Main	1	$60	($10)
B	1Q	Pvt	Sep	LL	$70	
C	1D	Pvt	Sep	LL	$55	($10)

Orchard View Inn   **(503) 472-0165**
16540 NW Orchard View Road, McMinnville, OR 97128
(Yamhill County wine region)

Set amidst luxuriant foliage, waterfalls, ponds, and the sounds of
nature, Wayne and Marie Schatter's unique octagonal home has the
remote quality of a true retreat, yet it is only minutes from valley
attractions.   One accommodation on the lower level has its own
entrance. Guests have the main floor all to themselves. The open
living area, with vaulted ceilings, large windows, and skylights,
strikes a harmonious chord with the surroundings. Choosing among
the Rose, Antique, and Iris Rooms is difficult indeed. Common areas
have an Oriental flavor -- antiques and art treasures from the Far East
contribute to the soothing environment. Sink into a big, soft sofa
facing a fireplace with a fieldstone hearth; absorb a vista of evergreen
forest, Mount Hood, and the Willamette Valley from the deck around
the inn's perimeter; and savor the sweet serenity.

No pets or small children; smoking outside only; full breakfast;
TV; AC; dining area and full kitchen exclusively for guests; credit
cards (V, MC).   With two-night minimum, rate for whole house is
$255/night. Brochure available.

ROOM	BED	BATH	ENTRANCE	FLOOR	DAILY RATES
					S - D (EP)
A	1K	Shd*	Main	1	$65 ($15)
B	1Q	Shd*	Main	1	$65 ($15)
C	1K	Pvt	Main	1	$70 ($15)
D	2T or 1K	Pvt	Sep	LL	$65 ($15)

Youngberg Hill Farm   **(503) 472-2727**
10660 Youngberg Hill Road, McMinnville, OR 97128
(Yamhill County wine region)

An awesome sight from the valley below, this imposing Victorian-style home offers guests an elegant haven with a separate entrance and its own common rooms and porches. Perched at the apex of a 700-acre farm, it overlooks vineyards, grazing sheep, forestlands, valley, and mountains, with amazing views from every room. Lovely turn-of-the-century details grace the interior and modern amenities make life extra comfortable for guests. Two of the spacious, tastefully furnished bedrooms have fireplaces. Hosts Norm and Eve Barnett, whose own quarters are on the other side of the house, provide special opportunities such as perusing their "winelovers cellar" and feasting on individually prepared dinners on selected evenings. Youngberg Hill Farm is, quite simply, a place you will never forget.

No pets or smoking; children over ten welcome; hearty farm breakfast; TV room; AC; walking trails on property; credit cards (V, MC); wheelchair access to Room A. $65 midweek rate; inquire about hunting season specials. Brochure available.

ROOM	BED	BATH	ENTRANCE	FLOOR	DAILY RATES	
					S - D	(EP)
A	1Q	Pvt	Main	1	$70-$75	
B	1Q	Pvt	Main	2	$70-$75	
C	1Q	Pvt	Main	2	$70-$75	
D	1Q	Pvt	Main	2	$70-$75	($25)
E	1Q	Pvt	Main	2	$70-$75	

Sonka's Sheep Station Inn (503) 863-5168
901 NW Chadwick Lane, Myrtle Creek, OR 97457
(West of I-5 and town of Myrtle Creek)

Sparkling fresh air, vivid green pastures, and the ever-changing beauty of stately trees mark the idyllic setting of the 360-acre working ranch surrounding Sonka's Sheep Station Inn. Outside pressures melt away as one settles into the tempo of ranch life, which can be thoroughly relaxing or busy with activities such as lambing, watching border collies herd flocks of sheep, or walking along the South Umpquah River. Louis and Evelyn Sonka sampled ranch homestays in New Zealand and decided to share similar experiences with guests at their own ranch. Accommodations have a country flavor, with sheepy accents throughout the decor. There are two rooms in the main house and a separate three-bedroom guest house. Hearty breakfasts are served, as are elegant dinners featuring locally raised foods. Authentic, rural hospitality doesn't get any better than this.

No pets; smoking outside only; full breakfast; credit cards (V, MC); airport pickup (Tri City). Brochure of this and other rural B&Bs available. Guest House = Rooms C, D, and E.

ROOM	BED	BATH	ENTRANCE	FLOOR	DAILY RATES S - D (EP)
A	1Q	Shd*	Main	2	$60
B	1D	Shd*	Main	2	$50
C	1Q	Pvt	Sep	1	$60
D	2T				$50
E	1D				$50

Secluded Bed & Breakfast   (503) 538-2635
19719 NE Williamson Road, Newberg, OR 97132
(Yamhill County wine region)

Oregon's growing stature as a wine-producing state is enhanced by a visit to its premier grape-growing region in Yamhill County. Whether you're making a quick stop between Portland and the coast or staying long enough to savor the fruits of the vine, Secluded Bed & Breakfast is an ideal stop. It's a woodsy retreat with quiet, natural surroundings and abundant seasonal wildlife.   Del and Durell Belanger are long-time residents of the county. Among other things, Durell is a skilled violin maker and Del a fabulous cook. They know some excellent places to send you for dinner, and later you'll have a great sleep in wonderful country silence.

No pets; smoking outside only; full breakfast; living room with fireplace, TV, VCR; AC; off-street parking; airport pickup (Newberg, McMinnville). Master suite with queen bed, private bath, and balcony available on request at $50; Master suite with shared bath, $45 on request. Brochure available.

ROOM	BED	BATH	ENTRANCE	FLOOR	DAILY RATES S - D (EP)
A	1D	Shd*	Main	2	$40
B	1D	Shd*	Main	2	$40

Springbrook Farm   **(503) 538-4606**
30295 North Highway 99 W, Newberg, OR 97132
(Yamhill County wine region)

Long maintained as a hazelnut farm, this orchard estate dates from 1912. Here a beautifully restored Carriage House offers delicious privacy in a landscape of mammoth old trees, a trout pond, gardens, orchard, meadow, and the adjoining Rex Hill Winery. Consisting of a spacious living room, a dining area, a wonderful kitchen, a romantic bedroom, and a bath, the attractive interior is graced with many Craftsman details, antiques, Oriental carpets, and a fresh, uncluttered look. The main house is a Crafstman-style dwelling of grand proportions, its interior alive with color, light, and art. In the guest wing, there are two ample bedrooms, both tasteful creations in cream and dark green, and a large bathroom off the hallway. The sitting room at the back of this wing is a delightful haven with lots of windows and heavenly country views.

No pets; infants allowed by arrangement; full breakfast; no smoking; AC; tennis courts and swimming pool on property; canoeing in pond; hot air ballooning at Rex Hill Winery; Spanish spoken. Weekly rate in Carriage House, $600. Brochure available.

ROOM	BED	BATH	ENTRANCE	FLOOR	DAILY RATES S - D (EP)
A	1Q	Pvt	Sep	2	$100 ($10)
B	1Q	Shd*	Main	2	$75
C	1Q	Shd*	Main	2	$75

Spring Creek Llama Ranch and Bed & Breakfast (503) 538-5717
14700 NE Spring Creek Lane, Newberg, OR 97132
(Yamhill County wine region)

Not far off the beaten path but seeming to be worlds away, Spring Creek Llama Ranch is set at the dead end of a private road on twenty-four acres of garden, field, and forest. Bed and breakfast takes place in a spacious contemporary home with cathedral ceilings and huge windows offering a feast of greenery. In this fresh atmosphere, enjoy a morning meal of home-baked treats and seasonal produce from the garden. A restful night is assured in one of two rooms: Spring Meadow, done in cheerful pastels and animal prints, or Red Cloud, a autumn-hued room with a large window overlooking a bank of fern, rhododendron, Douglas fir, and willow. Outside in the barn complex and yard, make friends with some of the Van Bossuyt family's llamas. It's easy to become totally enchanted while taking a guided Llama Walk along winding pathways through evergreen forest. You may even get to meet Red Cloud.

No pets, except other llamas; children welcome; no smoking; full breakfast; TV available; AC; patio; wineries, restaurants, antique shops, George Fox College, Champoeg State Park, and more nearby. Red Cloud Suite has two bedrooms (1Q & 2T) and a bath; 3 adults, $95; 4 adults, $105; inquire about family rates. Brochure available.

ROOM	BED	BATH	ENTRANCE	FLOOR	DAILY RATES S - D (EP)	
A	1D	Pvt	Main	1	$50	
B	1Q	Pvt	Main	2	$65	($20)

The Highlands   **(503) 756-0300**
608 Ridge Road, North Bend, OR 97459
(North of Coos Bay; five miles east of U.S. 101)

Here's a stunning, architecturally designed cedar home situated at a high elevation with a dramatic perspective of Haynes Inlet and the Oregon coastal range. But that's just for starters. Guests of Marilyn and Jim Dow are given the entire ground floor which includes a large, fully equipped kitchen, a spacious family room with a woodstove and a fantastic view, and two bedrooms with private baths (one with a whirlpool tub). Tasteful country furnishings have been well put together to impart a warm, homey, comforting feeling. The view alone might hold your attention, but there's also a TV and VCR for entertainment. Anglers shouldn't miss fishing for steelhead in the inlet below. The huge wrap-around deck is a fine place to sit and enjoy clean, fresh air and absolute serenity. A romantic Hot Springs spa on a secluded private deck makes a perfect ending to a busy day. Consider The Highlands a home base while you explore the area or a retreat to settle into for a while. It's a winner either way.

No pets; no children under ten; smoking outside only; full breakfast; day bed extra in Room A; goldfish pond on property; off-street parking; credit cards (V, MC); wheelchair access. Brochure available.

ROOM	BED	BATH	ENTRANCE	FLOOR	DAILY RATES S - D (EP)
A	1D	Pvt	Sep	1G	$63-$68 ($10)
B	1D	Pvt	Sep	1G	$58-$63

Jagger House Bed & Breakfast   **(503) 657-7820**
512 Sixth Street, Oregon City, OR 97045
(Just southeast of Portland, convenient to I-5 and I-205)

Here at the "official end of the Oregon Trail," you can soak up some history while enjoying the hospitable spirit, beautiful rooms, and extra privacy afforded by Jagger House. Owner Claire Met, who lives next door, is devoted to historic preservation and to making her guests feel at home. The house was built around 1880 in the Vernacular style. Inside, it's a study in American primitive coziness -- muslin or lace window coverings, colonial blues and reds, old pine pieces, stenciling, hand-dipped candles, old quilts, spongeware dishes -- and every detail is perfectly coordinated. The flavor of each guest room is summed up in its name: Garden Delight, Victorian Rose, and Country Charm. In the yard you'll find a romantic little picnic table under an arbor, wooden lawn chairs, and country gardens. Savor a quiet escape in heartwarming surroundings at Jagger House.

Children over twelve welcome; smoking outside only; full breakfast; guest telephone; museums, antique shops, historical walking tours nearby; bus transportation nearby; off-street parking; credit cards (V, MC); airport pickup by arrangement (Portland International). Brochure available.

ROOM	BED	BATH	ENTRANCE	FLOOR	DAILY RATES S - D (EP) +
A	1Q	Pvt	Sep	1	$60
B	1Q	Shd*	Main	2	$60
C	1Q & 1T	Shd*	Main	2	$55 ($10)

The Clinkerbrick House   **(503) 281-2533**
2311 NE Schuyler, Portland, OR 97212
(Near Lloyd Center, Convention Center, Memorial Coliseum)

In a quiet residential neighborhood just minutes from downtown Portland, discover the warm country comfort of The Clinkerbrick House. The 1908 Dutch Colonial offers all the pleasures of a welcoming, family environment, along with an extra measure of privacy for guests: a separate outside entrance, allowing one to come and go freely. The second-floor accommodations include a full kitchen/TV room and three spacious bedrooms. On the door of each room is a decoration hinting at the perfectly executed theme within. The Garden Room has a private bath, a small deck, and a botanical flavor. The Strawberry Room, with antiques and stenciled walls, shares a bath off the hallway with The Rose Room, a romantic haven done in pink roses and white wicker. Delicious full breakfasts are served in the bright, cheerful dining room. For the traveler who likes feeling independent and pampered at the same time, hosts Bob and Peggie Irvine have created the unique hospitality of The Clinkerbrick House.

No pets or smoking; full breakfast (special dietary needs accommodated); rollaway bed, $15; good area for walking or jogging; good public transportation; street and off-street parking; credit cards (V, MC). Brochure available.

ROOM	BED	BATH	ENTRANCE	FLOOR	DAILY RATES S - D (EP) +
A	1Q	Pvt	Sep	2	$50-$60
B	1Q	Shd*	Sep	2	$40-$50
C	1Q & 1T	Shd*	Sep	2	$40-$50 ($15)

187

Georgian House Bed & Breakfast (503) 281-2250
1828 NE Siskiyou, Portland, OR 97212
(Near Lloyd Center, Convention Center, and Coliseum)

Portland has only three true Georgian Colonial homes; one of them is Georgian House Bed & Breakfast. This authentic beauty, built in 1922, is red brick with white columns and dark blue shutters. It stands on a double corner lot in a fine, old, northeast Portland neighborhood. Proud owners Willie and Mike Ackley have expertly restored the home in its every exquisite detail. The tasteful use of interior colors serves to enhance classic features such as leaded glass windows, built-in china cabinets, heavy mouldings, oak floors, a sun porch, and a fireplace. A graceful stairway leads to the second-floor guest quarters. Each of the antique-furnished bedrooms, the East Lake and the Pettygrove, is a singularly charming creation. The romantic Lovejoy Suite is a light, spacious bed/sitting room with a canopy bed, French windows, a color TV, a ceiling fan, and a view of the lovely grounds. A wide deck and gazebo overlooking the backyard gardens has been added; lingering over breakfast here is indeed a pleasure -- one of many you'll experience at Georgian House.

No pets; children welcome; smoking outside only; full breakfast; TV/VCR in common area; robes provided; crib available; extra-long beds in Room B; guest rooms share one and one-half baths off hallway; good public transportation; train and airport connections; street and off-street parking; credit cards (V, MC). Brochure available.

ROOM	BED	BATH	ENTRANCE	FLOOR	DAILY RATES S - D (EP) +
A	1Q	Shd*	Main	2	$50-$65
B	2T or 1K	Shd*	Main	2	$50-$65
C	1Q	Shd*	Main	2	$50-$65

Hartman's Hearth   (503) 281-2210
2937 NE Twentieth Avenue, Portland, OR 97212
(Near Lloyd Center, Convention Center, Memorial Coliseum)

Christopher and Katie Hartman have made their home in a hand-some 1911 arts and crafts period house. It's in one of Portland's prettiest and most convenient intown neighborhoods, marked by stately shade trees and well-cared-for yards that burgeon with flowers in the spring. In cooler months, guests succumb to the lure of the hearth, the focal point of the living room. Throughout the interior, fabrics, colors, and textures are combined with an eclectic mix of antiques, traditional pieces, and contemporary art. Two guest rooms on the second floor derive their color schemes from subtle floral motifs. The suite comprising the third floor strikes a surprisingly different mood. Sleek and sophisticated, it has a muted art deco look. Tones of mauve and rose are used with grey and black in the huge space, which boasts a king-sized canopy bed, a black lacquered desk, and a bathroom with delightfully intricate tilework. Much thought has been given to the aesthetics of decor, lighting, music, and cuisine at Hartman's Hearth, making it a dream of a place to stay.

Three cats in residence; no pets; smoking restricted; no RV parking; full breakfast (special dietary needs accommodated); TV room with VCR; TV and AC in Room C; robes provided; sauna; spa; good area for walking or jogging; good public transportation; airport connections; off-street parking; all major credit cards. Brochure available.

ROOM	BED	BATH	ENTRANCE	FLOOR	DAILY RATES
					S - D (EP) +
A	2T	Shd*	Main	2	$45-$50
B	1Q	Shd*	Main	2	$50
C	1K	Pvt	Main	3	$70 ($10)

Portland Guest House   **(503) 282-1402**
1720 NE Fifteenth Avenue, Portland, OR 97212
(Closest B&B to Lloyd Center, Convention Center, and Coliseum)

An 1890 Victorian renovated with conspicuous care, Portland Guest House accommodates travelers who appreciate the historical sense it conveys, the many conveniences and comforts it offers, and the aesthetic pleasures of its decor. Innkeeper Susan Gisvold welcomes guests to enjoy the parlor, the dining room, and the garden. The interior is fresh, light, and airy, with plenty of white and discreet accents of mauve, gray, rose, and blue. Floral designs and tapestries share space with wonderful, carefully chosen art and antiques. Outfitted with heirloom linens, the guest rooms are especially appealing. There is a spacious family accommodation on the home's lower level, and the two rooms with a shared bath have private balconies.

No pets; children in family room only; smoking outside only; full breakfast; limited kitchen privileges; private phone in each room; FAX service, shopping, dining, and light rail service nearby; bus stop at the corner; off-street parking; major credit cards. Brochure available.

ROOM	BED	BATH	ENTRANCE	FLOOR	DAILY RATES	
					S - D	(EP) +
A	2T & 1Q	Pvt	Main	LL	$75	($10)
B	1D	Pvt	Main	2	$55-$60	
C	1Q	Pvt	Main	2	$55-$60	
D	1Q	Shd*	Main	2	$45-$50	
E	1D	Shd*	Main	2	$45-$50	

Gwendolyn's Bed & Breakfast (503) 332-4373
P.O. Box 913, Port Orford, OR 97465
(735 Oregon Street at coast highway - U.S.101)

In the quaint little fishing village of Port Orford, Gwendolyn's is a lavender bungalow guest house with four delightful bedrooms and lots of personality. Step inside and you'll be taken back to the magic and color of the twenties. Gwendolyn's is filled with vintage furniture, lace curtains, watercolor paintings, and hand-blown glass vases done by local artists. Restaurants are within walking distance and the beach and dock are only a block away. Port Orford is known for its wild rivers and its rugged, unspoiled ocean beaches. In the evening, sit by a warm fire in the parlor. Next morning, wake up to a country-style breakfast of crab or salmon quiche and fresh, locally-grown berries. Gwendolyn can guide you to the wealth of outdoor wonders and seasonal activities close by.

Cable TV; telephone; crab or salmon tasting in season; off-street parking; credit cards (V, MC); airport pickup (Cape Blanco).

ROOM	BED	BATH	ENTRANCE	FLOOR	DAILY RATES	
					S - D	(EP) +
A	1D	Pvt	Main	1	$45-$55	($10)
B	1D	Shd*	Main	2	$35-$45	($10)
C	2T	Shd*	Main	2	$35-$45	($10)
D	1Q	Pvt	Main	1	$55	($10)

HOME by the SEA   **(503) 332-2855**
P.O. Box 606-K, Port Orford, OR 97465
(444 Jackson Street)

Alan and Brenda Mitchell built their contemporary wood home on a spit of land overlooking a stretch of Oregon coast that could take your breath away. The arresting view may be enjoyed from both lovely bedrooms and from the Sunspace where the Mitchells get to know their guests. Queen-sized Oregon Myrtlewood beds and cable TV are featured in both accommodations, which make ideal quarters for two couples traveling together. It's a short walk to restaurants, public beaches, historic Battle Rock Park, and the town's harbor -- the home port of Oregon's only crane-launched commercial fishing fleet. Port Orford is a favorite of windsurfers as well of whale, bird, and storm watchers. It's an enchanting discovery, and so is HOME by the SEA.

No pets, children, or smoking; full breakfast; cable TV; laundry privileges; phone jacks in rooms; off-street parking; credit cards (V, MC).

ROOM	BED	BATH	ENTRANCE	FLOOR	DAILY RATES
					S - D (EP) +
A	1Q	Pvt	Main	2	$70 ($10)
B	1Q	Pvt	Main	2	$60

House of Hunter (503) 672-2335
813 SE Kane Street, Roseburg, OR 97470
(Bordering downtown Roseburg)

On a quiet residential street in the company of other historic
homes, House of Hunter is a classic Italianate built at the turn of the
century. In 1990 Walt and Jean Hunter made extensive renovations,
preserving the home's essential character while adding modern attrib-
utes to enhance its ease and comfort, resulting in a light, airy,
expansive atmosphere. The lovely guest rooms, each named for one
of the hosts' daughters, feature English wardrobe closets, hand-made
quilts, and antique accents. Inspired by their own B&B travels, the
Hunters offer their guests such treats as early morning coffee and
goodies delivered to the second floor alcove, followed by a full
breakfast served in the dining room. A warm welcome is always yours
at House of Hunter.

No pets; children over twelve welcome; smoking outside only; AC;
full breakfast; TV/VCR; laundry facilities; walk to downtown shops,
restaurants, and churches; off-street parking; airport shuttle (Roseburg). Brochure available.

ROOM	BED	BATH	ENTRANCE	FLOOR	DAILY RATES	
					S - D	(EP) +
A	1Q	Pvt	Main	2	$60-$65	($15)
B	1Q	Pvt	Main	2	$60-$65	($15)
C	2T	Shd*	Main	2	$45-$50	
D	1D	Shd*	Main	2	$45-$50	

Summer House
1221 North Franklin, Seaside, OR 97138
(North end of Seaside, one block from beach)

(503) 738-5740
1-800-745-BEST

In bustling Seaside, quiet is a luxury. A tranquil environment is one of the many assets of Summer House, a completely renovated vacation home with a history of beachside hospitality. It has a gray-shingled exterior, ample decking, and latticed and trellised garden areas burgeoning with flowers and vegetables. The interior is clean and modern with plenty of natural light and a subtle Southwest flavor. The Garden Room, a romantic haven on the main level, features a fireplace, a sitting area, a small refrigerator, and a TV. Other lovely rooms express different themes: Seashell, Sunset, and Whispering Seas. Host Jerry Newsome's breakfast cuisine is the essence of fresh-from-the-garden goodness. He and his wife, Leslee, provide superb, year-round hospitality at Summer House.

Dog in residence; no pets, children, or teenagers; no smoking; full breakfast; shopping, dining, ocean and river activities, beachcombing, whale and birdwatching, golfing, horseback riding, and more nearby; off-street parking; credit cards (V, MC). Weekend, holiday minimums. Brochure available.

ROOM	BED	BATH	ENTRANCE	FLOOR	DAILY RATES S - D (EP) +
A	1Q	Pvt	Main	1	$55
B	1Q	Pvt	Main	1	$75
C	1Q	Pvt	Main	2	$55
D	1Q	Pvt	Main	2	$55

Blue Haven Inn   **(503) 842-2265**
3025 Gienger Road, Tillamook, OR 97141
(South of town center, west of U.S. 101)

    Several attributes of the Tillamook area vie for first-place in my mind: some of the best oysters on the West Coast, the locally made cheeses, access to the remarkable Three Capes Loop of the Oregon coast, and the bucolic farmland scenery. A great place to stay while savoring these pleasures is Blue Haven Inn, a fully refurbished country home on two acres, with a healthy green lawn and a split-rail fence. Generously proportioned, somewhat formal common rooms have a light, open feeling and convey a sense of true welcome. Themes for the guest rooms -- Tara, Of the Sea, and La Femme -- are derived from the limited edition collectors' plates adorning the walls. Selected antiques and collectibles augment the home's decor. Guests at Blue Haven Inn enjoy sumptuous breakfasts in the dining room, leisure moments in the front porch swing, and the all-around gracious hospitality extended by hosts Joy and Ray Still.

    No pets; smoking outside only; full breakfast; fireplace and TV/VCR available; six miles to ocean; cheese factory, waterfalls, historic lighthouse, and more nearby; off-road parking. Brochure available.

ROOM	BED	BATH	ENTRANCE	FLOOR	DAILY RATES S - D (EP)
A	1Q	Pvt	Main	2	$60
B	1Q	Shd*	Main	2	$50
C	1D	Shd*	Main	2	$50

Walden House (503) 655-4960
P.O. Box 593, West Linn, OR 97068
(Just southeast of Portland, convenient to I-5 and I-205)

Located in the historic Willamette Falls area, this Queen Anne
Stick Victorian is surrounded by country gardens replete with flowers
and shrubs. In this friendly neighborhood of many beautifully restored turn-of-the-century dwellings, the home of Charles and Diane
Awalt is a National Register property of utmost authenticity. Furnishings were selected with care to suit the era and scale of the house.
Victorian colors predominate in an atmosphere of warm, polished
redwood and fir, stained glass, mouldings, and wainscoting with
wallpaper. The dining room has a marvelous garden view, a fitting
place for breakfast prepared with a gourmet's touch. Vintage table
and bed linens are used, and every room displays interesting collectibles. A large bath off the hallway features a long, deep clawfoot tub
and a lovely old braided rug. Relax on the wide veranda, in the
library, or in your carefully tailored bedroom. Walden House brings
the past to life as few places do.

Cats in residence; no pets; no young children; full breakfast; robes
provided; antiquing and river canoeing nearby; ample street parking.
Brochure available. *custom mattresses measuring 76" x 40"

ROOM	BED	BATH	ENTRANCE	FLOOR	DAILY RATES S - D (EP)
A	2T*	Shd	Main	2	$55-$60
B	1D	Shd	Main	2	$55-$60

The Willows Bed & Breakfast   (503) 638-3722

5025 SW Homesteader Road, Wilsonville, OR 97070
(Fifteen miles south of Portland, two miles east of I-5)

There's a gem of a bed and breakfast in the idyllic countryside just twenty minutes south of Portland. The historic Wilsonville area is marked by vast rolling hills, an assortment of crops and livestock, quaint old barns, and country roads. David and Shirlee Key have made their home on two gorgeous acres. The velvety lawn and luxuriant gardens are maintained to perfection, a creek crossed by two bridges meanders through the property, and one of the huge weeping willows supports a charming old wooden swing. This beauty is matched only by the gracious interior of the Keys' modern home. Guests have all to themselves a full garden-level suite with its own entrance. Like the rest of the house, it is furnished with utmost care. The larger bedroom features a brass bed, antiques, and an exquisite handmade quilt fashioned by Shirlee. A smaller bedroom has two good twin beds. There is a spacious living/dining area with a TV, desk, and phone. A handy refrigerator and beverage-brewing area are included in the bathroom. The standards of quality, hospitality, and value found at The Willows are simply unsurpassed.

No pets; children over twelve welcome; smoking outside only; full breakfast; AC; hosts recommend side trip to historic Aurora Colony; off-street parking. Brochure available.

ROOM	BED	BATH	ENTRANCE	FLOOR	DAILY RATES S - D (EP)
A	1Q & 2T	Pvt	Sep	LL	$45-$55 ($15)

Ziggurat Bed & Breakfast   **(503) 547-3925**
95330 Highway 101, Yachats, OR 97498
(Central Oregon coast, 6.5 miles south of Yachats)

Many coast aficionados would pick this unspoiled stretch of ocean wilderness near Cape Perpetua as an endless source of riches to explore. Here, with immediate beach access just thirty yards away, stands Ziggurat, true to its ancient Sumerian meaning, "terraced pyramid." A dwelling unique in every sense, its ambiance combines supreme comfort, constant communion with nature, fine contemporary art, and the most civilized hospitality imaginable. A first-floor guest suite has two beautiful bedrooms, a bath and a sauna off the hallway, an inviting library/living room, and a tiled solarium where one may sit with an ocean view. In the expansive second-floor dining area, relish the view along with full breakfasts featuring homemade breads. At the apex of the pyramid with windows on all sides is a superlative guest room one must see to believe. The same could be said of Ziggurat as a whole.

No pets; no children under fourteen; smoking outside only; full breakfast; decks; hiking, fishing, birding, tidepooling, and more nearby; off-street parking. Rate for whole suite, $110 for two, plus $15 EP up to five. Brochure available.

ROOM	BED	BATH	ENTRANCE	FLOOR	DAILY RATES
					S - D (EP) +
A	1Q	Shd*	Main	1	$65-$75
B	1Q	Shd*	Main	1	$65-$75
C	1Q	Pvt	Main	4	$75-$85

Please read "About Dining Highlights" on page *vii*.

ASHLAND

Alex's Plaza Restaurant, 35 North Main Street; (503) 432-8818; varied menu/ historic setting overlooking plaza/balcony seating/fireplace

New Sammy's Cowboy Bistro, 2210 South Pacific Highway, Talent; (503) 535-2779; country French

North Light Natural, 120 East Main Street; (503) 482-9463; vegetarian/ Oriental sautees to tofu delights

Thai Pepper, 84 North Main Street; (503) 482-8058

Winchester Country Inn, 35 South Second Street; (503) 488-1113; international fare/historic 1886 home overlooking gardens

BANDON

Bandon Boat Works, South Jetty; (503) 347-2111; seafood

Bandon Fish Market, Bandon Boat Basin; (503) 347-4282; seafood

BROOKINGS

Mama's Authentic Italian Food, 703 Chetco Avenue (U.S. 101); (503) 469-7611; southern Italian

Plum Pudding, 1011 Chetco Avenue (U.S. 101); no phone; homemade lunches

CANNON BEACH

Bistro Restaurant & Bar, 263 North Hemlock Street; (503) 436-2661; Northwest eclectic

Cafe de la Mer, 1287 South Hemlock Street; (503) 436-1179; Northwest/French

COOS BAY

Blue Heron Bistro, 100 Commercial; (503) 267-3933; Continental

COTTAGE GROVE

The Covered Bridge, 401 Main Street; (503) 942-1255; Continental/Italian

Thee Delicatessen Restaurant, 1435 Highway 99; (503) 942-4405; European

EUGENE

Ambrosia, 174 East Broadway; (503) 342-4141; fine Italian cuisine

Cafe Central, 384 West Thirteenth Street; (503) 343-9510; Northwest

Chanterelle, 207 East Fifth Street; (503) 484-4065; fresh fish/pasta

The Excelsior Cafe, 754 East Thirteenth Avenue; (503) 342-6963; nouvelle Northwest

The French Horn Cafe & Bakery, in L&L Market at 1591 Willamette, downtown Eugene; (503) 343-7473; soups/breads/takeout items

Jamie's Great Hamburgers, 2445 Hilyard; (503) 343-8488

L'Auberge, 770 West Sixth Street; (503) 485-8000; French regional

Mazzi's, 3377 East Amazon; (503) 687-2252; casual Italian

Mediterranean Cafe, 412 Pearl Street; (503) 342-8411; Middle Eastern

Oregon Electric Station, 27 East Fifth Street; (503) 485-4444; prime rib/seafood

Scampi's by Chef Don, 388 West Seventh Avenue; (503) 485-0601; international/live jazz on weekends

Zenon Cafe, 898 Pearl Street; (503) 343-3005; international/great desserts

GOLD BEACH

The Nor'Wester, Harbor at the Port of Gold Beach; (503) 247-2333; seafood

Port Hole Cafe, Port of Gold Beach; (503) 247-7411; breakfast/lunch/dinner; sandwiches/chowder/fish/pies

Rod 'N Reel, west of U.S. 101 at end of bridge, Wedderburn; (503) 247-6823; seafood/Continental

GRANTS PASS

Bistro, 1214 NW Sixth Street; (503) 479-3412

Buzz's Blue Heron Dinner Theater, 330 Merlin Avenue; (503) 479-6604

Hamilton House, 344 NE Terry Lane; (503) 479-3938; seafood/pasta/fowl/beef

Maria's Mexican Kitchen, 105 NE Mill Street; (503) 474-2429

Matsukaze, 1675 NE Seventh Street; (503) 479-2961; Japanese

Paradise Ranch Inn, 7000 Monument Drive; (503) 479-4333; Continental

Pongsri's, 1571 NE Sixth Street; (503) 479-1345; Thai

R-Haus Restaurant & Bistro, 2140 Rogue River Highway; (503) 476-4287

JACKSONVILLE

Jacksonville Inn Dinner House, 175 East California Street; (503) 899-1900; Continental/Northwest

McCully House Inn Restaurant, 240 East California Street; (503) 599-1942; creative American/historic home atmosphere

LAKE OSWEGO

Amadeus, Second and B Streets; (503) 636-7500; Continental

Le Lebon, 455 SW Second Street; (503) 697-1900; Lebanese

LINCOLN CITY

Bay House, 5911 SW Highway 101; (503) 996-3222; Continental/seafood

Dory Cove, 5819 Logan Road; (503) 994-5180; clam chowder/seafood

Kernville Steak & Seafood House, 186 Siletz Highway; (503) 994-6200

Kyllo's Seafood & Broiler, 2733 NW Highway 101; (503) 994-3179

Otis Cafe, Highway 18 at Otis Junction; (503) 994-2813; old-fashioned country

MC MINNVILLE

Augustine's, Highway 18; (503) 843-3225; Continental

Nick's Italian Cafe, 521 East Third Street; (503) 434-4471

Roger's Seafood Restaurant, 2121 East 27th Street; (503) 472-0917

Sir Hinkleman Funnyduffer Cafe, Wine & Antiques, 421 East Third Street; (503) 472-1309; picnics/lunch/catering

Umberto's, 828 North Adams Street; (503) 472-1717; traditional Italian

NEWBERG

Bahngaow's Newberg Inn, 2320 Portland Road; (503) 538-6637; Thai

Pasquale's Italian Restaurant, 111 West First Street; (503) 538-0910

NORTH BEND

Hilltop House Restaurant, 166 North Bay Drive; (503) 756-4160; seafood/steaks

OCEANSIDE

Roseanna's Oceanside Cafe, 1490 Pacific NW; (503) 842-7351; seafood/pasta

OREGON CITY

Fellows House, 416 South McLoughlin Boulevard; (503) 650-9322; lunch

La Hacienda, 76 Oregon City Shopping Center; (503) 656-2210; Mexican

PORTLAND

Alexis, 215 West Burnside Street; (503) 224-8577; Greek

Bread & Ink Cafe, 3610 SE Hawthorne Boulevard; (503) 239-4756; Continental

Cafe des Amis, 1987 NW Kearney Street; (503) 295-6487; lighter French/Continental

Elizabeth's Cafe, 3135 NE Broadway; (503) 281-8337; Continental

Genoa, 2832 SE Belmont Street; (503) 238-1464; fine Italian cuisine

Heathman Bakery & Pub, 901 SW Salmon; (503) 227-5700; designer pizza/brewpub

Indigine, 3723 SE Division Street; (503) 238-1470; Asian

Jake's Famous Crawfish, 401 SW Twelfth ; (503) 226-1419; Northwest seafood

Metropolis Cafe, 2015 NE Broadway; (503) 281-7701; European bistro

Old Wives Tales, 1300 East Burnside; (503) 238-0470; vegetarian/eclectic ethnic dishes

Papa Haydn, 5829 SE Milwaukie; (503) 232-9440; killer desserts

Winterborne, 3520 NE 42nd; (503) 249-8486; intimate dining/fine seafood

PORT ORFORD

The Silver Door, Sixth and Jackson Streets on U.S. 101; (503) 332-9885; lunches/homemade pies

Whale Cove Restaurant, U.S. 101 opposite Battle Rock Park; (503) 332-7575; Continental/seafood

SEAL ROCK

Yuzen Japanese, Highway 101; (503) 563-4766

SEASIDE

Christiano's Mexican & Seafood Specialties, 412 Broadway; (503) 738-5058

Emmanuel's Restaurant, 104 Broadway; (503) 738-7038; light Italian plus

TUALATIN

Rich's Restaurant, 18810 SW Boones Ferry Road; (503) 692-1460; seasonal bistro menu

WEST LINN

Bistro, 18740 Willamette Drive; (503) 636-9555; simple bistro dinners

YACHATS

La Serre, Second and Beach Streets; (503) 547-3420; breakfast/lunch/dinner; fresh fish/pasta/chicken/small to ample meals

I never travel without my diary. One should always have something sensational to read in the train.

—Oscar Wilde

How each friend represents a world in us, a world possibly not born until they arrive, and it is only by this meeting that a new world is born.

—Anaïs Nin

WASHINGTON

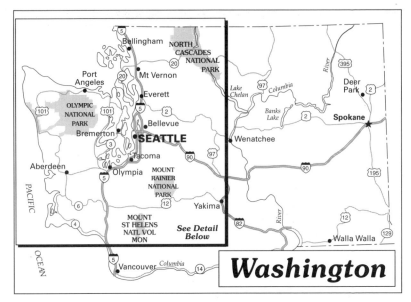

Washington

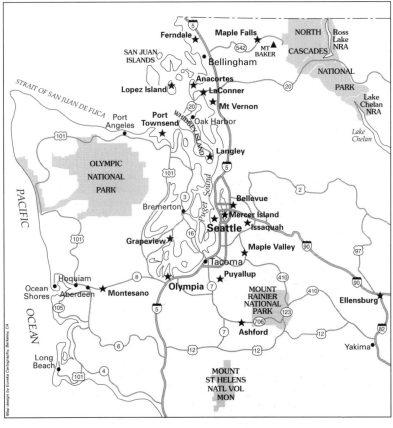

Albatross Bed & Breakfast (206) 293-0677
5708 Kingsway West, Anacortes, WA 98221
(Across from Skyline Marina on Fidalgo Island)

When this home was built in the twenties, almost at water's edge, it was well constructed of solid cedar and survives today as a gracious haven of hospitality. Cecil and Marilyn Short's Albatross Bed & Breakfast provides excellent views of the boat launch area, the sea, and the San Juan Islands. Each comfortable, commodious guest room has a bath, an original painting, a unique piece of needlework, a lap blanket, thick carpeting, and a quiet, restful atmosphere. There is a vast selection of books and games, and a spacious living room offers a fireplace, a TV/VCR, and an inspiring panorama. The Shorts do everything possible to ensure a pleasant stay for their guests, who appreciate especially the made-from-scratch breakfasts featuring local flavors. A sincere welcome and an array of thoughtful extras make staying here a rich experience indeed.

Cats in residence; smoking outside only; full breakfast; recreational opportunities, travel information available; transportation to ferries (one mile away); off-street parking; Spanish, French spoken. Winter rates. Brochure available.

ROOM	BED	BATH	ENTRANCE	FLOOR	DAILY RATES	
					S - D	(EP) +
A	1Q	Pvt	Main	1	$67-$72	($20)
B	1K	Pvt	Main	1	$67-$72	
C	1K	Pvt	Main	1	$67-$72	
D	1Q	Pvt	Main	1	$67-$72	($20)

Channel House   **(206) 293-9382**
2902 Oakes Avenue, Anacortes, WA 98221
(Overlooking Guemes Channel, five minutes from ferry docks)

Channel House is a joyous discovery for anyone traveling to this corner of the country. It's a home of unusual character; every guest room is uniquely situated for gazing out at the channel and the San Juan Islands. Shiny wood floors with Oriental rugs, fine antique furnishings, a library, and three fireplaces create an atmosphere of classic European elegance. Owners since 1986, Pat and Dennis McIntyre have preserved the flavor of the house while adding their own touches to make it their family home. Hosts are former restaurateurs who take pride in the quality and variety of the breakfasts they serve, usually before a crackling fire. Rooms E and F are in the Rose Cottage, adjacent to main house; the individually decorated quarters feature fireplaces and private baths with whirlpool tubs. A memorable treat for guests is outdoor hot-tubbing with a view of island sunsets. All in all, staying at Channel House is an experience to be savored.

No pets; children over twelve OK; no smoking; full breakfast; evening refreshments; off-street parking; credit cards (V, MC, D); ferry pickup. Off-season rates are $10 less. Brochure available.

ROOM	BED	BATH	ENTRANCE	FLOOR	DAILY RATES	
					S - D	(EP) +
A	1D & 2T	Pvt	Main	2	$69-$79	($20)
B	1Q	Pvt	Main	2	$69-$79	
C	1D	Pvt	Main	1	$69-$79	
D	1D	Pvt	Main	1	$59-$69	
E	1Q	Pvt	Sep	1	$89	
F	1Q	Pvt	Sep	1	$89	

Hasty Pudding House   (206) 293-5773
1312 Eighth Street, Anacortes, WA 98221   1(800) 368-5588
(Walking distance to downtown)

There's something very comforting about an older, stable neigh-borhood where people can stroll the sidewalks, picnic in a park, or visit the local museum. In this kind of setting, how appropriate to find a large, friendly-looking home that welcomes bed and breakfast travelers. Mike and Melinda Hasty have devotedly restored each room in their turn-of-the-century home, building on its considerable charac-ter and adding tasteful antique pieces in just the right places. Melinda has quite an eye for color; she's created an interior imbued with the feeling of a warm spring day. The sun room where you enter sets the tone for the rest of the house. It's like being in the prettiest of gardens -- pure poetry, any time of year.

No pets; no children under seven; no smoking; full breakfast; living room with fireplace; street and off-street parking; credit cards (V, MC, AE, D); ferry and airport pickup (Anacortes). Information available on seven local day trips as well as hiking, kayaking, cycling, and fishing and boating charters.

ROOM	BED	BATH	ENTRANCE	FLOOR	DAILY RATES S - D	(EP) +
A	1Q	Pvt	Main	2	$55	
B	2T or 1K	Pvt	Main	2	$59	
C	1Q	Pvt	Main	2	$69	($15)
D	1K	Pvt	Main	2	$75	($15)

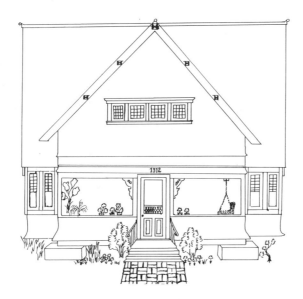

Old Brook Inn   **(206) 293-4768**
530 Old Brook Lane, Anacortes, WA 98221
(Off Route 20 West, four miles south of Anacortes)

At the end of a quiet country lane you'll find this gem of a home set amidst an ancient orchard. Old Brook Inn is Cape Cod in style, constructed of cedar and stone. The lush, nine-acre setting is replete with verdant trees and flowering plants; a babbling brook through the property and a delightful trout pond enhance the feeling of peace and tranquility. The interior is endowed with natural colors, striking artwork, and comfy places to sit and sleep. A light-infused room with a bay window on the first floor commands a lovely view of Fidalgo Bay. A huge second floor bed/sitting room that can sleep up to five people overlooks the ever-changing color and beauty of the orchard. You're welcome to pick your own strawberries, raspberries, and black-berries in season, or host Dick Ash will do it for you. You will undoubtedly find his home a gracious haven in the magical freshness of the country.

Cat in residence; living room, fireplace, and TV available to guests; off-street parking; credit cards (V, MC); airport pickup (Anacortes). Twin bed can be added to Room B.

ROOM	BED	BATH	ENTRANCE	FLOOR	DAILY RATES S - D (EP) +
A	1Q	Pvt	Main	1	$60
B	1Q & 2T	Pvt	Main	2	$70 ($10)

Growly Bear Bed & Breakfast   **(206) 569-2339**
37311 SR 706, Ashford, WA 98304
(One mile from entrance to Mount Rainier National Park)

Just before the park entrance to Mount Rainier National Park, an old wooden homestead house stands hidden by a shield of mammoth cedars. Old-growth cedar was used in the original 1890 building, which has undergone recent renovations. Susan Jenny has made it her home for many years and calls it and her nearby bakery Growly Bear. As rustic as its surroundings, the house offers three B&B rooms on the second floor, named after the original homesteaders, a nearby mountain peak, and a local river. The first two are cozy and cheery, sharing a bath off the hallway. The third is an expansive space with lots of windows, a sitting area with sofas, a private bath, and Growly Bear slippers in the closet! In each room, stuffed bears form a welcoming committee and a snack basket satisfies the munchies. Be lulled to sleep by the sound of Goat Creek, awake to the aroma of fresh bread from the nearby bakery ovens, and then enjoy the breakfast of your choice up the road at the Wild Berry Restaurant where tasty and fortifying meals are served.

No pets; children negotiable; no smoking; full breakfast; off-street parking; credit cards (V, MC, AE). Brochure available.

ROOM	BED	BATH	ENTRANCE	FLOOR	DAILY RATES S - D	(EP) +
A	1D	Shd*	Main	2	$50-$60	
B	1D	Shd*	Main	2	$50-$60	
C	1D	Pvt	Main	2	$70-$80	($15)

Jasmer's Guest House at Mount Rainier   **(206) 569-2682**
P.O. Box 347, Ashford, WA 98304
(Five miles from entrance to Mount Rainier National Park)

Tanna Barney-Osterhaus has transformed the one-time home of an old logging family, the Jasmers, into a guest house ideally suited for one guest couple at a time. The 500-square-foot attic floor has the original beadboard interior. The rich look of the wood, sloped ceilings, and lots of angles give the space a warm, romantic charm. A host of "rescued" mementoes from the early days at the foot of Mount Rainier offer myriad nostalgic images. A sitting area with a fireplace/woodstove adjoins an absolute love nest of a sleeping area. Tanna, who lives on the property with her husband, Luke, provides a luscious breakfast and all the information you could possibly need to make the most of your time at Mount Rainier. Lovely grounds and gardens include a spring-fed goldfish pond, burgeoning foliage and blossoms, and a pasture for Oscar, the llama. Jasmer's offers the perfect balance of pampering and privacy. It's a place to celebrate intimacy, historic surroundings, and nature all at the same time.

No pets; children over twelve welcome; smoking outside only; Continental plus breakfast; exclusive use of full kitchen and bathroom on main floor; off-street parking. Inquire about winter discounts.

ROOM	BED	BATH	ENTRANCE	FLOOR	DAILY RATES S - D (EP) +
A	1K & 1D	Pvt	Sep	2	$75 ($10)

Mountain Meadows Inn   **(206) 569-2788**
P.O. Box 291, Ashford, WA 98304
(Six miles from entrance to Mount Rainier National Park)

The enchantment of Mountain Meadows Inn starts the minute you turn off the main highway to the clearing where this 1910 Craftsman-style home stands in a meadow encircled by forest and country quiet. It overlooks a stream-fed pond edged with cattails. The sturdy, character-filled house features a kaleidoscope of heartwarming images and artistic touches. Host Chad Darrah, conductor on the Mount Rainier Scenic Railroad, displays a life-long collection of railroad paraphernalia. In 1991 he added two guest units (D and E) in a new building next door, and one has a full kitchen. Back at the main house, hearty breakfast fare is prepared on an old, wood-fired cook-stove. Other old-fashioned pleasures include gathering 'round the campfire in the evening, visiting on the wide front porch, or reading hearthside in the living room. The property is a magical place to explore, and, of course, the mountain beckons.

    Dog, cats, pigs, chickens, and ducks on property; no pets; children over ten welcome; no smoking in bedrooms; full breakfast; VCR in living room; player piano; pond has small dock, trout, and catfish; hiking trail to old National townsite; inquire about Scenic Railroad trips; off-street parking; credit cards (V, MC). Brochure available.

ROOM	BED	BATH	ENTRANCE	FLOOR	DAILY RATES S - D	(EP) +
A	1Q	Pvt	Main	1	$75	($15)
B	1K & 2T	Pvt	Main	1	$75	($15)
C	1Q	Pvt	Main	1	$75	($15)
D	1D & 1T	Pvt	Sep	2	$75	($15)
E	1D	Pvt	Sep	2	$75	($15)

Bellevue Bed & Breakfast   **(206) 453-1048**
830 - 100th Avenue SE, Bellevue, WA 98004
(Overlooking downtown Bellevue)

Cy and Carol Garnett make their home at the end of a dead-end street on a hillside overlooking city and mountains. It's convenient to freeways, but very quiet, and just a short walk from the east shore of Lake Washington. Guests have their own entrance on the lower level of the house, offering extra privacy for a family, two couples, or a group. The 1200-square-foot suite consists of a spacious living room with wide picture windows all around and a large cable TV, a full kitchen, two bedrooms with private baths, and a laundry room. The Garnetts are gracious, caring hosts who want people to feel comfortable in their home. Whatever you desire -- be it restful privacy, assistance with your plans, or conversation -- it can be easily arranged at Bellevue Bed & Breakfast.

No pets or smoking; children over ten welcome; full breakfast; phone in guest quarters; good public transportation and airport connections; off-street parking; wheelchair access; credit cards (V, MC). Weekly and winter rates; seventh consecutive night free. Brochure available.

ROOM	BED	BATH	ENTRANCE	FLOOR	DAILY RATES	
					S - D	(EP)
A	1D	Pvt	Main	LL	$50-$55	($15)
B	1D	Pvt	Main	LL	$50-$55	($15)

Petersen Bed & Breakfast　　　　　　　**(206) 454-9334**
10228 SE Eighth, Bellevue, WA 98004
(Fifteen minutes east of Seattle)

Though some think of Bellevue simply as part of suburban Seattle, it has come into its own in recent years as a major business and shopping area with its fair share of fine dining establishments and horticultural displays. In a quiet, established neighborhood, Eunice and Carl Petersen open their warm and inviting home to bed and breakfast guests. On the lower (daylight) level of the house you'll find two pretty, relaxing rooms with down comforters, plush carpeting, and tasteful decorator touches. Spend leisure moments on the large deck -- perhaps in the steamy spa -- that overlooks beautifully landscaped grounds. After a wonderful night's rest, enjoy a generous home-style breakfast in the atrium kitchen. Then you should be able to face the day with a smile.

Smoking outside only; full breakfast; TV; VCR; hot tub; one mile from Bellevue Square shopping; good public transportation; off-street parking. Waterbed in Room A.

ROOM	BED	BATH	ENTRANCE	FLOOR	DAILY RATES S - D (EP) +
A	1Q	Shd*	Main	LL	$40-$45
B	2T or 1K	Shd*	Main	LL	$40-$45

213

Murphy's Country Bed & Breakfast　　　**(509) 925-7986**
Route 1, Box 400, Ellensburg, WA 98926
(Near junction of I-90 and Highway 97)

Ellensburg, situated in a wide, picturesque valley in central Washington, is cattle and horse country. The annual rodeo, western parade, and county fair draw folks from all over. Hiking in state parks, golfing, and cross-country skiing are also popular. Doris Murphy offers some of the area's most pleasant lodging in her stately home, situated on three rural acres. With a foundation of native stone, it is a house with a feeling of substance. From the lovely front porch, enter a commodious living room with high ceilings, an abundance of beautiful woodwork, and an inviting hearth. Also on the main floor are a formal dining room where Doris, a professional baker, serves breakfast, and a guest lounge with a TV. Second floor accommodations include two spacious bedrooms attractively decorated in peach and aqua. A large bathroom and a half-bath are shared by guests. Turn-of-the-century style combined with twentieth-century comfort make Murphy's Country Bed & Breakfast an altogether memorable place to stay.

Dog in residence; no pets; limited accommodations for children; horses accommodated in corral, $15; no smoking; full breakfast; museums, art galleries, historical buildings, river rafting, cattle drives, berry-picking, and fishing nearby; off-street parking; credit cards (AE, D). Brochure available.

ROOM	BED	BATH	ENTRANCE	FLOOR	DAILY RATES S - D (EP) +
A	1Q	Shd*	Main	2	$50-$55
B	1Q	Shd*	Main	2	$50-$55

Anderson House Bed & Breakfast   **(206) 384-3450**
P.O. Box 1547, Ferndale, WA 98248
(2140 Main Street)

David and Kelly Anderson's extensive renovations have brought out the best in this interesting old house, and the beautifully landscaped yard with its distinctive lampposts makes a welcoming impression. Inside, perfectly chosen furnishings strike just the right balance between comfort and aesthetics. Luxurious carpeting, wallcoverings, and fabrics, plus a stunning Bavarian crystal swan chandelier mark the decor. With humor and thoughtfulness, the Andersons make guests feel relaxed and pampered. Accommodations are of the highest quality, as is the cuisine. Each of the bedrooms is charming, but the Tower Suite (D) is especially unique; the huge space has a sloped ceiling, lots of angles, touches of wood and brick, an alcove with a day bed, a refrigerator, and a TV. It has one drawback: You may never come out to enjoy the rest of the Andersons' splendid hospitality.

No pets; children over twelve welcome; smoking outside only; extensive list of amenities; several restaurants in walking distance; forty-one minutes to downtown Vancouver, B.C.; thirty minutes to Victoria ferry; off-street parking; all major credit cards. $10 for extra person in room. Brochure available.

ROOM	BED	BATH	ENTRANCE	FLOOR	DAILY RATES S - D (EP) +
A	1D	Shd*	Main	2	$45
B	2T	Shd*	Main	2	$45
C	1Q	Pvt	Main	2	$55
D	1K & 2T	Pvt	Main	2	$75

Hill Top Bed & Breakfast   **(206) 384-3619**
5832 Church Road, Ferndale, WA 98248
(A mile west and one-third mile north of town center)

   Doris and Paul Matz didn't skimp on windows when they built
their sturdy brick home. It affords an expansive view out across the
Nooksack River Valley to Mount Baker and the Cascades -- truly one
of the finest there is. Doris admits to an addiction to quiltmaking, and
her museum-quality quilts appear throughout the house, enhancing the
colonial theme. In addition to a guest room with a private bath on the
main floor, the entire ground floor with its own patio entrance is
available for guests. It's a nice, private place to come home to after a
day of exploring Birch Bay, nearby islands, Lynden, or Mount Baker.

   Families welcome; smoking outside only; one and one-half baths,
plus shared shower, on lower floor; TV, fireplace, kitchenette, and
sitting area in Fireside Room (B); Room C sleeps up to four with sofa
bed and cable TV; playpen available; badminton, croquet, games,
puzzles, and books available; off-street parking; credit cards (V, MC);
Norwegian spoken.   10% discount for three nights or more, or for
seniors over 65. *Closed for Christmas*. Brochure available.

ROOM	BED	BATH	ENTRANCE	FLOOR	DAILY RATES	
					S - D	(EP) +
A	1Q	Pvt	Main	1	$39-$44	
B	1Q	Pvt	Sep	LL	$54	($20)
C	1K	Pvt 1/2	Sep	LL	$49	($10)

Llewop Bed & Breakfast   **(206) 275-2287**
Box 97, Grapeview, WA 98546
(Southwest Puget Sound, off Highway 3)

This huge contemporary home rests on a wooded knoll overlooking an orchard, Case Inlet, and Stretch Island, with the summit of Mount Ranier showing on clear days. It is endowed with many windows, skylights, and decks, so it's easy to feel at one with the incredible beauty of the environment. There are three bedrooms for guests, all as lovely as can be. Room A has a spacious private deck with full view. Guests are welcome to sit around the living room fireplace, explore the property, swim, play pickleball, or unwind in the whirl-pool spa (tub in bathroom on main floor). Most of all, Llewop is a place for restoration and relaxation. The Powell family wants you to enjoy their home as much as they enjoy sharing it.

No pets; families welcome; smoking on decks; full breakfast; TV; extra beds; bathtub spa; pickleball court; golf course and restaurant four miles away; off-street parking. Clergy discount.

ROOM	BED	BATH	ENTRANCE	FLOOR	DAILY RATES S - D (EP)
A	1D	Shd*	Main	2	$45-$60 ($20)
B	2T	Shd*	Main	2	$45-$60 ($20)
C	2T	Pvt	Main	1	$45-$60 ($20)

The Wildflower   **(206) 392-1196**
25237 SE Issaquah-Fall City Road, Issaquah, WA 98027
(Twenty-five-minute drive east of Seattle)

Awakening to the pleasure of light streaming through tall ever-greens into a room with walls of honey-colored logs is a homespun, back-to-nature experience. Throughout her authentic log home, Laureita Caldwell displays her grandmother's marvelous quilts. One on the wall of each bedroom suggests its theme -- Strawberry, Fern, Daisy, and Rose. The antique-furnished abode is unusually restful and cozy. Guests often linger in the dining room by the wood-burning stove where delicious, made-from-scratch breakfasts are served. Stroll out to the gazebo in a meadow on the property where small weddings are sometimes held. Or take some time to explore nearby Gilman Village, a major eastside attraction. Whatever your inclination, be assured: A relaxing sojourn in the forest may be yours at The Wildflower.

Cat and dog in residence; no pets; no children under twelve; smoking outside only; full breakfast; hiking trails, fine restaurants, Salmon Days in October, and Snoqualmie Falls nearby. Brochure available.

ROOM	BED	BATH	ENTRANCE	FLOOR	DAILY RATES S - D	(EP) +
A	1Q	Pvt	Main	2	$55	
B	1Q	Pvt	Main	2	$55	
C	1D & 1T	Shd*	Main	2	$55	($15)
D	1Q	Shd*	Main	2	$55	

The White Swan Guest House   **(206) 445-6805**
1388 Moore Road, Mount Vernon, WA 98273
(Six miles from La Conner, on Skagit River)

Peter Goldfarb made a major shift in life style when he moved from New York City to the quiet countryside of the Pacific Northwest, but adapted to hosting quite easily. He bought a handsome Victorian home, badly in need of attention, and gave it his all. Keeping its charm and character intact, Peter's inspired renovations turned it into the jewel it is today. My favorite aspect of the decor is the bold use of color throughout the house. Vivid hues of a country garden create a cheerful environment, a lift to the spirit on dull days. Comfortable rooms are uniquely decorated, featuring Peter's large collection of antique samplers. Outside, English-style country gardens with seating areas and lots of flowers enhance the grounds. To the rear of the property is a wonderful, private Garden Cottage (D) with its own kitchen, deck, and gorgeous views of the farmlands. Mother Nature has richly endowed the surrounding landscape -- it's great for walking along the river, cycling, and observing wildlife. Any way you look at it, The White Swan is a find.

Dogs in residence; smoking outside only (porch); homemade chocolate chip cookies all day; three rooms share two baths on second floor; cottage also has double futon sofa bed; off-street parking; credit cards (V, MC).

ROOM	BED	BATH	ENTRANCE	FLOOR	DAILY RATES	
					S - D	(EP) +
A	K	Shd*	Main	2	$60-$70	
B	1Q	Shd*	Main	2	$60-$70	
C	1Q	Shd*	Main	2	$60-$70	
D	1Q	Pvt	Sep	1 & 2	$100 ($25)	

219

Inn at Swifts Bay   **(206) 468-3636**
Route 2, Box 3402, Lopez Island, WA 98261
(Two miles from ferry dock on Port Stanley Road)

A few days on Lopez Island can satisfy many tastes.   It's the friendliest place in the San Juans (be sure to wave!), so you'll feel welcome right off.   Cyclists and nature lovers consider it an ideal getaway.   Those who appreciate luxury and superb cuisine will find the Inn at Swifts Bay much to their liking.   The Tudor-style inn is classy, stylish, and oh, so comfortable. Hosts Christopher and Robert provide every amenity a guest might need and then some. An understated elegance marks the decor. When you're not out exploring the island, you'll find a choice of areas to relax that are just for guests: your tastefully appointed bedroom, the living room by the fireplace, the outdoor hot tub (sign up ahead for complete privacy), or the sunning area. Mornings will find you at your very own table enjoying a breakfast that is nothing short of sensational.   Then take a stroll down to the private beach across the road and let the day unfold.

No pets, children, or smoking; full breakfast; TV/VCR with good selection of movies (winter only); guest phone; small fridge with complimentary mineral water and ice; hot tub; bicycles for rent by reservation; off-street parking; credit cards (V, MC, D); pickup at ferry dock, airstrip, or seaplane dock. Brochure available.

ROOM	BED	BATH	ENTRANCE	FLOOR	DAILY RATES S - D (EP) +
A	1Q	Shd*	Main	1	$75
B	1Q	Shd*	Main	1	$75
C	1Q	Pvt	Main	1	$95
D	1Q	Pvt	Main	2	$115

Yodeler Inn   **(206) 599-2156**
P.O. Box 222, Maple Falls, WA 98266
(Twenty-six miles east of Bellingham in Mount Baker foothills)

Yodeler Inn seems a natural part of the ambiance in the little Alpine village of Maple Falls. With the omnipresence of Mount Baker, the surrounding area is a vacation wonderland with year-round adventures to pursue. Here Jeff and Bethnie Morrison aim to provide "a relaxing environment to sleep, eat, and play in." Their homey inn has five bedrooms, three bathrooms, a hot tub, and a spacious living room with a fireplace. Also available is an intimate private cottage on the property. It's a pleasant surprise to find several good restaurants, and one great one, nearby. Some local activities include Alpine and cross-country skiing, river rafting, hiking, mountain climbing, fishing, and photography. Your hosts can suggest many more.

Two cats in residence; smoking outside only; full breakfast; kitchenette in cottage (no breakfast served); VCR/TV available; off-street parking; credit cards (V, MC). 20% discount after first night. Brochure available.

ROOM	BED	BATH	ENTRANCE	FLOOR	DAILY RATES S - D (EP) +
A	1D	Shd*	Main	2	$55
B	1D & 1T	Shd*	Main	2	$55
C	1D	Shd*	Main	2	$55
D	1D	Shd*	Main	2	$55
E	1D	Shd*	Main	2	$55
F	1Q	Pvt	Sep	1	$55

Maple Valley Bed & Breakfast   **(206) 432-1409**
20020 SE 228, Maple Valley, WA 98038
(Twenty-five miles due east of Sea-Tac International Airport)

After a demanding week at work or a day of hard traveling, how satisfying to find that perfect haven in the country for a few days of pampered relaxation -- Maple Valley Bed & Breakfast. Jayne and Clarke Hurlbut have fashioned a rustic family home of outstanding warmth and charm. Built by Clarke, it stands in a clearing in the woods, surrounded by a carpet of neat green lawn. The later addition of an "eagles' aerie" lends a fairytale quality. Walls of warm cedar, a huge stone fireplace, open-beamed ceilings, and many interesting angles give the house its singular appeal, and two gabled guest rooms on the second floor couldn't be more endearing. The decor is country Americana, very well done. Each room has lacy curtains, antiques, and nostalgia pieces, as well as French doors that open to a large deck. Featured in Room A are a handhewn four-poster log bed and a pedestal sink; in Room B, beautiful heirloom quilts cover the beds. An upstairs sitting room and adjoining TV area are great for reading, playing games, working puzzles, and viewing the wildlife pond through binoculars. Attention to detail is the essence of what's so special at Maple Valley Bed & Breakfast. Far be it from me to spoil all the surprises.

Outdoor peacocks, chickens, cats, and dog; no pets; smoking outside only; full breakfast; cots available; barbecue area; basketball; hiking; nature walks; outdoor weddings; off-street parking.

ROOM	BED	BATH	ENTRANCE	FLOOR	DAILY RATES S - D (EP) +
A	1Q	Shd*	Main	2	$40-$45 ($15)
B	1D & 1T	Shd*	Main	2	$45-$50 ($15)

Duck-In   (206) 232-2554
4118 - 100th Avenue, SE, Mercer Island, WA 98040
(East side of island on waterfront)

Removed from urban frenzy, on the bank of Lake Washington, this inviting, cozy cottage makes a great little getaway spot. Take it easy in lounge chairs on the sloping green lawn, grill some fish for dinner, or even send out for pizza -- you'll probably want to stay put for a while. Guests have the cottage to themselves. Full of homey touches, it's comfy as can be. There are two bedrooms separated by a bath-room and an office. Facing the water is the living/dining room. You'll find nice table linens, a well-stocked kitchen, and all kinds of thoughtful amenities (picnic basket, sewing basket, binoculars, books and games, etc.). Hosts Ron and Ruth Mullen encourage snooping in every nook and cranny, really making yourself at home. At the Duck-In, you'll have plenty of privacy in a waterfront setting with all the necessary comforts and many unexpected ones.

No pets; smoking outside only; TV; desk and private phone; full kitchen with stove, dishwasher, and microwave Brochure available.

ROOM	BED	BATH	ENTRANCE	FLOOR	DAILY RATES
					S - D (EP) +
A	1D & 1T	Pvt	Main	1	$95 ($10)

Mercer Island Hideaway   **(206) 232-1092**
8820 SE 63rd Street, Mercer Island, WA 98040
(Three miles south of I-90, off Island Crest Way)

It's only a fifteen-minute drive from Seattle or Bellevue, but when you cross a bridge over Lake Washington to Mercer Island, it seems like another world. The Williams' home, Mercer Island Hideaway, is a place of quiet luxury. It is tucked into the lush green landscape that adjoins the wilderness of 120-acre Pioneer Park. No matter which of the attractive accommodations you stay in, it will be like "sleeping in a forest," as one guest put it. The home has been beautifully renovated throughout and is kept in immaculate condition. Anyone with an interest in music will be at home here. The spacious living room has tall windows and a cathedral ceiling. It holds two grand pianos, a reed organ, and a harpsichord, any of which Mary Williams will play on request. She and Bill excel in making every guest feel special. Their personal warmth enhances the outstanding hospitality at Mercer Island Hideaway.

No pets, smoking, or RV parking; full breakfast; TV; off-street parking. Room B is a suite with patio entrance. Two-night minimum. *Sometimes unavailable January-March.* Brochure available.

ROOM	BED	BATH	ENTRANCE	FLOOR	DAILY RATES	
					S - D	(EP) +
A	1K or 1Q	Pvt	Main	1	$75	
B	2T or 1K	Pvt	Sep	LL	$75	

Mole House Bed & Breakfast   **(206) 232-1611**
3308 West Mercer Way, Mercer Island, WA 98040
(West shore of island)

It would take an album full of pictures to capture the many facets of Mole House. The rambling contemporary Northwest home overlooks Lake Washington, Seattle, and the Olympic Mountains. It is made up of several distinct sections that are harmoniously linked together by the hosts' collection of art, antiques, and family heirlooms. Don, a native of Seattle, and Petra, who emigrated from West Germany in 1986, extend caring hospitality in a refined atmosphere. Here you can have all the privacy you need, invite friends in for a visit, or enjoy the interesting company of Don and Petra. The three guest accommodations are on different levels of the house. The Eagle has its own sitting room, The Garden Suite has a sitting room and opens onto a patio, and The Apartment is a totally self-contained space with a deck and a panoramic view of the lake. Park-like surroundings, soft music, and elegant breakfasts contribute to the sensual delight of staying at Mole House. It is in every respect a rare find.

No pets; well-behaved children welcome; no smoking; full breakfast; sofa bed, telephone, TV, and kitchen with stocked fridge in Room C; patios, decks, and gardens; ten minutes to Seattle, twenty to airport; good public transportation and airport connections; off-street parking; German and Spanish spoken. Brochure available.

ROOM	BED	BATH	ENTRANCE	FLOOR	DAILY RATES S - D (EP)
A	1D	Pvt	Main	1	$50
B	1D	Pvt	Main	LL	$50
C	1D	Pvt	Main & Sep	2	$60 ($5)

The Abel House (206) 249-6002
117 Fleet Street South, Montesano, WA 98563 1(800) 235-ABEL
(Downtown area)

Second only to the imposing Grays Harbor County Courthouse in grandeur, The Abel House was built in 1908 as the home of William H. Abel, who enjoyed a distinguished career as a defense and trial attorney in the nearby courthouse. Among the rooms of the four-floor mansion now owned by Vic Reynolds are eight bedrooms, a game room, a well-stocked library, a formal dining room, and a comfortably appointed living room. Lustrous woodwork, box-beamed ceilings, massive brick fireplaces, and original fixtures enhance the interior. An unusual Tiffany chandelier, commissioned to hang over the dining table, befits the baronial setting. Guests may relax on the wide covered veranda, stroll through the glorious gardens, or set out to cover small, friendly Montesano on foot. To stay at The Abel House is to experience one of the community's best assets first hand.

Dog in residence; no pets; smoking in designated areas; color cable TVs in rooms; ample street parking; credit cards (V, MC). Inquire about discounts. Brochure available.

ROOM	BED	BATH	ENTRANCE	FLOOR	DAILY RATES S - D (EP) +
A	2T	Shd*	Main	2	$50
B	1Q	Shd*	Main	2	$50
C	1Q	Shd*	Main	2	$50
D	1D	Shd*	Main	2	$60

Sylvan Haus   **(206) 249-3453**
P.O. Box 416, Montesano, WA 98563
(417 Wilder Hill Drive, overlooking Montesano)

What an appropriate name Mike and JoAnne Murphy picked for their B&B: settings don't get much more sylvan than this. The view from the home's lofty elevation through towering evergreens takes in downtown Montesano and a wide valley checkered with farmlands. Sylvan Haus has contemporary lines and rustic wood construction. It's built on three levels and has many windows, as well as several decks and fireplaces. A guest suite with plenty of natural light occupies one end of the second level; it has two bedrooms and a bath to accommodate up to four people. On the lower level, guests have a bedroom, a bath, and easy access to a large recreation room with TV, VCR, and pool table. Bountiful breakfasts are served in the dining room where a colorful collection of pharmaceutical bottles (Mike's a pharmacist) is displayed -- and, of course, there is the view. For casual comfort in quiet country surroundings, Sylvan Haus is just the ticket.

No pets; no children under fourteen; smoking outside only; full breakfast; hot tub; Lake Sylvia State Park (with trout fishing) nearby; off-street parking. Rate for using both bedrooms in suite (A) is $80. Brochure available.

ROOM	BED	BATH	ENTRANCE	FLOOR	DAILY RATES S - D (EP) +
A	1Q & 2T	Pvt	Main	2	$50
B	1Q	Pvt	Main	1	$50

Whispering Firs Bed & Breakfast   (206) 428-1990
1957 Kanako Lane, Mount Vernon, WA 98273
(In hills just east of I-5 between the two La Conner exits)

When you arrive at the hilltop where Vic and Linda Benson live, you're in for something special. Their rambling contemporary home on 250 acres is rustic yet luxurious. Tinkling sounds from a rock fountain greet you in the foyer, where the walls display mounted wildlife trophies. The expansive living area for guests has cathedral ceilings, a huge stone fireplace, a sunken conversation area, and an astonishing view across the Skagit Valley to the San Juan Islands! On either side of this vast space, deluxe guest accommodations offer exceptional comfort, amenities, and privacy. Relax on the spacious deck to the sounds of a spouting fountain fed by a water wheel in a mountain stream. Peaceful seclusion in a majestic woodland setting -- that's Whispering Firs.

Families welcome; full country breakfasts and harvest dinners offered by Linda, a nationally acclaimed cook; smoking outside only; waterbeds and conventional beds available; spa on deck; hiking, swimming, fishing, horseshoes, volleyball, and basketball on property; off-street parking; airport pickup (Barker, Skagit Regional). Brochure available.

ROOM	BED	BATH	ENTRANCE	FLOOR	DAILY RATES S - D (EP) +
A	2Q	Pvt	Main	1	$70
B	1K	Pvt	Main	1	$80
C	1Q	Pvt	Main	1	$60

Pickerings' Landing

7825 Urquhart Street NW, Olympia, WA 98502
(Just outside Olympia, in lower Puget Sound)

(206) 866-4537
(Keep trying!)

After driving along unhurried, woodsy back roads, arriving at Pickerings' Landing is like finding the treasure at rainbow's end. The pristine white house is set in a commanding position with a view straight up Dana Passage. The home and landscaped grounds are a vision of stunning beauty. The front yard slopes down to a beach where you can dig for clams, hunt for agates and shells, and observe a variety of shorebirds. The home is extremely comfortable, with two lovely guest rooms and many windows to allow sweeping vistas of waterways and Mount Rainier. Jo and Chris Pickering feel that they have "something too good not to share," and I certainly agree. If you plan a visit to Pickerings' Landing, be sure to allow enough time to explore the area, enjoy the home and its surroundings, and get to know your genial hosts.

No pets; children over ten welcome; limited smoking; TV; AC; laundry privileges; boating; other meals (from the garden's bounty) by arrangement; off-street parking; Pacific Ocean is one hour west; Mount St. Helens National Park, one hour south; Seattle, an hour and a half north.

ROOM	BED	BATH	ENTRANCE	FLOOR	DAILY RATES S - D (EP)
A	1D	Shd*	Main	1	$50
B	1D	Shd*	Main	LL	$50

Holly Hill House   **(206) 385-5619**
611 Polk Street, Port Townsend, WA 98368
(Historic Uptown District)

　　This Christmas-card-perfect 1872 Victorian stands on a corner lot with tall holly trees and other plantings from long ago, including an amazing Camperdown elm. Since Bill and Laurie Medlicott became the home's proud owners, they've been digging into its fascinating history and, with the slightest prompting, will entertain you with stories, the funniest of which center around Lizette and Billie. Two guest rooms are named in their honor, one with a view of the garden, the other with a view of Admiralty Inlet and the Cascades. Equally attractive newer rooms in the Carriage House include the Morning Glory and the Skyview. In the large country kitchen, Laurie creates sumptuous breakfasts that are served with a gracious air in the formal dining room. Both here and in the living room, notice the original stippled woodwork that was the rage in the house's heyday. Some furnishings are antiques, some reproductions, but the accent is on liveability. Hosts call it "a home, not a museum," and that's exactly how it feels.

　　No pets; children over twelve welcome; smoking outside only; no RV parking; full breakfast; historic buildings, Fort Worden State Park, interesting shops and restaurants nearby; off-street parking; credit cards (V, MC); ferry pickup. Brochure available.

ROOM	BED	BATH	ENTRANCE	FLOOR	DAILY RATES	
					S - D	(EP) +
A	1Q & 1T	Pvt	Main	2	$82	($26)
B	1Q	Pvt	Main	2	$90	
C	1Q	Pvt	Sep	1	$76	
D	1Q	Pvt	Sep	1	$82	

Hart's Tayberry House
(206) 848-4594

7406 - 80th Street East, Puyallup, WA 98371
(Puyallup/Tacoma area)

The authenticity of this Victorian charmer is almost palpable, so it's surprising to learn that the home is in fact a reproduction. The original no longer stands, but it was built by a leading pioneer in the area. Unusual care was taken in its re-creation here on a hillside overlooking rich farmlands. Intricately carved exterior woodwork and a wrap-around porch with a gazebo are a perfect prelude to the turn-of-the-century details inside. Upstairs, the front Balcony Room offers fresh air and a view. The smaller but oh-so-sweet Heart Room is just down the hall. A bathroom off the hallway has an old-fashioned chain-pull toilet and a clawfoot tub. A spacious suite spans the back of the house. Lovingly combined wallpapers, rugs, linens, and furnishings give each room a romantic warmth. A friendly, hospitable stay in quiet rural surroundings awaits you at Hart's Tayberry House.

No pets; children over twelve welcome; smoking outside only; small refrigerator in suite; AC; elevator; walk to city park and tennis courts; off-street parking. Discount to seniors. Brochure available.

ROOM	BED	BATH	ENTRANCE	FLOOR	DAILY RATES S - D (EP) +
A	1Q	Shd*	Main	2	$50
B	1D	Shd*	Main	2	$40
C	1Q	Pvt	Main	2	$60 ($10)

Capitol Hill House Bed & Breakfast
(206) 322-1752
2215 East Prospect, Seattle, WA 98112
(Capitol Hill)

Mary Wolf's stately brick home is on a quiet, tree-lined street in one of Seattle's most prestigious older neighborhoods. Standing on a lovely corner lot, it is handsome indeed. Here you'll find luxurious accommodations with antiques, objects of art, tapestries, and Oriental rugs collected over the years. Two pretty guest rooms and an attractive master suite occupy the second floor. Mary keeps things just so for guests and enjoys setting a beautiful table where breakfast is graciously served. Refined comfort in a convenient location near the University of Washington, Volunteer Park, and downtown Seattle can be yours at Capitol Hill House Bed & Breakfast.

No pets; no smoking on second floor; nursery facilities for infants; ages 0-3 free, then crib at $10; older children by prior arrangement; full breakfast; extra-long rollaway bed, $15; TV in master suite (C); ample street parking; good public transportation and airport connections.

ROOM	BED	BATH	ENTRANCE	FLOOR	DAILY RATES S - D (EP) +
A	1D	Shd*	Main	2	$40-$45
B	2T	Shd*	Main	2	$45-$50
C	2T or 1K	Pvt	Main	2	$50-$55

Capitol Hill Inn　　　　　　　　　**(206) 323-1955**
1713 Belmont Avenue, Seattle, WA 98122
(Two blocks from Broadway shops and restaurants)

To capture all the richness below the surface of this capacious 1903 intown residence was a challenge requiring vision, determination, and no small measure of chutzpah. So endowed, mother and daughter Katie and Joanne Godmintz forged ahead until every room in the house had been thoroughly revived. Elaborately carved woodwork, custom-designed Victorian wall coverings, period light fixtures, and regal colors provide a proper setting for the large-scale European antiques highlighting the dramatic decor. Eccentric collectibles, exquisite bed linens, lavish breakfast specialties -- the list of delights goes on and on. At Capitol Hill Inn, the sense of style (like the sense of fun) never misses.

Toy poodle in residence; no pets or children; smoking outside only; deluxe Continental breakfast; seven blocks from Convention Center; good public transportation and airport connections. Brochure available.

ROOM	BED	BATH	ENTRANCE	FLOOR	DAILY RATES
					S - D (EP) +
A	1D	Pvt 1/2	Main	2	$79
B	1Q	Pvt 1/2	Main	2	$79
C	1Q	Pvt	Main	2	$89
D	1D	Pvt	Main	2	$89
E	1D	Shd*	Main	3	$75

Marit Nelson   **(206) 782-7900**
6208 Palatine Avenue North, Seattle, WA 98103
(Woodland Park area)

This cozy brick Tudor-style home is in a quiet north Seattle neighborhood with good access to freeways and public transportation. Here Marit Nelson offers her special version of Scandinavian hospitality. There's a very homey atmosphere, the kind that makes you feel like settling in for a while. A whimsical note is struck by the collection of stuffed bears flanking the stairs that lead to the three guest rooms (only two are used at any one time). Care has been taken to make each room comfy and attractive. Room B has a delightful view of water, mountains, and sunsets. A variety of guidebooks to Seattle and environs ensures that you'll find plenty to do, rain or shine. Breakfasts are delicious and beautifully served, a savory beginning to any day.

No pets, smoking, or RV parking; families welcome; full breakfast; walking distance to Green Lake and Woodland Park Zoo; ten minutes to downtown and University of Washington; two blocks to bus stop; ample street parking; Norwegian spoken. Member Washington Bed & Breakfast Guild and Seattle Bed & Breakfast Association. Brochure available.

ROOM	BED	BATH	ENTRANCE	FLOOR	DAILY RATES S - D (EP) +
A	1Q	Shd	Main	2	$50-$60
B	1D	Shd	Main	2	$50-$60
C	2T	Shd	Main	2	$50-$60

Mildred's Bed & Breakfast (206) 325-6072
1202 Fifteenth Avenue East, Seattle, WA 98112
(Capitol Hill, facing east side of Volunteer Park)

If ever a place could tug at your heartstrings, Mildred's would do it. It's the ultimate trip-to-Grandmother's fantasy come true. A large white Victorian possessed of a friendly charm, it's the perfect setting for Mildred Sarver's caring hospitality. Three guest rooms on the upper floor couldn't be prettier. Sitting alcoves, lace curtains, and antiques add to the ambiance of warmth and security. Off the hallway are a half bath and a very nice full bath with a skylight view. For longer stays, there's a self-contained apartment suite (D) on the ground floor with its own entrance, kitchen, bath, living room, and bedroom. Mildred's special touches and lavish breakfasts make her guests feel truly pampered.

No pets; smoking in restricted areas; full breakfast; TV available; fireplace in living room; sofa bed in living room of suite (D); park across street (site of Seattle Art Museum) good for walking or jogging; ample street parking; good public transportation and airport connections; all major credit cards.

ROOM	BED	BATH	ENTRANCE	FLOOR	DAILY RATES S - D (EP) +
A	1D	Shd*	Main	2	$55-$65 ($15)
B	1D	Shd*	Main	2	$55-$65 ($15)
C	2T or 1K	Shd*	Main	2	$55-$65 ($15)
D	1D	Pvt	Sep	1G	$85

Prince of Wales   **(206) 325-9692**
133 Thirteenth Avenue East, Seattle, WA 98102
(Capitol Hill)

From this handsome turn-of-the-century home you can easily walk or take public transportation to the city's conference sites and all the downtown attractions you'll want to visit. Equally well-suited for convention, business, or vacation travelers, Prince of Wales has home-like comfort with a regal air. Interior colors hint at the owners' past on the eastern seaboard: navy, white, burgundy, and gray, with shades of pink added in the upstairs guest quarters. Conveniences such as a private telephone line and a laundry room with an iron can come in handy when you're on the road. A delicious full breakfast rounds out the generous hospitality offered by hosts Naomi and Bert. But most impressive of all is the view -- a stunning panorama of the city skyline, Olympic Mountains, and Puget Sound, with the Space Needle in the foreground. Three of the four guest rooms feature this ever-present reminder that you couldn't be anywhere but Seattle.

Two cats in residence; no pets or smoking; no RV parking; full breakfast; fireplace in living room; private garden; good public transportation and airport connections; off-street and street parking; credit cards (V, MC).

ROOM	BED	BATH	ENTRANCE	FLOOR	DAILY RATES S - D (EP) +
A	1D	Shd*	Main	2	$55
B	2T	Shd*	Main	2	$60
C	1Q	Pvt	Main	2	$70 ($10)
D	1Q	Pvt	Sep	3	$80 ($10)

Hillside House (509) 535-1893
East 1729 Eighteenth, Spokane, WA 99203 days: 534-1426
(South Hill)

There's something wonderful about a mature residential neighborhood with quiet, tree-shaded streets and houses of individual character. Hillside House graces such a setting, just three miles from downtown on Spokane's South Hill. While appearing deceptively small from the front, it is actually spacious inside. A large living room spanning the glassed-in back of the house overlooks the lush leafiness of a wooded hillside; it feels more like being outdoors on a terrace than enclosed in a room. Myriad artistic touches add to the vibrant interior. The use of fabrics, wallpapers, carpeting, and furnishings is both original and tasteful, lending a rich, textured look. A stairwell lined with art leads to the second floor guest rooms, which are as attractively appointed as the rest of the house. A guest once claimed to have slept on "the world's most comfortable bed" here. Hosts JoAnn and Bud cater to the needs of each guest, providing hospitality in the truest sense. In this spirit, they keep their B&B "small by intent."

Cat in residence; no pets; smoking outside only; full breakfast; common room with telephone and library; parks, museums, recreational and cultural attractions nearby; credit cards (V, MC); ample street parking. Brochure available.

ROOM	BED	BATH	ENTRANCE	FLOOR	DAILY RATES S - D (EP) +
A	2T	Shd*	Main	2	$45-$48 ($10)
B	1D	Shd*	Main	2	$45-$50 ($10)

Love's Victorian Bed & Breakfast   (509) 276-6939
North 31317 Cedar Road, Deer Park, WA 99006
(Fifteen minutes north of Spokane)

Using nineteenth century plans, Bill and Leslie Love fashioned their three-story home, an authentic Victorian gray and mauve reproduction with white gingerbread trim. To encounter it in the woods set among tall pines is a dramatic surprise. One's initial delight is heightened upon entering the heartwarming interior. A stairway leads from the main floor to the guest quarters above; follow the stenciled heart design up the stairwell to an ambiance of pure Victorian romance. The Turret Suite features an antique bed, a gas fireplace, a sitting area, a balcony, and a bathroom with a clawfoot tub and shower and a pedestal sink. Annie's Room honors Leslie's grandmother and features her bed and dresser; the bath has a clawfoot tub and shower. Both elegant accommodations have Victorian patterned wallpaper and coordinating carpets. This B&B is not only incredibly romantic -- it's a family home filled with Love.

Dog and cats on premises; no pets; children by prior arrangement; smoking outside only; full breakfast; TV, VCR, and stereo in guest sitting room; AC; robes provided; private solarium/hot tub room; bicycles available; fishing, skiing (cross-country trails five minutes away), hiking, festivals, and museums nearby; off-street parking; credit cards (AE); inquire about birthday celebrations, garden weddings, and receptions. Brochure available.

ROOM	BED	BATH	ENTRANCE	FLOOR	DAILY RATES S - D (EP) +
A	1Q	Pvt	Main	2	$78 ($10)
B	1Q	Pvt	Main	2	$60-$65

Marianna Stoltz House   (509) 483-4316
East 427 Indiana, Spokane, WA 99207
(Central Spokane, historic Gonzaga University area)

Phyllis and Jim Maguire have the good fortune to live in the 1908 American foursquare classic home in which Phyllis grew up. She named it Marianna Stoltz in honor of her mother. Now one of Spokane's historic landmarks, it has the feel of a big, old-fashioned family home that's comfortable through and through. Period furnishings, handsome woodwork, leaded glass cabinets, and a lovely tile fireplace enhance the gracious interior. Accommodations are all on the second floor, and guests are welcome to come and go as they please; the front entrance is theirs alone. Beds are covered with the wonderful collection of old quilts that Phyllis so generously shares. Fond memories of Marianna Stoltz House might include visiting or reading on the wide, wrap-around porch, sipping a nightcap of home-made raspberry cordial, or breakfasting on cheese strada or Dutch babies. These and other pleasures await you at this popular intown B&B.

No pets; no children under twelve; smoking outside only; full breakfast; TV available; AC; choice of shower or clawfoot tub; good public transportation and airport connections; off-street parking; credit cards (V, MC, AE). Brochure available.

ROOM	BED	BATH	ENTRANCE	FLOOR	DAILY RATES	
					S - D	(EP) +
A	1K	Shd*	Main	2	$45-$55	($10)
B	2T	Shd*	Main	2	$45-$55	
C	1Q	Pvt	Main	2	$45-$55	
D	1Q	Pvt	Main	2	$45-$55	

Eagles Nest Inn   **(206) 321-5331**
3236 East Saratoga Road, Langley, WA 98260
(One and one-half miles from village, overlooking Saratoga Passage)

Nancy and Dale Bowman's ingeniously designed home is set amidst fir and cedar with commanding vistas of Saratoga Passage, Camano Island, and Mount Baker. A pleasing contrast of contemporary and traditional gives the interior an ambiance that is refined, comfortable, and aesthetically satisfying. Abundant windows and open space help to bring the outside in; you feel secluded and close to nature while being pampered beyond expectation. Each of the four spacious guest rooms has a sitting area and a TV/VCR. The Saratoga Room has majestic views and triple French doors leading to a private balcony; The Forest Room has a large bay window with a view through the trees, plus a skylight; The Eagles Nest is perched at the top of the house with a private balcony and a dramatic 360-degree panorama. The newest accommodation is the delightful Garden Room on the ground floor. Breakfast selections from Nancy's wide-ranging repertoire start the day off right. Stroll about the grounds, paddle your own canoe, soak in the spa under the stars, savor the privacy of your romantic room -- beautiful memories are yours for the making at Eagles Nest Inn.

No pets or children; smoking outside only; full breakfast; guest lounge/library; 350 video selections; robes provided; decks; spa; "bottomless" cookie jar; off-street parking; credit cards (V, MC).

ROOM	BED	BATH	ENTRANCE	FLOOR	DAILY RATES S - D (EP) +
A	1K	Pvt	Main	3	$95-$105
B	1K	Pvt	Sep	3	$85-$95 ($40)
C	1Q	Pvt	Main	4	$95-$105
D	1Q	Pvt	Sep	1G	$75-$85 ($40)

Log Castle Bed & Breakfast   **(206) 321-5483**
3273 East Saratoga Road, Langley, WA 98260
(Beachside overlooking Saratoga Passage)

An authentic taste of the Northwest awaits you at this unique island home. Away from the road at water's edge, the fairytale log castle is full of the Metcalfs' family history. It was built using wood from the property and has evolved over the years into a rustic, homey retreat for

B&B guests. Aged, handhewn wood imbues the interior with a mellow warmth, and there are countless one-of-a-kind details. A panorama of water, beach, mountains, and pasture is yours from a porch swing, from your bedroom, or from the living room with its huge stone fireplace, cathedral ceilings, and comfy places to sit. Guest rooms are loaded with charm. An east-facing room has French glass doors to a private deck; the room above has a nifty woodstove and a porch with a swing. The second-story turret room has two big windows overlooking beach and mountains; the turret room above has windows on five sides and is warmed by a 1912 woodstove. Breakfast is a multi-course feast. To work it off, you may want to make your way along the beach to the village of Langley. At Log Castle, there's a peaceful, restorative atmosphere where cares slowly melt away.

Dog, ducks, and geese on property; no indoor pets; children over ten welcome; smoking outside only; no RV parking; full breakfast; TV in living room; canoe available; off-street parking; credit cards (V, MC, D).

ROOM	BED	BATH	ENTRANCE	FLOOR	DAILY RATES
					S - D (EP) +
A	1Q	Pvt	Main	1	$80
B	2T or 1K	Pvt	Main	2	$90
C	2T or 1K	Pvt	Main	2	$100 ($20)
D	1D	Pvt	Main	3	$100 ($20)

DINING HIGHLIGHTS: WASHINGTON

Please read "About Dining Highlights" on page *vii*.

ABERDEEN

Bridges Restaurant, 112 North G Street; (206) 532-6563; seafood/prime rib/pasta

ANACORTES

Boomer's Landing, 209 T Avenue; (206) 293-5109; seafood

Charlie's, 5407 Ferry Terminal Road; (206) 293-7377; prime rib/steaks/seafood

GERE-A-DELI, 502 Commercial Avenue; (206) 293-7383; deli/pasta/pastries

La Petite, 3401 Commercial Avenue; (206) 293-4644; European

Slocum's Restaurant, 2201 Skyline Way; (206) 293-0644; innovative seafood

ASHFORD

Alexander's Country Inn, Highway 706 E; (206) 569-2300; Continental

The Wild Berry, Highway 706 E; (206) 569-2628; hearty, mountain fare

BELLEVUE

Landau's Restaurant, 500 - 108th Avenue NE; (206) 646-6644; Northwest/Continental

The New Jake O'Shaughnessey's, 401 Bellevue Square, NE Sixth and Bellevue Way; (206) 455-5559; peachwood broiled poultry/meats/seafood

BELLINGHAM

Il Fiasco, 1308 Railroad Avenue; (206) 676-9136; Italian

La Belle Rose, 1801 Roeder Avenue; Harbor Center; (206) 647-0833; French

Le Chat Noir, 1200 Harris, The Marketplace; (206) 733-6136; French

Pacific Cafe, 100 North Commercial; (206) 647-0800; Asian/Northwest

Pepper Sisters Restaurant, 1222 North Garden; (206) 671-3414; Southwest

BOW

The Oyster Bar, 240 Chuckanut Drive; (206) 766-6185; Northwest seafood

Oyster Creek Inn, 190 Chuckanut Drive; (206) 766-6179; oysters/seafood

ELLENSBURG

The Blue Grouse, 1401 Dollar Way (Exit 106 off I-90); (509) 925-4808; American

Donaghadee's, 801 Euclid Way; (509) 962-5050; American/meats/poultry/pasta

Giovanni's on Pearl, 402 North Pearl; (509) 962-2260; Italian/ seafood/Ellensburg lamb/steaks

Valley Cafe, 105 West Third; (509) 925-3050; seafood/pasta

FERNDALE

Douglas House, 2254 Douglas Drive; (206) 384-5262; seafood/steak/chicken/lobster bisque/daily specials

GLACIER

InnisFree Restaurant, 9393 Mount Baker Highway; (206) 599-2373; seasonal fresh/innovative Northwest dishes

Milano's, 9990 Mount Baker Highway; (206) 599-2863; Italian

HOQUIAM

Levee Street Restaurant, 709 Levee Street; (206) 532-1959; imaginative seafood plus

ISSAQUAH

Lombardi's, 719 NW Gilman Boulevard; (206) 391-9097; Italian

Mandarin Garden, 40 East Sunset Way; (206) 392-9476; Chinese

KIRKLAND

Cafe Juanita, 9702 NE 120th Place; (206) 823-1505; Italian

LA CONNER

Barkley's of La Conner, Second and Washington Streets; (206) 466-4133; Northwest

Black Swan Cafe, 505 South First Street; (206) 466-3040; Mediterranean/Northwest

Calico Cupboard, 720 South First Street; (206) 466-4451; bakery items/sandwiches/soups/desserts/all from scratch

LANGLEY

Cafe Langley, 113 First Street; (206) 221-3090; Greek/Continental

LOPEZ ISLAND

Bay Cafe, Lopez Village; (206) 468-3700; eclectic

MONTESANO

Savory Faire, 135 South Main Street; (206) 249-3701; breakfast/lunch/occasional dinner

MOUNT VERNON

Wildflowers, 2001 East College Way; (206) 424-9724; Skagit Valley/Northwest

PORT TOWNSEND

Fountain Cafe, 920 Washington Street; (206) 385-1364; seafood/pasta

Lanza's Ristorante, 1020 Lawrence; (206) 385-6221; Italian

Manresa Castle Dining Room, Seventh and Sheridan; (206) 385-5750; Northwest

Silverwater Cafe, 126 Quincy; (206) 385-6448; Continental

SEATTLE

Cafe Sport, 2020 Western Avenue; (206) 443-6000; new American/Pacific Rim

Dahlia Lounge, 1904 Fourth Avenue; (206) 682-4142

Le Gourmand, 425 NW Market Street; (206) 784-3463; upscale Northwest

Rain City Grill, 2359 Tenth Avenue East; (206) 325-5003; Northwest seafood

Rover's, 2808 East Madison Street; (206) 325-7442; French/Northwest

Santa Fe Cafe, 5910 Phinney Avenue North; (206) 783-9755; Southwest

Scandie's, 2301 NW Market Street; (206) 783-9755; Scandinavian

Siam on Broadway, 616 Broadway East; (206) 324-0892; Thai

SEQUIM

The 3 Crabs, 101 Three Crabs Road; (206) 683-4264; local seafood

SNOQUALMIE

Old Honey Farm Inn Restaurant, 8910 - 384th Avenue SE; (206) 888-9899; Northwest

SPOKANE

Clinkerdagger, West 621 Mallon (Flour Mill); (509) 328-5965; seafood/steak/chicken

The Onion, West 302 Riverside; (509) 747-3852 - and - North 7522 Division, (509) 482-6100; soups/salads/burgers/dinners

Luigi's Italian Restaurant, North 113 Bernard; (509) 624-5226

Milford's Fish House and Oyster Bar, North 719 Monroe Street; (509) 326-7251

Patsy Clark's, West 2208 Second Street; (509) 838-8300; Continental

Peking Garden, East 3420 Sprague; (509) 534-2525; Mandarin Chinese

C.I.Shenanigan's, 322 North Spokane Falls Court; (509) 455-5072; seafood/prime rib

The Thai Cafe, 410 Sprague Road; (509) 838-4783

TACOMA

The Pacific Rim Restaurant, 100 South Ninth Street; (206) 627-1009

Stanley and Seaforts Steak, Chop, and Fish House, 115 East 34th Street; (206) 473-7300; seafood

BRITISH COLUMBIA

British Columbia

TWEEDSMUIR PROVINCIAL PARK

Prince George

COAST MOUNTAINS

WELLS GRAY PROV PARK

Kinbasket Lake

YOHO NATL PARK

STRAIT

Port Hardy

MALCOLM IS

Sointula

VANCOUVER

STRATHCONA PROV PARK

PACIFIC OCEAN

GARIBALDI PROVINCIAL PARK

VANCOUVER

Nanaimo

ISLAND

GEORGIA

OF

Victoria

Revelstoke

Kamloops

Monashee Pass

Vernon

Kelowna

Summerland

Penticton

Hope

Nelson

Rossland

KOOTENAY MOUNTAINS

See Detail Below

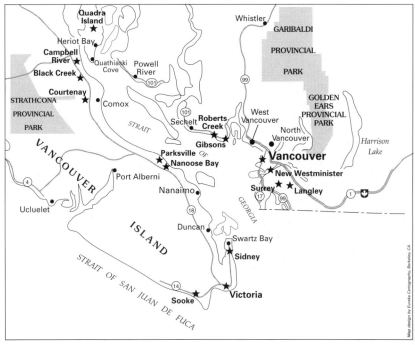

Quadra Island

Heriot Bay

Campbell River

Black Creek

Courtenay

STRATHCONA PROVINCIAL PARK

VANCOUVER

Quathiaski Cove

Powell River

Comox

STRAIT

Port Alberni

Ucluelet

ISLAND

Whistler

GARIBALDI PROVINCIAL PARK

GOLDEN EARS PROVINCIAL PARK

Harrison Lake

Sechelt

Roberts Creek

Gibsons

West Vancouver

North Vancouver

Vancouver

New Westminister

Surrey

Langley

Parksville

Nanoose Bay

Nanaimo

GEORGIA

OF

Duncan

Swartz Bay

Sidney

STRAIT OF SAN JUAN DE FUCA

Sooke

Victoria

Country Comfort   **(604) 337-5273**
P.O. Box 3, Black Creek, B.C. V0R 1C0
(8214 Island Highway between Courtenay and Campbell River)

If you like a rural atmosphere but appreciate modern conveniences and handy access to the highway, Ron and Elaine Bohn's Country Comfort has it all -- on fifty beautiful acres! It is equally satisfying for overnighters or for those who make it home base while exploring parks and beaches, fishing waters, Mount Washington, and Forbidden Plateau. The three neat guest rooms are done in pastel shades, and each has a different quilt theme. Elaine's handcrafted items enhance the cheerful decor, and her variety of breakfasts include farm fresh eggs, homemade bread, jams, and muffins. Guests are welcome in the main living areas but may enjoy the exclusive use of a downstairs family room for watching TV, reading, or visiting. An all-around generous spirit marks the hospitality found at Country Comfort.

No smoking in bedrooms; beach, golf course, boat marina, stores, restaurants, tennis court, petting zoo, and mini-golf nearby; off street parking. EP rates apply to children aged six to twelve; no charge for younger children. Brochure available.

ROOM	BED	BATH	ENTRANCE	FLOOR	DAILY RATES S - D (EP)
A	1Q	Shd*	Main	1	$30-$45 ($10)
B	1D	Shd*	Main	1	$30-$45 ($10)
C	1D	Shd*	Main	1	$30-$45 ($10)

Rates stated in Canadian funds

Pier House Bed & Breakfast   **(604) 287-2943**
670 Island Highway, Campbell River, B.C. V9W 2C3
(Heart of Campbell River facing ocean and harbor)

Pier House, circa 1924, is distinguished as the oldest house in town and the home of its first provincial policeman. Furnished with antiques of the period, it is an utterly charming combination of old curiosity shop, museum, and "Grandma's house." The allure of the library is most immediate: There are floor-to-ceiling bookshelves packed with vintage hardbacks, a dictionary on a stand, a globe, an old short-wave radio, and myriad other relics that beg to be examined. It's a place to settle in for a good read or a visit. Guest rooms, too, are long on character. Mementoes, art, and reading matter create the sense that the residents of yesteryear have just stepped out for a bit. Tunes from the old Victrola may accompany breakfast set with bone china and unique serving pieces now found only in antique shops. Pleasant surprises and touches of whimsy abound in the easygoing warmth of the Pier House.

No pets or children; smoking outside only; full breakfast; restaurants, pubs, shops, harbor, fishing pier, and Quadra Island ferry nearby; off-street parking; credit cards (V, MC).

ROOM	BED	BATH	ENTRANCE	FLOOR	DAILY RATES S - D (EP) +
A	1Q	Pvt 1/2	Main	1	$45-$55
B	1D	Shd*	Main	2	$50-$60 ($12)
C	1D	Shd*	Main	2	$40-$50
D	2T	Shd*	Main	2	$50-$60

Rates stated in Canadian funds

248

Willow Point Guest House   **(604) 923-1086**
2460 South Island Highway, Campbell River, B.C. V9W 1C6
(On left when heading north, south of town center)

This contemporary home offers not only easy access to the fishing activities of the "Salmon Capital of the World," but shipshape accommodations and top-notch hosts. Valerie and George Bright extend a style of hospitality that is friendly, courteous, and tailored to each guest's requirements. If you need to make a fishing charter, there will be a 4:00 a.m. breakfast and a packed lunch waiting (if required). Return later to a warm, clean place for some civilized comfort. You'll sleep in one of three impeccably furnished bedrooms on the home's upper level. All front windows face a breathtaking view of mountains and Discovery Passage. A full English breakfast -- or, if you choose, a lighter breakfast -- is served in a manner perfectly suited to the refined ambiance of Willow Point Guest House.

Cat in residence; no pets; no children under twelve; no smoking; no RV parking; full or light breakfast; refreshments offered on arrival; extra charge for packed lunch; TV and fireplace available to guests; fishing charters arranged; off-street parking; credit cards (V); airport pickup (Campbell River). Brochure available.

ROOM	BED	BATH	ENTRANCE	FLOOR	DAILY RATES S - D (EP)
A	1D	Shd*	Main	2	$40-$50
B	2T or 1K	Shd*	Main	2	$40-$55
C	2T or 1K	Pvt	Main	2	$50-$60 ($15)

Rates stated in Canadian funds

249

Greystone Manor   **(604) 338-1422**
Site 684, Comp. 2, R.R.6, Courtenay, B.C. V9N 8H9
(On Comox Bay, across from mainland Powell River)

You can reach this outdoor recreation mecca, the Comox Valley, via the Sunshine Coast or the highway from Nanaimo or Port Hardy. One of the oldest homes in the Comox Valley, Greystone Manor is set in one and a half acres of waterfront with views across Comox Bay to the mainland coast mountains. This is a perfect place to relax and use as a base for sampling the region's many activities. Hosts Mike and Mo Shipton moved to Canada from England in 1991. Both are keen gardeners, which is reflected in their colorful flower beds, hanging baskets, and window boxes. Mo enjoys cooking and serves a full breakfast including freshly baked muffins and scones. Watch the seals, herons, and bald eagles from the deck or take a stroll down to the beach. Winter skiing at two resorts, summer salmon fishing, and hiking are among the area's most popular attractions. When you're not busy outdoors, you'll appreciate all the homey comforts of Greystone Manor.

No pets or smoking; full breakfast; fireplace; off-street parking.

ROOM	BED	BATH	ENTRANCE	FLOOR	DAILY RATES S - D (EP) +
A	2T	Shd*	Main	2	$40-$50
B	1D	Shd*	Main	2	$40-$50
C	1D	Shd*	Main	2	$40-$50
D	1Q	Shd*	Main	2	$40-$50

Rates stated in Canadian funds

Ocean View Cottage   **(604) 886-7943**
R.R.#2, S46-C10, Gibsons, B.C. V0N 1V0
(On Sunshine Coast, west of Highway 101 just north of Gibsons)

When Bert and Dianne Verzyl designed their home and guest cottage on three rural acres, the view took top priority -- and rightfully so. The cliffside setting looks out across the Georgia Strait with Vancouver Island in the background. There are two neat quest rooms with private baths in the main house; they're at the opposite end from the hosts' quarters, and one has a great view. Set well away from the main house, the contemporary wood cottage is generously proportioned and completely self-contained. It has a full kitchen, a bedroom, a sofa bed, a cot, cable television, skylights, plenty of comfortable seating, a deck with table and chairs, and expansive windows to bring in the mesmerizing panorama. A few days at Ocean View Cottage should prove peaceful, restful, and utterly undemanding.

No pets or smoking; full breakfast; shopping, dining, golfing, hiking, fishing, scenic cruises, and sandy beaches nearby; off-street parking; Dutch and French spoken; airport pickup (Tyee at Sechelt). Brochure available.

ROOM	BED	BATH	ENTRANCE	FLOOR	DAILY RATES	
					S - D	(EP)
A	1Q	Pvt	Main	1	$45-$55	
B	2T	Pvt	Main	1	$45-$55	
C	1D	Pvt	Sep	1	$65	($20)

Rates stated in Canadian funds

251

Sonora Bed & Breakfast   **(604) 763-0969**
1732 Sonora Drive, Kelowna, B.C. V1Y 8K7
(Central Kelowna)

The neat, well-kept neighborhood in which you'll find Sonora Bed & Breakfast is near the hub of Okanagan Valley activity. Even so, it's quiet here, and the mountains in the background lend a countrified air. Kurt and Edith Grube's two story home offers a clean, comfortable, friendly environment. A large guest room on the first floor, tastefully decorated in neutral tones, has a brick hearth, a woodstove, and enough space for five people. Sharing a bathroom off the hallway is another bedroom, done in soft, elegant peach tones with a crown canopy over the bed. An upstairs bedroom with a homey atmosphere has a private bath down the hall. Edith's artistic touches adorn a wall here or a door there throughout the house. Her sumptuous breakfasts are often served on the garden sun deck with a beautiful mountain view.

No pets; smoking outside only; full breakfast; TV/VCR available; AC; sofa bed also in Room C; tennis courts and major golf course nearby; off-street parking; German spoken; airport and bus depot pickup. Off-season rates. Brochure available.

ROOM	BED	BATH	ENTRANCE	FLOOR	DAILY RATES S - D (EP)
A	2T	Pvt	Main	2	$40-$55
B	1Q	Shd*	Main	1G	$40-$50
C	1D & 1T	Shd*	Main	1G	$40-$60

Rates stated in Canadian funds

252

Jill & Royce Fisher   **(604) 534-1104**
5033 - 209 Street, Langley, B.C.   V3A 5Y4
(Just west of downtown Langley)

Staying at the Fishers' spacious split-level house puts you close to the U.S.-Canadian border, historic Fort Langley, and Vancouver (thirty minutes away by Skytrain). And while you're there, enjoy the friendly warmth of the Fishers' hospitality.   Jill is from Ontario, Royce from New Zealand; they've traveled widely but have grown very fond of the place they now call home. Guests here feel the freedom to really relax and put their feet up in a variety of places: the family room, living room, sun room, sun deck, or enclosed back yard. Two bedrooms off the hallway share a full bath at the end. One room has pale aqua walls with a pink and white print border and coordinating bed linens; the other is highlighted by dark wood antiques and lovely bed quilts. No matter where you sleep, the first thing your feet touch when you arise is a sheepskin on the floor at your bedside, a gentle experience that is but one aspect of the overall pleasure guests enjoy at the Fishers' home.

No pets; smoking outside only; fireplace, TV/VCR available; robes provided; swimming pool and horseback riding center nearby; off-street parking.

ROOM	BED	BATH	ENTRANCE	FLOOR	DAILY RATES S - D (EP)
A	1D	Shd*	Main	2	$40
B	2T	Shd*	Main	2	$40

Rates stated in Canadian funds

Muench's Bed & Breakfast (604) 888-8102
21333 Allard Crescent, Langley, B.C. V3A 4P9
(Thirty minutes southeast of Vancouver on Fraser River)

In a quiet, rural setting near historic Fort Langley, Bernie and Mina Muench live on the original homestead that the Muenches settled in the 1860s. Guests may fish from a bar in the Fraser River right at the back of the property. Beautiful mountains loom in the background as you look out over the river from this exceptionally lovely home. Among its many assets are an indoor pool, spa, and sauna, a fireplace, a piano, and the warmth that natural wood imparts to the interior. You'll find walnut, cedar, oak, teak, and birch in the various rooms. The tasteful decor and physical comfort of the home are appealing indeed, but it's the heartwarming hospitality experienced at the hands of Bernie and Mina that you'll remember most.

No pets; no smoking in bedroom area or living room; rates include Continental breakfast and are $2 less without breakfast, $2 more with full breakfast; other meals optional; Room C is a two-section family unit; crib available; good area for walking; three museums at Fort Langley; off-street parking.

ROOM	BED	BATH	ENTRANCE	FLOOR	DAILY RATES S - D (EP) +
A	2T	Shd	Main	1	$32-$39
B	1D	Shd	Main	1	$32-$39
C	2D & 1T	Shd	Main	LL	$25-$34

Rates stated in Canadian funds

The Brown House   **(604) 468-7804**
Box 62, Park Place, R.R.#2, Nanoose Bay, B.C. V0R 2R0
(Between Nanaimo and Parksville)

In a lovely garden setting with a rural flavor, The Brown House offers a roomy ground-floor suite for up to four guests. Enter from the carport where you've parked and you're in your own living room, decorated in earth tones and highlighted by a rustic, brick-hearthed fireplace. At the back of the suite is the quiet double bedroom and a bathroom with a shower. In this clean, pleasant environment you may enjoy breakfast, which is delivered each morning, at a table with a blue-water view out the front. Wander across the road to the shore and boat launch area or take a little drive to a popular sandy beach and picnic area. Golfing, island hopping, all manner of water recreation, and many easy day trips make Nanoose Bay a natural vacation destination. Anyone looking for extra privacy and extra good value will find The Brown House the natural place to stay.

No pets, children, or smoking; color cable TV; queen sofa bed in living room; wheelchair access; off-street parking; airport pickup (Qualicum). Second couple using sofa bed, $35. Brochure available.

ROOM	BED	BATH	ENTRANCE	FLOOR	DAILY RATES S - D (EP)
A	1D	Pvt	Sep	1G	$50 ($20)

Rates stated in Canadian funds

The Lookout   **(604) 468-9796**
Box 71, Blueback Drive, R.R.#2, Nanoose Bay, B.C. V0R 2R0
(Between Nanaimo and Parksville at 3381 Dolphin Drive)

Whether you've come to Nanoose Bay to play the challenging 18-hole Fairwinds Golf Course, to pause enroute to the dramatic West Coast, or just to relax in comfort at water's edge, The Lookout provides ideal headquarters. It offers close-up views of islands, the sea, and coastal mountains from the wide deck, from the living/dining area, or from the luxurious vantage point of the Captain's Suite (a favorite of honeymooners). Enhanced by its peaceful wooded setting, the home's interior is imbued with lively colors and plenty of light. Friendly hosts Marj and Herb Wilkie serve breakfast -- "what you want, when you want it" -- indoors or out, but always with the sea in sight. They'll understand if all you want to do is sit on the deck for hours watching the endless parade of wildlife and watercraft.

No pets; no children under seven; smoking outside only; full breakfast; Suite has TV and deck access; TV in Room C; pool, tennis courts, etc. at nearby Schooner Cove Resort; stables nearby; off-street parking. Self-contained, ground-floor apartment with TV/VCR available by week or in winter at $400/week for 2 or $600 for 4. *Closed November 1 to April 1.* Brochure available.

ROOM	BED	BATH	ENTRANCE	FLOOR	DAILY RATES S - D	(EP)
A	1Q	Shd*	Main	2	$55	
B	1T	Shd*	Main	2	$40	($10)
C	1Q	Pvt	Main	1	$70	

Rates stated in Canadian funds

Oceanside   **(604) 468-9241**
Box 26, Blueback, R.R.#2, Nanoose Bay, B.C. V0R 2R0
(Between Nanaimo and Parksville)

    In a secluded spot far removed from any main highway, Oceanside is set among tall trees overlooking the sandy beach of Schooner Cove. The beach feels as if it could be yours alone. The well-protected setting is enhanced by beautiful, mature landscaping. The home is as carefully tended as the grounds, creating a neat and inviting environment. Two clean, pleasant B&B rooms are located on the main floor. One has a private half-bath, a deck, and a view of the water; the other overlooks the garden. On the lower level is a large, self-contained vacation suite with all the conveniences one could hope for, a private deck, and easy access to the beach. A favorite activity of nature lovers is watching the myriad wildlife that visit the bay -- whales, eagles, otters and seals are spotted regularly. Hosts Lee and Leone Chapman can suggest a variety of interesting sights, restaurants, and things to do close by. They are sold on their location, and you will be, too.

    No pets; smoking outside only (decks); no RV parking; reasonably priced fishing charters offered by host; off-street parking. Vacation suite with full kitchen, fireplace, and color TV sleeps up to eight at $75 to $150; weekly rates. *Closed December-March.* Brochure available.

ROOM	BED	BATH	ENTRANCE	FLOOR	DAILY RATES S - D (EP) +
A	1Q	Shd*	Main	1	$50
B	1K	Pvt 1/2	Main	1	$65

Rates stated in Canadian funds

257

Gilgan's Bed & Breakfast   **(604) 521-8592**
333 Third Street, New Westminster, B.C. V3L 2R8
(Just southeast of Vancouver)

The municipality of New Westminster has many heritage homes from the turn of the century when it was, for a time, the capital of British Columbia. Some of the most notable architects of the day left their mark here along streets where the homes seem to be maturing as gracefully as the trees. One such home in the Queen's Park area is Gilgan's Bed & Breakfast; it's been fully refurbished and updated with modern conveniences. A spacious suite on the lower level has high ceilings, plenty of light, and a sitting area with a fireplace. There is another smaller room off the hallway and a separate guest entrance for easy access to the backyard sun deck, heated pool, and hot tub. The hospitality offered by the Gilgans is as gracious as one might expect in this distinctive neighborhood; the extra privacy is quite nice, too.

No pets or smoking; full breakfast; extra beds available; great area for walking; good selection of restaurants close by; ten-minute walk to Skytrain, then thirty minutes to downtown Vancouver; off-street parking; airport pickup (Vancouver).

ROOM	BED	BATH	ENTRANCE	FLOOR	DAILY RATES S - D (EP)
A	1Q	Pvt	Sep	LL	$60 ($10)
B	1D				$50

Rates stated in Canadian funds

Marina View Bed & Breakfast   **(604) 248-9308**
895 Glenhale Crescent, Parksville, B.C. V9P 1Z7
(Between Parksville and Qualicum Beach)

In a spectacular setting overlooking the Strait of Georgia, the islands, and the mountains beyond is Marina View Bed & Breakfast. It's a home full of modern luxuries where the main floor is almost entirely turned over to guests. From one guest room, from the large deck, and from the expansive solarium, you might catch the unforgettable sight of Alaskan cruise ships sailing past the marina into showy sunsets. Use the handy binoculars to spot eagles, shorebirds, seals, otters, and the occasional whale. A comfortable guest lounge offers TV, games, and bumper pool. Bedrooms feature bay windows with cushioned window seats. There is handy access to the shoreline where serious beachcombing might ensue, and host Dea Kern has worked out many intriguing day trips for people keen to explore. She can even charter you a fishing expedition and send you off with a delicious breakfast to enjoy on the boat. At Marina View, the setting and the personalized service stand out.

No pets or small children; smoking outside only; full breakfast; rollaway bed available; off-street parking; airport pickup (Qualicum). Brochure available.

ROOM	BED	BATH	ENTRANCE	FLOOR	DAILY RATES S - D (EP)
A	2T	Shd*	Main	1	$40-$60 ($20)
B	1D	Shd*	Main	1	$40-$55 ($20)
C	1Q	Pvt	Main	1	$65 ($20)

Rates stated in Canadian funds

259

Hamilton Bed & Breakfast   **(604) 949-6638**
Box 1926, Port Hardy, B.C. V0N 2P0
(9415 Mayor's Way, northwest section of town)

    The uninformed traveler tends to think of Port Hardy merely as a jumping-off point for the trip up the Inside Passage to Prince Rupert. But many outdoor enthusiasts are aware of Port Hardy's unique attributes. The area boasts excellent diving conditions; great waters for catching hefty halibut, salmon, and cod; and access to the wild, open ocean, raging surf, and white beaches of the island's West Coast (a day trip to San Josef Bay is a *must*). Touring the local copper mine and the Port Hardy Museum with its impressive collection of native artifacts is also popular. Lorne and Betty Hamilton offer clean and tidy accommodations in their quiet residential area, about a fifteen-minute walk from the waterfront. Both helpful and accommodating, the Hamiltons have hosted backpackers, business travelers, vacationers, outdoor lovers, sportsmen, and international students. Their home is a welcoming place for a good night's sleep at the remote tip of Vancouver Island.

    No pets; children by arrangement; smoking outside only; TV available; transportation to ferry dock or airport; off-street parking. Inquire about off-season rates for business travelers.

ROOM	BED	BATH	ENTRANCE	FLOOR	DAILY RATES S - D (EP)
A	1Q	Shd	Main	LL	$30-$45
B	2T	Shd*	Main	1	$30-$45
C	1D	Shd*	Main	1	$30-$40

Rates stated in Canadian funds

Bonnie Bell Bed & Breakfast (604) 285-3578
Box 331, Campbell River, B.C. V9W 5B6
(On West Road, two and one-half miles from ferry dock)

When John and Trudy Parkyn designed the home of their dreams, respect for the natural setting was their prime concern. Entirely hidden from other houses and the road, this B&B is set in the leafy privacy of alder and fir overlooking Gowlland Harbour, where loons and seals may be sighted. In every aspect, the ambiance is simple and pure, clean and uncluttered. The traditionally-styled home combines country freshness with handcrafted construction. The living and dining area has an open-beamed ceiling and high windows all around. White walls, a brick hearth, and an array of fine woodwork are enhanced by a few well-chosen antiques and heirlooms. Second-floor guest quarters with tree and water views consist of two wonderful bedrooms, a large, old-fashioned bathroom, a reading nook, and an enclosed porch. If you choose, you may charter a boat, the Bonnie Bell, skippered by John. And after a tranquil night's sleep, arise to an ample breakfast prepared by Trudy on the wood-fired cookstove; it can be plain or fancy, depending on your appetite. I suggest you let Trudy use her imagination -- you won't be sorry.

Dog in residence; children and pets welcome; smoking on porch; full breakfast; off-street parking. Brochure available.

ROOM	BED	BATH	ENTRANCE	FLOOR	DAILY RATES S - D (EP)
A	2T	Shd*	Main	2	$25-$50
B	1D	Shd*	Main	2	$25-$50

Rates stated in Canadian funds

261

Hyacinthe Bay Bed & Breakfast   **(604) 285-2126**
Box 343, Heriot Bay, B.C. V0P 1H0
(East coast of island, seven miles from ferry dock)

The contemporary home of Janice Kenyon and Ross Henry features dramatic open-beam cedar construction, a wide, wrap-around deck with a hot tub, and huge windows that frame a spectacular view of Hyacinthe Bay. Light bathes the interior, where traditional furnishings, family heirlooms, and Oriental rugs on polished wood floors create a most appealing contrast of old and new. A guest bedroom and bath on the main floor have been outfitted for maximum comfort and ease; there's extra sleeping space in the loft. The deck is a great place for sunbathing, stargazing from the hot tub, or enjoying a leisurely breakfast. Janice, a cookbook author, prepares a delectable specialty each morning and can provide a thermos of coffee to take to the beach. You may wish to share the good company of Janice and Ross, a physician; bask in the serene beauty of Hyacinthe Bay; take a hike up Chinese Mountain; spend time in quiet repose; or all of the above. A time of relaxation and renewal awaits you at this Quadra Island retreat.

No pets; children welcome; no smoking; full breakfast; picnic lunches or suppers on request; TV and VCR for movies (rentals nearby); barbecue; hot tub; fishing charters arranged; off-street parking; French and German spoken. Brochure available.

ROOM	BED	BATH	ENTRANCE	FLOOR	DAILY RATES S - D (EP)
A	2T	Pvt	Main	1	$50-$60 ($10)

Rates stated in Canadian funds

Joha House   **(604) 285-2247**
Box 668, Quathiaski Cove, Quadra Island, B.C. V0P 1N0
(Less than one mile from ferry dock)

After spending ten summers on beautiful Quadra Island, Joyce and Harold Johnson moved from California to take up full-time residency. Their unbridled enthusiasm is justified, as any visitor quickly learns. The contemporary wood home is oriented toward a breathtaking view of Quathiaski Cove, tiny Grouse Island, and the Inside Passage. Watch occasional cruise ships and regular ferries, or spot eagles and herons. Accommodations at Joha House include a self-contained, private garden suite and two B&B rooms on the upper level. Bedrooms are full of country charm with attractive quilts providing each color scheme. The living/dining area features custom-designed stained-glass windows and a fireplace of smooth local stones with hand-hewn yellow cedar trim. It's a splendid setting for enjoying a tasty breakfast in full view of nature's glory. With the Johnsons' help, discover the many joys of Quadra Island.

No pets; children welcome in suite; smoking permitted on deck; full breakfast; robes provided; woodstove and sofa bed in suite; dock for guest boats; good collection of literature on hiking, whale-watching trips (July-September), and other local activities; fishing charters arranged; off-street parking; ferry pickup for walkers. Three-night minimum in suite; inquire about weekly beach house rentals. Brochure available.

ROOM	BED	BATH	ENTRANCE	FLOOR	DAILY RATES S - D (EP)
A	1D	Shd*	Main	2	$45-$50
B	1Q	Shd*	Main	2	$50-$55
C	1Q	Pvt	Sep	LL	$65 ($12)

Rates stated in Canadian funds

L&R Nelles Ranch (604) 837-3800
P.O. Box 430, Revelstoke, B.C. V0E 2S0
(Highway 23 South)

Set amid the majesty of the Selkirk Mountains is L&R Nelles Ranch, located just a few miles out of delightfully refurbished downtown Revelstoke. Just being in this spectacular area affords a sense of wonder and exhilaration, and no one could love it more than Larry and Rosalyne Nelles. B&B guests are greeted with a warm, open, down-to-earth reception that makes them feel like members of the family. You'll find no urban cowboys here, but a realistic picture of life on a working horse ranch. For those so inclined, Larry offers wilderness trail rides of varying lengths at reasonable prices. Many photos and trophies displayed in the house attest to his expertise as a horseman. An expert skier as well, he knows intimately the area's variety of skiing opportunities. Rosalyne's full ranch breakfasts are sure to satisfy the most powerful of appetites. An enjoyable family atmosphere, comfortable accommodations, and breathtaking natural beauty are in store for you at L&R Nelles Ranch.

Small dog in residence; overnight horse accommodation; no smoking in bedrooms; full breakfast; TV/ VCR; crib and rollaway bed; doll museum with over 300 dolls and treasures on premises; numerous outdoor activities nearby. EP rate for adults in same room, $15. Brochure available.

ROOM	BED	BATH	ENTRANCE	FLOOR	DAILY RATES S - D (EP) +
A	1D	Shd*	Main	2	$35-$45 ($10)
B	2T	Shd*	Main	1G	$35-$50 ($10)
C	2D	Pvt	Main	1G	$35-$45 ($10)
D	1D	Shd*	Main	1G	$35-$45 ($10)
E	1D	Shd*	Main	2	$35-$45 ($10)

Rates stated in Canadian funds

Bed & Breakfast at Roberts Creek   **(604) 885-5444**
R.R.#2, S18-C7, Gibsons, B.C. V0N 1V0
(Off Highway 101 on Hanbury Road in Roberts Creek)

Walls of huge logs imbue the interior of the Cattanachs' home on five wooded acres with golden warmth. Trees on the property were felled to build this rustic dwelling where the feeling of domestic security is almost tangible. On the main floor, there's an antique wood cookstove, a floor-to-ceiling natural stone hearth and woodburning stove, and a view of grazing horses from the dining room. Upstairs, guests have their own sitting room, a bathroom off the hallway, and two bedrooms full of cozy charm. A crib can be provided, and there are books, games, and a television. Families find the arrangement particularly comfortable, but most anyone would take pleasure in the snug country ambiance of Bed & Breakfast at Roberts Creek.

No pets; smoking restricted; full breakfast; golfing, dining, horseback riding, picnicking, and good beaches nearby; off-street parking.

ROOM	BED	BATH	ENTRANCE	FLOOR	DAILY RATES S - D (EP)
A	1D	Shd*	Main	2	$35-$45 ($10)
B	2T	Shd*	Main	2	$35-$45 ($10)

Rates stated in Canadian funds

By the Sea Bed & Breakfast **(604) 886-2302**
General Delivery, Roberts Creek, B.C. V0N 2W0
(Near waterfront, Sunshine Coast)

In a woodsy setting facing the sea, the Gurrs' split-level home offers guest quarters on the upper floor that can be closed off for complete privacy. The light, airy space is done in ivory and lilac and has an ensuite bath, two beds, bookshelves, a desk, a TV, sliding glass doors, and a balcony. The view is yours to savor every moment if you wish, even during breakfast in the dining room downstairs. There is easy access to the beach where you'll no doubt want to linger on mild days. Escape to the peaceful seclusion of By the Sea Bed & Breakfast, secure in the knowledge that you've found one of the best values around.

No pets; child over ten welcome; no smoking; full breakfast; TV; off-street parking; golfing, horseback riding, dining, picnicking, other beaches, kayaking, boat charters, and Festival of the Written Arts (mid-August) nearby.

ROOM	BED	BATH	ENTRANCE	FLOOR	DAILY RATES S - D (EP)
A	1Q & 1T	Pvt	Main	2	$40-$45 ($10)

Rates stated in Canadian funds

Country Cottage Bed & Breakfast   **(604) 885-7448**
General Delivery, Roberts Creek, B.C. V0N 2W0
(On Sunshine Coast, off Highway 101 just north of Gibsons)

You'll find Country Cottage Bed & Breakfast in the tiny hamlet of Roberts Creek. The heart warms at first glimpse of this small, butterscotch-colored farmhouse, trimmed in red, with flower gardens flanking the walkway. In the yard are fruit trees, a vegetable garden, sheep grazing contentedly, and chickens roaming about. The interior was lovingly created by hosts Loragene and Philip Gaulin. The look of rich wood, colorful handloomed rugs, nostalgic collectibles, and family heirlooms brings to mind the simple pleasures of an earlier time. Upstairs, the Rose Room evokes in every detail a Victorian rose garden, and a delightful solarium/half-bath is attached. Loragene's legendary breakfasts, prepared on a wood-burning cookstove, are served with exquisite care in the old-fashioned country kitchen. Incurable romantics like to escape to their own little world in the sweetest cottage imaginable, just to the right of the farmhouse. It has an iron bed, a pull-out sofa, a full kitchen, cable TV, a woodstove, colorful rugs, and decor in blues and reds. The extraordinary charm of Country Cottage is the result of a clear vision perfectly realized.

Dog and cat in main house; no pets; children over nine welcome; no smoking; full breakfast; afternoon tea and scones; for bathing, Rose Room shares full bath on main floor; fifteen-minute walk to beach and excellent restaurant; off-street parking; French spoken.

ROOM	BED	BATH	ENTRANCE	FLOOR	DAILY RATES S - D (EP)
A	1D	Pvt 1/2	Main	2	$50-$60
B	1D	Pvt	Sep	1	$70-$80 ($15)

Rates stated in Canadian funds

The Willows Inn   **(604) 885-2452**
Box 1036, Sechelt, B.C. V0N 3A0
(On Beach Avenue, off Highway 101 at Roberts Creek)

Imagine getting away to a meticulously handcrafted little cottage in the woods with its own yard enclosed by a rose-clad split-rail fence. The 500-square-foot dollhouse has beautiful hardwood floors and cabinetry, skylights, ceiling fans, a full tiled bath with a host of little luxuries, a table for two by a picture window, a glass-front woodstove, and a small kitchen area where coffee, tea, and goodies are kept. Peachy-pink walls cast a warm glow to an interior accented by evergreen, white, and brass. After a restful night in a bed of exceptional comfort, a home-cooked breakfast is delivered to your doorstep at the time of your choosing. John and Donna Gibson, whose luxurious log home is at the front of the property, have created this heartwarming haven in the forest where their guests are pampered in countless ways. The Willows Inn is a place to make some romantic dreams come true.

No pets; no smoking; country Continental breakfast; no RV parking, but guest car parking right beside cottage; color TV; sink and small fridge; fine dining, salmon fishing (information available), beaches, shops, and galleries nearby; airport pickup (Tyee).

ROOM	BED	BATH	ENTRANCE	FLOOR	DAILY RATES S - D (EP)
A	1Q	Pvt	Sep	1	$55-$65 ($10)

Rates stated in Canadian funds

Heritage Hill Bed & Breakfast (604) 362-9697
P.O. Box 381, Rossland, B.C. V0G 1Y0
(Three blocks from town center)

It was the beauty and grandeur of the Kootenays that first brought Jill and Chris Perry to Rossland. Skiing at nearby Red Mountain is among the finest anywhere, and hikers are thrilled to explore the many marked trails in the area. The Perrys found a turn-of-the-century character home and set about restoring its Tudoresque, old-world charm. Common areas are endowed with polished hardwood floors, heavy-beamed ceilings, and stained-glass windows. Choose a book from the library to curl up with by the living room fireplace; in the morning, convene in the formal dining room for one of Jill's full English breakfasts. As night falls in the Canadian Rockies, welcome slumber in one of the newly renovated, comfortable rooms at Heritage Hill. And no matter what you do when you visit the Kootenays, don't forget your camera!

Cat in residence; children over five welcome; no pets; smoking restricted; full breakfast; TV available; transportation to ski area arranged; off-street parking. Brochure available.

ROOM	BED	BATH	ENTRANCE	FLOOR	DAILY RATES S - D (EP) +
A	2T	Shd*	Main	2	$35-$60
B	1D	Shd*	Main	2	$35-$60
C	1D	Shd*	Main	2	$35-$60
D	1Q	Shd*	Main	2	$35-$60

Rates stated in Canadian funds

Orchard House Bed & Breakfast (604) 656-9194
9646 Sixth Street, Sidney, B.C. V8L 2W2
(Central Sidney)

Lovely gardens and old trees punctuate this orchard land of yester-year that once extended to water's edge. The Craftsman-style heritage home was built in 1914 by the son of the town's founder. Its friendly appearance hints at the welcoming spirit within. Handsome interior features include ample woodwork, leaded and stained glass, built-in cabinetry, and a quaint fireplace of small beach stones and shells. On the main floor, the spacious Rose Room and Duck Room share a bath down the hall. Charming upstairs quarters are all wood, angles, and sloped ceilings. The Lace Room and the Tree Room share a hallway bath and a cozy woodstove in the common area. Breakfasts are large, healthy, and homemade. Hosts Joan and Gerry enjoy their lovingly preserved home -- and so will you.

No pets; no children under twelve; smoking outside only; full breakfast; walk to parks, tennis courts, shops, restaurants, and Ana-cortes ferry terminal; short drive to Swartz Bay ferries, airport, and Butchart Gardens; under half an hour from Victoria; off-street park-ing. Brochure available.

ROOM	BED	BATH	ENTRANCE	FLOOR	DAILY RATES S - D (EP)
A	1Q	Shd*	Main	1	$59-$69 ($15)
B	1Q	Shd*	Main	1	$59-$69 ($15)
C	1D	Shd*	Main	2	$49-$59 ($15)
D	1D	Shd*	Main	2	$49-$59 ($15)

Rates stated in Canadian funds

Ocean Bliss   **(604) 973-6537**
P.O. Box 253, Sointula, B.C.   V0N 3E0
(On Malcolm Island off Port McNeill, Vancouver Island)

I was urged by others to make the extra effort of managing an
unscheduled visit to Sointula; it turned out to be pure serendipity.
Sointula is a small fishing village that was settled at the turn of the
century by Finns seeking an existence of peace and harmony. "Pro-
gress" has been, thankfully, slow in coming to this outpost of unri-
valed beauty and serenity. Similar to an English country cottage in
appearance, Ocean Bliss overlooks Rough Bay, an ever-changing vista
of sloops and fishing boats, sky and mountains, shorebirds and eagles.
Inside, there's a wonderfully eclectic mix of fine artwork, Oriental
rugs, antiques, books, and music. A fireplace in the living room
warms the open dining room and kitchen as well, and you're free to
enjoy it all. Guest quarters are in a cozy back bedroom with exclusive
use of the main floor bathroom. (Hosts' quarters are upstairs.)
Nicholas and Anita Galitzine are very kind hosts and interesting
company. Their Ocean Bliss is a treasure to be savored by the
fortunate souls who find it.

Dog in residence; smoking outside only; full breakfast; hiking,
crabbing, fishing, diving, and whale-watching nearby; ferry pickup.
For a more rustic experience, inquire about the private, self-catering
cabin (Ocean Breeze) on the property.

ROOM	BED	BATH	ENTRANCE	FLOOR	DAILY RATES S - D (EP)
A	2T	Pvt	Main	1	$30-$45

Rates stated in Canadian funds

271

Bed & Breakfast by the Sea (604) 642-5136
6007 Sooke Road, R.R.#1, Sooke, B.C. V0S 1N0
(One and one-half miles east of Sooke Village)

The sheer physical beauty of the setting is overwhelming. Facing Sooke Basin (part of the Pacific), the land is heavily forested with Douglas fir and western red cedar and bordered by a creek to the west and an inlet and private beach to the east. Here Marjorie and Dalton Schrank offer the quiet, gentle environment of their home where guest accommodations, located well away from the hosts' sleeping quarters, consist of two bedrooms sharing a bath off the hallway. One is prettily done in white and lilac; navy blue prevails in the other. Guests also have exclusive use of a large, luxurious living room with a brick fireplace and an expansive ocean view. Or, for total privacy, choose the sunny, secluded cottage just steps from the water with its own beach. It has a full kitchen, a bed with a view, and extra sleeping space for up to six people. Sighting herons, swans, otters, deer, and rabbits is common at Bed & Breakfast by the Sea. So is the joy of pure relaxation.

Dog in residence; no pets in main house; no smoking; full breakfast; cable TV and rollaway beds in cottage; VCR available; barbecue and picnic area; off-street parking.

ROOM	BED	BATH	ENTRANCE	FLOOR	DAILY RATES S - D	(EP)
A	1D	Shd*	Main	1	$70-$75	
B	1Q	Shd*	Main	1	$70-$75	
C	1Q & 1D	Pvt	Sep	1	$95	($15)

Rates stated in Canadian funds

Burnside House   **(604) 642-4403**
1890 Maple Avenue, Box 21, R.R.4, Sooke, B.C. V0S 1N0
(Off Route 14, just past Sooke Village)

A glimpse of the Sooke region's pioneer heritage can be yours at Burnside House, circa 1870. The renovated Georgian farmhouse originally belonged to Michael Muir, fourth son of John Muir, Sr., who initiated Sooke's lumbering industry. It is ideally located for exploring historical sites, arts and crafts stores, and the area's exceptional parks. Hosts Renata and Heinz von Tilly are proud of the fact that the renovation and decoration of Burnside House received a Hallmark Society Award of Merit. They offer guests a choice of five generously proportioned bedrooms sharing two full baths on the second floor, some with water and mountain views. On the main floor, there is an attractive living/dining room exclusively for guests. The Tillys' style of hospitality is summed up in their irresistible slogan: "We'd love to spoil you."

Children eight and older welcome; no smoking preferred; full country breakfast; antique shop on property; golfing, swimming, hiking trails, salt and fresh water fishing, seal and whale-watching nearby; picnic lunches and bicycles available; off-street parking; German spoken; credit cards (V, MC). 10% surcharge for one-night stays. Brochure available.

ROOM	BED	BATH	ENTRANCE	FLOOR	DAILY RATES S - D (EP) +
A	2T	Shd*	Main	2	$60-$65
B	1Q	Shd*	Main	2	$65-$70
C	1D	Shd*	Main	2	$60
D	1Q	Shd*	Main	2	$70-$75
E	1D	Shd*	Main	2	$50

Rates stated in Canadian funds

Malahat Farm
(604) 642-6868

Anderson Road, R.R. #2, Sooke, B.C. V0S 1N0
(Eight miles west of Sooke)

A genuine Canadian farm vacation awaits you at a fully restored heritage house near Sooke. Surrounded by acres of bucolic farmland, the wonderful vintage home has two accommodations of the highest caliber on each floor. Upstairs there is a guest lounge and two of the most inviting bedrooms imaginable, outfitted with antiques, down comforters, ruffled curtains, and bathrooms with whiter-than-white clawfoot tubs. The same is true of the bath in the main-floor bed/sitting room that has a fireplace and a four-poster bed. Another bedroom with a big snowball tree at the window has a brass bed, a bay window, a corner fireplace, and a bath with a shower. Host Diana Clare's abundant breakfasts are the quintessence of farm-fresh, homemade goodness and feature her own organic produce. Visitors love the silence and tranquility of the farm. They thrill to see how bright stars can be in an ink-black sky. But most of all, they're touched by the caring hospitality at the very heart of Malahat Farm.

Dogs, cat, and farm animals on property; no pets or children; full country breakfast; claw foot tubs have hand-held showers; fridge, beverage-brewing center, and sitting area in guest lounge; bicycles available; beachcombing, bird and whale-watching, hiking, and picnicking in nearby parks; salmon charters arranged.

ROOM	BED	BATH	ENTRANCE	FLOOR	DAILY RATES	
					S - D	(EP) +
A	1Q	Pvt	Main	2	$80-$85	($20)
B	1Q	Pvt	Main	2	$80-$85	($20)
C	1Q	Pvt	Main	1	$90-$95	($20)
D	1Q	Pvt	Main	1	$90-$95	($20)

Rates stated in Canadian funds

Heritage House   **(604) 494-0039**
Box 326, Summerland, B.C. V0H 1Z0
(Walking distance from town center at 11919 Jubilee Road)

Marsha Clark's heritage home was built in 1907, around the time Summerland was founded. The sparkling white frame house with a blue door stands on a hill surrounded by stately old trees, with mountains in the background and a view out over the town. Ever so inviting is the wrap-around veranda, ideally suited for sitting, visiting, reading, or enjoying Marsha's wonderful, home-cooked breakfasts. Guests have a choice of three bright, spacious, second-floor rooms that share two large bathrooms (with a choice of shower or tub). The front room, done in pale yellow with antiques, can sleep three people or a family. The overall feeling of the house combines a sense of dignity, admirable simplicity, and informal comfort. The hospitality is easygoing and accommodating. From this secure home base, all the wonders of the Okanagan are yours to explore year-round.

No pets; smoking outside only; full breakfast; robes provided; laundry privileges; off-street parking. Brochure available.

ROOM	BED	BATH	ENTRANCE	FLOOR	DAILY RATES S - D (EP)
A	1Q & 1T	Shd*	Main	2	$40-$50 ($15)
B	1Q	Shd*	Main	2	$40-$50
C	2T	Shd*	Main	2	$40-$50

Rates stated in Canadian funds

275

Bed & Breakfast on the Ridge (604) 591-6065
5741 - 146 Street, Surrey, B.C. V3S 2Z8
(Off Highway 10, south Surrey)

Panorama Ridge is home to Dale and Mary Fennell, who appreciate its quiet, rural flavor along with its good access to the U.S.-Canadian border crossing, ferries, the airport, shopping centers, Skytrain to Vancouver (thirty minutes), and major freeways. Their large contemporary home is set on a wooded half acre, where the country ambiance is ever-present whether you're going for a walk, relaxing on the wide sun deck that encircles the house, or enjoying the hospitality indoors. Cathedral ceilings and lots of skylighting give the whole interior a bright, airy feeling. On the upper level, guests may read or watch TV in their own sitting area. Furnishings lean toward modern comfort, with a sprinkling of antiques for counterpoint. Bed & Breakfast on the Ridge is an easygoing place where a family could feel as much at home as a business traveler or a vacationing couple.

No smoking in bedrooms; TV/VCR available in recreation room; crib and playpen available; off-street parking; airport pickup (Vancouver). Brochure available.

ROOM	BED	BATH	ENTRANCE	FLOOR	DAILY RATES S - D (EP)
A	1Q	Pvt	Main	1	$55
B	1Q	Shd*	Main	2	$30-$40
C	2T	Shd*	Main	2	$30-$40
D	1Q & 1T	Shd*	Main	2	$30-$40 ($10)

Rates stated in Canadian funds

White Heather Guest House   **(604) 581-9797**
12571 - 98 Avenue, Surrey, B.C. V3V 2K6
(Twenty minutes from U.S.-Canada border at Blaine)

A sincere welcome awaits you at White Heather Guest House, home of Glad and Chuck Bury. The quiet southeast suburb of Vancouver offers good bus service, as well as a fun and easy trip downtown by Sky Train. At afternoon tea time, you may wish to enlist the help of your seasoned hosts in planning your stay. They consistently search out cream-of-the-crop experiences to share with guests. Whether you're looking for the perfect restaurant -- ethnic, family, or special occasion -- or for attractions that are most worth visiting, the Burys offer sound advice. Full English breakfasts, cooked to perfection by Chuck, are served in a sunny, garden-like room with a dramatic view of snow-capped mountains. Spend leisure moments relaxing or visiting on the patio overlooking the back garden. All this, plus a good night's sleep, makes White Heather Guest House a most hospitable place to stay.

No pets; family accommodation by arrangement; no smoking; no RV parking; full breakfast; fireplace and TV available; games room with toys and piano; licensed chauffeur available; off-street parking; pickup from airport or cruise ships. Inquire about EP rates.

ROOM	BED	BATH	ENTRANCE	FLOOR	DAILY RATES S - D (EP) +
A	1Q	Pvt 1/2	Main	1	$40-$45
B	1D	Shd*	Main	1	$35-$40

Rates stated in Canadian funds

277

Beachside Bed & Breakfast   (604) 922-7773
4208 Evergreen Avenue, West Vancouver, B.C. V7V 1H1
(West of Lion's Gate Bridge, just south of Marine Drive)

It would be difficult to top this Vancouver location: Just steps from the door you're on a sandy beach sniffing the salt air, watching gulls circle overhead, and feeling buoyant. The contemporary waterfront home offers fantastic views from the dining room where breakfast is served, from the outdoor whirlpool spa and deck, and from the deluxe suite at the rear of the ground-level guest floor. Soothing pastel colors blend with the seaside setting, and fresh fruit and flowers, delightful artwork, and comfortable furnishings enhance the accommodations. Hosts Gordon and Joan Gibbs want you to enjoy the quiet, relaxing ambiance of their home as well as the interesting local activities and day trips that they thoughtfully describe in the literature placed in each room. Gordon and Joan promise "a warm, friendly Canadian welcome." Believe me, that's only the beginning.

Dog in residence; no pets; no children under eight; no smoking; TV available; full breakfast; off-street parking; credit cards (V, MC). Brochure available.

ROOM	BED	BATH	ENTRANCE	FLOOR	DAILY RATES S - D (EP) +
A	1Q & 1T	Pvt	Sep	1G	$85-$95 ($20)
B	1Q	Pvt	Sep	1G	$95-$105
C	1Q	Pvt	Sep	1G	$125-$135

Rates stated in Canadian funds

Laburnum Cottage   **(604) 988-4877**
1388 Terrace Avenue, North Vancouver, B.C. V7R 1B4
(Off Capilano Road, enroute to Grouse Mountain)

    The home of Delphine Masterton is tucked away in a quiet corner of a gracious older neighborhood that is wonderful for walking. Despite its feeling of seclusion, it's convenient to downtown Vancouver, Horseshoe Bay, Grouse Mountain, and other attractions. Laburnum Cottage is set in a half-acre English garden so breathtaking that one feels privileged to experience its serene beauty. A meandering stream crossed by a little red bridge, an exquisite array of pampered plants, and a pond with a rippling fountain delight the senses and the soul. The enchantment of the garden permeates the guest quarters. A refined English charm marks the interior of the main house, where lovely bedrooms on the second floor overlook the garden. Set in its midst is the Summerhouse Cottage (pictured), a self-contained haven with a romantic brass bed and a fresh, light atmosphere. There is another, larger cottage (E) that sleeps up to six. It's all here: lodging for most any occasion and first-rate hospitality to match the magnificent setting.

    Cat in residence; no pets; smoking outside only; full breakfast; good public transportation; nine-hole golf course, public tennis courts nearby; off-street parking; French and German spoken; credit cards (V, MC).

ROOM	BED	BATH	ENTRANCE	FLOOR	DAILY RATES S - D (EP) +
A	1Q	Pvt	Main	2	$95 ($30)
B	1Q	Pvt	Main	2	$95 ($30)
C	1Q	Pvt	Main	2	$95 ($30)
D	1D	Pvt	Sep	1	$125 ($30)
E	1Q	Pvt	Sep	1	$125 ($30)

Rates stated in Canadian funds

279

Castle on the Mountain   (604) 542-4593
Site 10, Comp. 12, R.R.#8, Vernon, B.C. V1T 8L6
(Upper Okanagan Valley at 8227 Silver Star Road)

This large Tudor-style home is located on the southern exposure of Silver Star Mountain, seven miles from city center. The elevation not only allows a sweeping view of valley, lakes, and the lights of Vernon, but gives you a head start in getting to the ski slopes at Silver Star (seven miles away). In this choice setting, Castle on the Mountain offers a unique lodging experience. Hosts Sharon and Eskil Larson are artists/craftspeople; they have an ever-changing collection in their in-home gallery studio where guests enjoy browsing. Tea service is offered on the deck. The entire ground floor provides accommodations. There's a living room with places to relax by the fire; a kitchen area for light meals; two bedrooms that share a bathroom with a shower; and one bedroom with private bath, Jacuzzi tub, and shower -- views are phenomenal from this huge turret-shaped and multiwindowed room (C). The third floor has one comfortable guest room, a bath with a large shower, and a private "crow's nest" balcony. All in all, Castle on the Mountain is spectacular.

Smoking outside only; allergy-free environment; full breakfast; TV; phone; outdoor spa; picnic area; summer hiking, beaches, and fruit-picking; winter skiing (Alpine and Nordic) and snowmobiling; off-street parking; wheelchair access; credit cards (V, MC, AE).

ROOM	BED	BATH	ENTRANCE	FLOOR	DAILY RATES S - D (EP) +
A	1D	Shd*	Sep	1G	$50-$60
B	1D	Shd*	Sep	1G	$50-$60
C	1Q & 1T	Pvt	Sep	1G	$65-$75 ($20)
D	1K & 1T	Pvt	Main	3	$65-$75 ($20)

Rates stated in Canadian funds

Bayridge Guest Lodge   **(604) 658-8592**
5175 Beckton Road, Victoria, B.C. V8Y 2C2   **FAX:(604) 658-5109**
(Near Cordova Bay)

In a setting that feels peaceful and remote yet is only fifteen minutes from downtown, Ernst and Lydia Kaufmann offer a variety of suites in their modern guest lodge. Staying here is almost like having your own apartment: The Kaufmanns keep things in tip-top condition and provide comforts and extra touches unique to quarters custom-built with travelers' needs in mind. Join other guests in the spacious lounge for the hearty breakfast specialties that Ernst cooks and Lydia serves. People desiring extra privacy, great views, and roomy, immaculate accommodations are sure to appreciate Bayridge Guest Lodge.

No pets or children; smoking restricted; full breakfast; TV and refrigerator in each suite; some kitchenettes; queen sofa bed in D and E; sandy beach, parks, restaurants, Fable Cottage, and new Cordova Bay Golf Course (18 holes, driving range, restaurant, and lounge) nearby; deluxe personalized tours conducted by Ernst; off-street parking; German and Spanish spoken; major credit cards. Brochure available.

ROOM	BED	BATH	ENTRANCE	FLOOR	DAILY RATES	
					S - D	(EP) +
A	1Q	Pvt	Main	1	$75	
B	1Q & 1D	Pvt	Main	1	$69	($18)
C	1Q & 1T	Pvt	Main	1	$59	($18)
D	1Q	Pvt	Main	LL	$81	($18)
E	1Q	Pvt	Main	LL	$81	($18)

Rates stated in Canadian funds

Bender's Bed & Breakfast (604) 477-6804
4254 Thornhill Crescent, Victoria, B.C. V8N 3G7
(One mile from University, five miles from downtown)

Bender's suburban location is near University of Victoria, Mount Douglas Park, Cordova Bay, and shopping centers, yet only five miles from the heart of town. The clean, comfortable accommodations here are easy on the budget and offer variety and flexibility -- very helpful for families or larger groups. Guests in the bedrooms on the lower level of the house may enjoy a large sitting room with a stone fireplace and a TV. Upstairs, guests tend to gather in the living room. The neighborhood is safe, quiet, and good for walking. Mrs. Bender has a lot of regular guests who appreciate her easy, come-and-go-as-you-please manner and the all-around good value she offers.

No pets or smoking; full breakfast; TV in Rooms A and E; off-street and street parking. Brochure available.

ROOM	BED	BATH	ENTRANCE	FLOOR	DAILY RATES S - D	(EP)
A	1D	Pvt	Main	1	$50	
B	1D	Shd*	Main	1	$40	
C	1D	Shd*	Main	1	$40	
D	1D & 1T	Shd*	Main	LL	$45	($20)
E	1D & 1T	Pvt	Main	LL	$55	($20)
F	1Q	Shd*	Main	LL	$50	

Rates stated in Canadian funds

Camellia House   **(604) 370-2816**
1994 Leighton Road, Victoria, B.C. V8R 1N6
(Near Oak Bay)

One glance at this picture-perfect little house tells you that someone cares a lot about it.   It's pale yellow trimmed in blue with
well-tended gardens out back and a rainbow of garden colors throughout. What the small-scale wonder lacks in size it more than makes up
for in charming details.   There is a bright, lovely bedroom with
ensuite bath on the main floor overlooking the back yard.   Two
upstairs rooms are especially cozy and pretty, with a shared bath off
the hallway and an intimate seating area that beckons one to relax with
a cuppa tea.   Each room has been so carefully fashioned that its
personality is almost tangible. Jo Brooks and Jo Caragata have endowed Camellia House with endearing scenes at every turn, amenities
too numerous to mention, and comforts aplenty. A pleasing variety of
breakfast specialties rounds out the flawless hospitality they provide.

No pets, children, or smoking; full breakfast; TV/VCR available;
swimming nearby; near bus route; fifteen-minute walk to Oak Bay
waterfront; ample street parking; some Japanese and Spanish spoken;
credit cards (V, MC). Brochure available.

ROOM	BED	BATH	ENTRANCE	FLOOR	DAILY RATES S - D (EP)
A	1Q	Pvt	Main	1	$70-$80
B	1D	Shd*	Main	2	$55-$65
C	2T	Shd*	Main	2	$55-$65

Rates stated in Canadian funds

Carriage Stop Bed & Breakfast　　　　　　**(604) 383-6240**
117 Menzies Street, Victoria, B.C. V8V 2G4
(Short walk from beach and downtown)

　　Close proximity to the heart of Victoria is just one of the assets of
Carriage Stop Bed & Breakfast. Jane McAllister's blue heritage home
has a gabled roof, interesting angles, and lots of character. The
charm of its age comes through, while renovations have given the
interior a clean, new feeling of light and openness. With this background, the well-chosen artwork shows up to good advantage. One of
the guest rooms is on the first floor; two rooms and a bath on the
second floor make ideal quarters for several people traveling together.
Besides the convenient location and agreeable atmosphere, you'll get
expert advice on picking that special restaurant to suit your mood,
your palate, and your purse. At Carriage Stop, the best of old and new
come together in an ambiance of casual comfort.

　　Two cats in residence; no pets; no children under twelve; smoking
outside only; no RV parking; full breakfast; robes provided; common
room with fireplace and TV; patio in summer; credit cards (V, MC);
good public transportation and airport connections. Off-season rates.

ROOM	BED	BATH	ENTRANCE	FLOOR	DAILY RATES S - D (EP)
A	1D & 1T	Shd	Main	1	$50-$60 ($15)
B	1D	Shd*	Main	2	$50-$60
C	1D & 1T	Shd*	Main	2	$50-$60 ($15)

Rates stated in Canadian funds

Charlotte's Guest House   (604) 595-3528
338 Foul Bay Road, Victoria, B.C. V8S 4G7
(Off Crescent Road waterfront)

The namesake of Charlotte's Guest House was an elegant Persian cat once owned by hosts Rose Marie and Bruce Arlidge. They do her memory proud by offering visitors a great sense of privacy and comfort. Located within steps of Gonzales Bay, Charlotte's has a separate guest entrance to the ground-floor accommodations. The two bedrooms, set well apart, are especially spacious, nicely furnished, and tranquil. There is a snack room off the hallway where guests may have coffee, tea, or take-out food. The hosts' passion for gardening is obvious in the well-tended grounds around the giant outcroppings of rock that characterize the local landscape. Observe the gardens close-up, from the deck, or during breakfast upstairs in the dining room, which also has a heady view across Juan de Fuca Strait to the Olympics. The Arlidges are helpful but unobtrusive, and the value they offer is exceptional.

No pets; smoking restricted; full breakfast; TV in each room; many local walks and drives; on bus route; off-street and street parking; limited wheelchair access. Brochure available.

ROOM	BED	BATH	ENTRANCE	FLOOR	DAILY RATES S - D (EP)
A	1D	Pvt	Sep	1G	$60
B	2T	Pvt	Sep	1G	$60

Rates stated in Canadian funds

The Crow's Nest   **(604) 383-4492**
71 Linden Avenue, Victoria, B.C. V8V 4C9   **FAX: (604) 383-3140**
(Just east of Beacon Hill Park and a half-block from waterfront)

This 1911 heritage home was designed by Samuel Maclure, a leading architect of the time, in his American Chalet style. It has large, sunny rooms, an abundance of impressive woodwork, beveled and stained glass, and polished fir floors covered with Oriental rugs. Original light fixtures lend an Arthurian charm. Furnishings are largely English and Flemish antiques. A second-floor guest room at the front of the house and another at the back share a split bath off the hallway. Kit and Dene Mainguy are superb hosts. Kit has honed his skills as a former hotelier down to a smaller, more personal scale. He serves a most savory English breakfast in the formal dining room. He and Dene intuit guests' needs very well and accommodate them in every way possible.

Dog and cat in residence; no pets; infants and children over eight welcome; restricted smoking; full breakfast; special diets accommodated; robes provided; rollaway beds available; Dallas Road waterfront, shops, bistros, and tearooms nearby; ten-minute bus ride or thirty-minute walk to town; ample street parking; French spoken. Brochure available.

ROOM	BED	BATH	ENTRANCE	FLOOR	DAILY RATES S - D (EP)
A	1Q	Shd*	Main	2	$65-$80 ($15)
B	2T or 1K	Shd*	Main	2	$65-$80 ($15)

Rates stated in Canadian funds

The Haterleigh   (604) 384-9995

243 Kingston Street, Victoria, B.C. V8V 1V5
(Two blocks from inner harbor, three from Empress Hotel)

Winner of the prestigious Hallmark Award for restoration, this 1901 heritage home is superbly detailed, from the gingerbread carving outside to the elaborate mouldings, plaster archways, and leaded glass inside. High ceilings and delicate shades of paint and wallpaper make the large rooms extra light and airy. With names like Roses and Lace, Victoriana, Secret Garden, and Day Dreams, you can begin to imagine the array of romantic accoutrements that lend character and charm to each one. The Haterleigh makes you want to celebrate whether you have an occasion or not. Hosts hold themselves to this maxim: "Every room lovingly restored, every meal tastefully prepared, every service graciously provided." And it shows.

Cat in residence; no pets or smoking; full breakfast; some Jacuzzi tubs; off-street parking; credit cards (V, MC). "2 nights for 1" weekend special; off-season rates. Brochure available. *extra-long double beds in A, B, and D

ROOM	BED	BATH	ENTRANCE	FLOOR	DAILY RATES S - D (EP) +
A	1D*	Pvt	Main	2	$70
B	1D*	Pvt	Main	2	$90
C	1K	Pvt	Main	1	$110
D	1D*& 1Q	Pvt	Main	2	$130 ($20)
E	1Q	Pvt	Main	2	$125
F	1Q	Pvt	Main	1	$135

Rates stated in Canadian funds

Hibernia Bed & Breakfast   **(604) 658-5519**
747 Helvetia Crescent, Victoria, B.C.   V8Y 1M1
(Near Cordova Bay)

Aideen Lydon, who hails from Galway Bay, is Irish through and through -- and so is her home. As it is in the old country, hospitality here is lively, warm, and generous. The two-story brick home, set at the end of a cul-de-sac, is surrounded by extensive grounds with lovely old trees, vines and flowers, and country quiet. Inside, its ample character is enhanced by lots of wood paneling, Oriental rugs, antiques, artwork, and family memorabilia. The guest lounge downstairs, offering television, a grand piano, books, and games, is especially cozy and inviting. Relax here or in the garden -- and you're welcome in the main living area as well. Aideen's many repeat guests come back for the comfortable beds, the huge, delicious breakfasts, and (most of all) a visit with their quintessential Irish hostess.

No pets; smoking outside only; full breakfast; location central to ferries, airport, Butchart Gardens, and city; Fable Cottage, lakes, parks, golf, tennis, dining, and country walks nearby; off-street parking. Brochure available.

ROOM	BED	BATH	ENTRANCE	FLOOR	DAILY RATES S - D (EP)
A	1Q	Pvt	Main	1	$40-$60
B	1D	Pvt	Main	1	$40-$60
C	2T	Pvt	Main	2	$40-$60

Rates stated in Canadian funds

The Inn on St. Andrews   **(604) 384-8613**

231 St. Andrews Street, Victoria, B.C. V8V 2N1
(James Bay area, near Beacon Hill Park)

The glorious gardens surrounding this heritage property do justice to its stature and grace. Built in 1913 by Edith Carr, eldest sister of the famous Canadian artist and author Emily Carr, the grand home is lovingly tended by proud owner Joan Peggs. Starting with its innate fine craftsmanship, elegant woodwork, stained and beveled glass, and gracious proportions, she has used ivory, pale green, peach, and pink in fashioning an interior that is at once light, welcoming, and sooth-ing. Common areas -- living room, delightful sun room, formal dining room, and TV room -- seem truly meant to be enjoyed as one's own. Large, bright bedrooms are located off the central second-floor landing. At Joan's beautifully preserved inn, guests usually reach such a level of at-homeness that they return whenever possible to its familiar embrace.

Smoking outside only; full breakfast; walk to heart of town, ocean front, and Beacon Hill Park; near bus route; ample street parking; credit cards (MC, en route). Off-season rates. Brochure available.

ROOM	BED	BATH	ENTRANCE	FLOOR	DAILY RATES	
					S - D	(EP) +
A	1D	Shd*	Main	2	$50-$65	($15)
B	1Q	Shd*	Main	2	$50-$65	
C	2T	Shd*	Main	2	$50-$65	($15)

Rates stated in Canadian funds

289

Laird House   **(604) 384-3177**
134 St. Andrews Street, Victoria, B.C. V8V 2M5
(James Bay area, near Beacon Hill Park)

An exceptional place to stay in the quiet and lovely James Bay section of Victoria is the inviting 1912 heritage-style home of Ruth Laird. It has been restored and decorated with the utmost attention to detail. In fact, one gets the feeling that every square inch of Laird House was fashioned to offer visual delight and comfort to its inhabitants. On the main floor, a guest living room and parlor exude quality; coffered ceilings and impressive woodwork are enhanced by beautiful floral motifs in rose, green, and cream. Tea and sherry are available to sip by the fireplace as soft music soothes the senses. On the second floor, two most attractive bedrooms (one with a fireplace and balcony) are full of special touches including fresh flowers and fruit. Two shared bathrooms are stocked with amenities while another room contains a guest refrigerator, sink, coffee, tea, and cookies. Elegant three-course breakfasts are served in the prettiest dining room imaginable -- a sterling way to start your glorious day in Victoria!

Cat in residence; no pets, children, or smoking; no RV parking; full breakfast; robes and hair dryers provided; walk to heart of town, ocean front, and Beacon Hill Park; near bus route; off-street parking; credit cards (V, MC).

ROOM	BED	BATH	ENTRANCE	FLOOR	DAILY RATES S - D (EP) +
A	1D	Shd*	Main	2	$55-$65
B	1Q	Shd*	Main	2	$55-$65

Rates stated in Canadian funds

Manley's Bed & Breakfast   (604) 384-9844
239 Superior Street, Victoria, B.C. V8V 1T4
(James Bay area, near inner harbor and Empress Hotel)

Flexibility is key at Dorothy Manley's well-located older home. Mrs. Manley, who's from England, is a long-time "B&B person" and believes in hospitality that poses few restrictions. She has outfitted the house with a variety of options for lodgers: There are beds of all sizes with down comforters, smoking and non-smoking rooms, shared and private baths, and some rooms where children are welcome. There is a spacious sun deck behind the large, bright dining room where full English breakfasts are served. Travelers from far and near appreciate the gracious treatment and relaxed atmosphere found at Manley's.

Dog in residence; no smoking in dining room and some guest rooms; cribs and cots available; off-street and street parking; credit cards (V, MC). EP rate for children under twelve, $8; off-season and extended stay rates. Brochure available.

ROOM	BED	BATH	ENTRANCE	FLOOR	DAILY RATES	
					S - D	(EP) +
A	1Q	Pvt	Main	1	$65	($15)
B	2T	Shd*	Main	2	$45-$55	($15)
C	1Q & 1T	Shd*	Main	2	$45-$55	($15)
D	1Q	Shd*	Main	2	$45-$55	($15)
E	2T	Pvt	Sep	LL	$65	($15)
F	1Q	Pvt	Sep	LL	$65	($15)

Rates stated in Canadian funds

Rose Cottage
(604) 381-5985

3059 Washington Avenue, Victoria, B.C. V9A 1P7
(One and one-half miles northwest of inner harbor)

A stay at this charming 1912 guest house takes you into a world of the turn-of-the-century seaport of Victoria. The guest parlor with an oak-manteled fireplace, as well as the large dining room with a library wall, are done in a nautical theme featuring period furnishings and paintings of clipper ships. Host Robert Bishop has sailed extensively in the South Pacific and has many stories to tell; his wife, Shelley, makes fine, full breakfasts that include homemade muffins, scones, jams, and organic eggs. There are four bright, cheery guest rooms with high ceilings. The Blue Room (A) even has a small mother-in-law or childrens' room adjacent. Shared split baths offer the choice of a shower or a wonderful soak in a large, cast iron clawfoot tub. Without a doubt, Rose Cottage offers an authentic experience in the finest tradition of bed and breakfast.

No pets; children welcome; baby-sitting available; large yard with tree house; smoking outside only (veranda); full breakfast; ample street parking; credit cards (V, MC); good public transportation and airport connections. Off-season weekly rates. Brochure available.

ROOM	BED	BATH	ENTRANCE	FLOOR	DAILY RATES S - D (EP)
A	1Q & 1D	Shd*	Main	2	$65-$75 ($18)
B	1Q	Shd*	Main	2	$65-$75
C	1D	Shd*	Main	2	$65-$75
D	1Q	Shd*	Main	1	$65-$75

Rates stated in Canadian funds

Sealake House   **(604) 658-5208**
5152 Santa Clara Avenue, Victoria, B.C. V8Y 1W4
(Overlooking Elk Lake)

Set on a rural lane amidst a half-acre of country gardens, this 1905 home has been carefully refurbished by the Laidmans. Their private sleeping quarters are all on the second floor; guests have a choice of three lovely rooms on the main floor as well as their own sitting room and a large full bath off the hallway. An understated country warmth marks the interior. Particularly charming is the character dining room where breakfast is presented, often on pieces from a collection of English antique china. On nice mornings, guests dine on the porch to take in the view of the lake and wooded surroundings. Wildlife such as rabbits, deer, birds, and squirrels visit regularly. Beyond the Laidmans' property, there are excellent places to hike, cycle, run, and enjoy water sports. At Sealake House, experience friendly hospitality in a restful atmosphere, with many area attractions only minutes away.

No pets; families welcome; smoking outside only; full breakfast; guest sitting room; Cordova Bay and Butchart Gardens nearby; fifteen-minute drive to heart of Victoria; off-street parking. Off-season rates.

ROOM	BED	BATH	ENTRANCE	FLOOR	DAILY RATES S - D (EP)
A	1D	Shd*	Main	1	$45-$60 ($15)
B	1Q	Shd*	Main	1	$45-$60 ($15)
C	1Q	Shd*	Main	1	$45-$60 ($15)

Rates stated in Canadian funds

The Sea Rose   **(604) 381-7932**
1250 Dallas Road, Victoria, B.C. V8V 1C4
(On sea front)

On a corner lot facing the famous view across Juan de Fuca Strait
to the snow-capped Olympics, this revitalized 1921 home far exceeds
its modest outward appearance. Inside, common areas are possessed
of a beautifully refurbished Craftsman-like charm. Each of the four
spacious, luxurious view suites is outfitted with a modern private
bath, fridge, wet bar, and TV. All are light, airy, and particularly
soothing. Guests may come and go as they please using the separate
entrance adjacent to the rear parking lot. Host Karen Young keeps the
premises immaculate top to bottom, dispenses all manner of assistance
to guests, and prepares a palate-pleasing hot breakfast each morning.
The Sea Rose is a pristine retreat offering genial hospitality, a great
location, and exceptional comfort.

No pets, children, or smoking; full breakfast; coin-op laundry
available; on bus route; off-street parking. Inquire about off-season
and senior rates. Brochure available.

ROOM	BED	BATH	ENTRANCE	FLOOR	DAILY RATES S - D (EP) +
A	1Q	Pvt	Sep	2	$80
B	2T or 1K	Pvt	Sep	1G	$95 ($20)
C	1Q	Pvt	Sep	1G	$95 ($20)
D	1Q	Pvt	Sep	3	$110 ($20)

Rates stated in Canadian funds

Seaview Bed & Breakfast　　　　　　　　**(604) 383-7098**
1144 Dallas Road, Victoria, B.C.　V8V 1C1　**FAX:(604) 385-1962**
(On sea front near Beacon Hill Park)

Think back to your most satisfying bed and breakfast experience in England -- or imagine what it would be like. In other words, think of the very *essence* of bed and breakfast: warm, lively hosts, a comfortable bed, and a hearty breakfast. Add to this a breathtaking view of the Olympic Mountains and lights of Port Angeles across the Strait of San Juan de Fuca. From Pat and Alec Gordon's seaside home, stroll along the waterfront, explore adjacent Beacon Hill Park, or make the five-minute drive to city center (many people walk). These words from a former guest of the Gordons appeared in the *San Francisco Examiner:* "The hosts...provide comfortable beds and a superb breakfast, with congeniality, a rare sense of humor, and an unusual willingness to help out a tired or frustrated tourist." I couldn't have said it better myself.

Small dog in residence; no pets or smoking; full English breakfast; TV in each room; Room B has sun porch; ample street parking; ferry pickup at city harbor; bus from Swartz Bay ferry. Hosts also operate a B&B reservation service listing homes in the neighborhood from $55 to $95.

ROOM	BED	BATH	ENTRANCE	FLOOR	DAILY RATES	
					S - D	(EP)
A	1Q & 1T	Pvt	Main	1	$55-$75	($20)
B	1Q	Pvt	Main	2	$55-$75	

Rates stated in Canadian funds

Sonia's Bed & Breakfast by the Sea   **(604) 385-2700**
175 Bushby Street, Victoria, B.C. V8S 1B5
(East of Beacon Hill Park, one block from waterfront)

Sonia McMillan is as clear on her own identity as she is on that of her lodging establishment, so there's no mistaking this B&B for anyone else's. As she'll readily tell you, she doesn't do antiques and she requires full payment in advance. In return, she offers quality lodgings at a good value; her breakfasts are as bountiful as the rest of the hospitality. Guests are invited to make themselves at home in the living room, the family room, or the deck (with ocean view) -- they're even free to use the good crystal from the display cabinet. Dusty, the African Grey parrot, usually hangs out in the family room and becomes a friend of guests who so choose. People who stay at Sonia's appreciate the extent to which she and her husband, Brian, open their comfortable home to guests. They have a *great* time, too.

No children under thirteen; smoking outside only; full breakfast; TV/VCR and fireplace in family room; good access to long walks along waterfront; on bus route; off-street and street parking. Off-season rates March & April. Brochure available. *Closed October-February.*

ROOM	BED	BATH	ENTRANCE	FLOOR	DAILY RATES S - D (EP)
A	1Q	Pvt	Main	1	$70
B	1Q	Pvt	Main	1	$70
C	1K	Pvt	Main	1	$75

Rates stated in Canadian funds

Sunnymeade House Inn   (604) 658-1414

1002 Fenn Avenue, Victoria, B.C. V8Y 1P3
(At Cordova Bay; central to ferries, Butchart Gardens, and city)

The country English-style home of Nancy and Jack Thompson is, in a word, exceptional. The picture-perfect garden and patio are as well maintained as the house itself, and the Thompsons have clearly anticipated everything a guest might need or desire. A hallway leads from the foyer on the main floor up to the guest quarters. There is a lounge for guests, along with four bedrooms, a bed/sitting room (D), and three baths. Luxurious, tastefully appointed rooms have their own vanity/sinks, luggage racks, and other niceties. Luscious full breakfasts are served, with a choice of menu items. For a warm welcome, elegant accommodations, and first-rate hospitality, Sunnymeade House Inn is simply unsurpassed.

No pets; smoking outside only; full breakfast; extra-long bed in Room A; walking distance from beach, fine restaurants, and the new world-class Cordova Bay Golf Course; regular bus service to Victoria and Swartz Bay ferry; off-street parking; credit cards (V). Room F is a bed/sitting room, available in season. Inquire about EP, weekly, and monthly rates. Brochure available.

ROOM	BED	BATH	ENTRANCE	FLOOR	DAILY RATES
					S - D (EP) +
A	1D	Shd*	Main	2	$65-$69
B	1Q	Shd*	Main	2	$69-$79
C	1D	Shd*	Main	2	$65-$69
D	1D & 1T	Shd*	Main	2	$69-$79
E	1Q	Pvt	Main	2	$79-$89
F	1Q	Pvt	Main	1	$89-$99

Rates stated in Canadian funds

297

Top O'Triangle Mountain

(604) 478-7853

3442 Karger Terrace, Victoria, B.C. V9C 3K5 **FAX:(604) 478-2245**

(Between Victoria and Sooke)

Staying out of the city has its advantages -- peace and quiet, a slower pace, ease of parking -- but this B&B offers much more. Top O'Triangle Mountain is just twenty-two minutes out of Victoria, but the view from this elevation is wondrous: the city and inner harbor, Port Angeles, the Olympic Mountains, and a spectacular light show at night. The house is built of interlocking cedar logs, and the warmth of wood permeates the interior. There are plenty of windows, decks all around, and a solarium where ample breakfasts are served. The three guest accommodations, all with private baths, include a room on the main floor and, on the ground floor, a mini-suite and a suite with a TV/sitting room. Comfort and silence ensure a sound sleep. Hosts Henry and Pat Hansen encourage unrestricted relaxation and sincerely want guests to think of their B&B as home.

No pets; families welcome; no smoking in rooms or dining area; full breakfast; off-street and street parking; credit cards (V, MC). Room A has a water and mountain view, a sliding glass door to the deck, TV, and ensuite bath; it is available June-August only; otherwise, another room on the main floor is used. Brochure available.

ROOM	BED	BATH	ENTRANCE	FLOOR	DAILY RATES S - D (EP)	
A	1Q	Pvt	Main	2	$85	
B	1Q	Pvt	Main	1G	$75	($15)
C	1Q	Pvt	Main	1G	$60	

Rates stated in Canadian funds

The Vacationer   **(604) 382-9469**
1143 Leonard Street, Victoria, B.C.   V8V 2S3   **384-6553**
(Two blocks from beach, bordering Beacon Hill Park)

One glance at this B&B and you feel the promise of something good inside. Pass the manicured front lawn and flower beds, enter the front door, and you'll receive the heartiest of welcomes from hosts Anne and Henry DeVries. They raised their family here and now keep their home in top shape for B&B guests. The spacious living room with a fireplace of stone is so comfortable that you might feel like inviting friends in for a visit -- and you are welcome to do so. The adjacent dining area is the scene of beautifully presented, four-course breakfasts. Anne prides herself on coming up with a different specialty each morning, no matter how long you stay. Three pretty bedrooms with excellent mattresses and color TVs, along with two bathrooms, occupy the second floor. Hosts offer the use of their secluded back yard, bicycles, and a separate phone line. They have a wealth of budget-stretching tips that should help to maximize your resources while visiting lovely Victoria.

No pets, children, or smoking; full breakfast; robes provided; tennis courts nearby; walking distance from downtown; off-street parking; Dutch and German spoken; credit cards (V, MC); free pickup from downtown, ferries, and bus depot. Off-season rates. Host also operates a B&B reservation service offering a variety of other accommodations. Brochure available.

ROOM	BED	BATH	ENTRANCE	FLOOR	DAILY RATES S - D (EP)
A	1Q	Shd*	Main	2	$45-$70 ($20)
B	1Q	Shd*	Main	2	$45-$70
C	2T	Shd*	Main	2	$45-$70

Rates stated in Canadian funds

Viewfield Inn (604) 389-1190

1024 Munroe Street, Victoria, B.C. V9A 5N9

(Ten-minute drive from city, northwest of inner harbor)

With the ambiance of a small private estate, this 1895 country Victorian was expanded in 1989 to accommodate guests. The blend of old and new works unusually well here. An air of peaceful seclusion is created by a velvety lawn met by beautiful rock and flower gardens with tall shrubs at the outer edges. Tall trees in the background hide all but a marvelous view across the strait to the entrance of the inner harbor and on to the Olympic Peninsula. The inn's guest quarters include a sitting/dining room endowed with warm Victorian charm as well as such amenities as a wet bar, fridge, TV/VCR and movies, and an array of parlor games, books, and puzzles. Two luxuriously appointed, antique furnished bedrooms were individually designed to be as lovely as they are comfortable. Fresh flowers, wonderful breakfasts, the park-like setting, and the view are just a few of the good memories hosts Larry and Valarie Terry hope you'll take with you from Viewfield Inn.

No pets, children, or smoking; full breakfast; walk to Olde England Inn, Fleming Beach, and Macauley Point Park; off-street parking; credit cards (V, MC). One bedroom suite, $140. Brochure available.

ROOM	BED	BATH	ENTRANCE	FLOOR	DAILY RATES S - D (EP)
A	1Q	Pvt	Sep	2	$80
B	1Q	Pvt	Sep	2	$95

Rates stated in Canadian funds

The Weathervane   (604) 592-0493
1633 Rockland Avenue, Victoria, B.C. V8S 1W6
(Near Craigdarroch Castle, four minutes to downtown)

Decades of antique collecting and interest in fine cuisine come together in splendid style at the character-laden home of John, Sue, and David Cabeldu. The interior is a tasteful blend of venerable furnishings, Oriental carpets, old prints, lovely paintings, and English chintz, with botanical themes recurring throughout the decor. Spacious guest accommodations are deliciously luxurious, featuring goosedown quilts and private baths. Some rooms have superb views toward the sea, while a deluxe suite also has a Jacuzzi tub, balcony, and sitting area. A living room for guests has a fireplace and is the picture of old-world civility, and the dining room table is properly set for the sumptuous morning meals John prepares. For first-class service and surroundings, The Weathervane shines.

No pets; children over ten welcome; no smoking; full breakfast; fridge, tea, and coffee center; private garden; tennis rackets available; near bus route; off-street parking; wheelchair access, Room B. Brochure available.

ROOM	BED	BATH	ENTRANCE	FLOOR	DAILY RATES
					S - D (EP) +
A	1K	Pvt	Main	2	$120-$125($20)
B	1K	Pvt	Main	1	$100-$105($20)
C	1Q	Pvt	Main	2	$85-$90 ($20)
D	1Q	Pvt	Main	2	$85-$90 ($20)

Rates stated in Canadian funds

Wellington Bed & Breakfast   **(604) 383-5976**
66 Wellington Street, Victoria, B.C. V8V 4H5
(Just east of Beacon Hill Park and a half-block from waterfront)

With her marvelous talent for design, Inge Ranzinger has coaxed every charming nuance out of her Fairfield character home. Its interior is fresh, artistic, and classy. In the main-floor common areas, tones of mauve, pink, and aquamarine contrast with lots of white -- a splendid setting for pretty patterned rugs, myriad collectibles and art objects, and very homey furnishings. Equal flair marks the upstairs guest quarters. The White Room is a vision of palest lilac, white, fresh and dried flowers, and lovely works of glass. The Hearth Room has colonial blue wallpaper, lace curtains, and a fireplace; The Antique Room is a bit smaller and more traditional. Inge and her daughter, Sue, offer hospitality to match the inspired design of Wellington Bed & Breakfast.

Cat in residence; no pets; no smoking; no children under twelve; full breakfast; ensuite bath in Room C; bath across hall from Room B; bath on first floor for Room A; Dallas Road waterfront, shops, bistros, and tearooms nearby; ten-minute bus ride or thirty-minute walk to town; off-street and street parking; German and Spanish spoken. Off-season rates.

ROOM	BED	BATH	ENTRANCE	FLOOR	DAILY RATES S - D (EP) +
A	1Q	Pvt	Main	2	$45-$60
B	1K	Pvt	Main	2	$55-$80
C	1Q & 1T	Pvt	Main	2	$55-$80 ($15)

Rates stated in Canadian funds

Wooded Acres Bed & Breakfast　　　　　　**(604) 478-8172**
4907 Rocky Point Road, R.R.#2, Victoria, B.C. V9B 5B4
(Between Victoria and Sooke)

The rural municipality of Metchosin is becoming known as a center for organic farming and for arts and crafts. It is particularly fitting to find here Wooded Acres Bed & Breakfast where "made-from-scratch" finds full expression. In a majestic forest setting, Elva and Skip Kennedy's home was built with logs from their property, and the mellow beauty of cedar, oak, and fir has tremendous appeal. The warm, snuggly atmosphere is enhanced by a rustic stone fireplace, heavy beams at the ceilings, country antiques, and intriguing displays of artifacts recovered from the local area. On the second floor, one party of guests at a time enjoys complete privacy. There's a choice between two very charming bedrooms, a hallway with an old-fashioned ice box for guests' use, a large bathroom with a clawfoot tub, and a huge private spa in a room exposed to the wilderness on one side. Breakfast is a literal feast of home-baked specialties, fresh brown eggs, old-fashioned slab bacon, and Elva's own jams and jellies. Country goodness is reflected in every facet of the romantic escape to be found at Wooded Acres.

No pets; children over ten welcome; full breakfast; golf, hiking, tennis, and beachcombing nearby; off-street parking. Two couples, $150. Brochure available.

ROOM	BED	BATH	ENTRANCE	FLOOR	DAILY RATES S - D (EP) +
A	2Q	Pvt	Main	2	$85

Rates stated in Canadian funds

303

Please read "About Dining Highlights" on page *vii*.

CAMPBELL RIVER

Charron's, 1376 Island Highway; (604) 286-0009; Continental

Gourmet-by-the-Sea, 4378 South Island Highway, Oyster Bay; (604) 923-5234; fresh seafood/creative Continental

Le Chateau Briand, 1170 Island Highway; (604) 287-4143; Continental

The Royal Coachman Inn, 84 Dogwood Street; (604) 286-0231; Continental

The Willows Neighbourhood Pub, 521 Rockland Road; (604) 923-8311

COURTENAY

La Cremaillere Restaurant, 975 Comox Road; (604) 338-8131; French

LANGLEY

J.R. Barbecue House, 20270 Fraser Highway; (604) 530-0886

The Seahorse at Ken Oddy's, 20563 Douglas Crescent; (604) 534-3131; West Coast specialties

NANOOSE BAY

Schooner Cove Resort, 3521 Dolphin Drive; (604) 468-7691; varied menu/fresh local seafood/pub fare

NEW WESTMINSTER

des Gitans, 83 Sixth Street; (604) 524-6122; Swiss

PARKSVILLE

Kalvas Restaurant, 180 Molliet; (604) 248-6933; seafood/European

PENTICTON

Theo's, 687 Main Street; (604) 492-4019; Greek

PORT HARDY

Brigg Seafood House, Market and Granville Streets; (604) 949-6532

Snuggles, Pioneer Inn; (604) 949-7575; seafood/steaks over alder coals

Sportsman's Steak & Seafood House, Market Street; (604) 949-7811

QUADRA ISLAND

Isaqwaluten Lodge, Cape Mudge; (604) 285-2042; West Coast/salmon barbecues

QUALICUM BEACH

Tudor Tea Rooms Restaurant, 3336 West Island Highway; (604) 752-6053; English lunch/tea/dinner

REVELSTOKE

Black Forest Inn, TransCanada Highway West; (604) 837-3495; Bavarian dishes and seafood

The 112, Regent Inn, 112 East First Street; (604) 837-2107; Continental

ROBERTS CREEK

The Creekhouse, Roberts Creek Road and Beach Avenue; (604) 885-9321; Continental

SECHELT

Blue Heron Inn, East Porpoise Bay Road; (604) 885-3847; waterfront dinners

SIDNEY

Blue Peter Pub & Restaurant, 2270 Harbour Road; (604) 656-4551; waterfront seafood

Cafe Mozart, 2470 Beacon Avenue; (604) 655-1554; fine dining

Rumrunner Pub, 9881 Seaport Place; (604) 656-5643; waterfront seafood

The Stonehouse Pub, 2215 Canoe Cove; (604) 656-3498; pub fare in old English character house

SOOKE

The Breakers, West Coast Road, Jordan River; (604) 646-2079; varied seafood

Good Life, A Bookstore Cafe, 2113 Otter Point Road; (604) 642-6821; fresh local specialties

Mom's Cafe, 2036 Shields Road; (604) 642-3314; hearty house-made dishes

Sooke Harbour House, 1528 Whiffen Spit Road; (604) 642-3421; Pacific Northwest/in fresh local seafood/ fine dining

SUMMERLAND

Shaugnessy's Cove, 12817 Lakeshore Drive; (604) 494-1212; seafood restaurant/pub

The Stone House, 14015 Rosedale Avenue; (604) 494-4022

VANCOUVER

Bishop's, 2183 West Fourth Avenue; (604) 738-2025; contemporary home cooking

Cin Cin, 1154 Robson Street; (604) 688-7338; Mediterranean

Favorito Pasta Trattoria, 552 West Broadway; (604) 876-3534; Italian

Kameros Restaurant, 2422 Marine Drive, West Vancouver; (604) 922-5751; Greek

Kettle of Fish, 900 Pacific Street; (604) 682-6661; fresh seafood

La Toque Blanche, 4368 Marine Drive, West Vancouver; (604) 926-1006; Continental

Le Crocodile, 818 Thurlow Street; (604) 669-4298; French

Lorenzo Ristorante Italiano, Ltd., 3605 West Fourth Avenue; (604) 731-2712

Maria's Taverna, 2324 West Fourth Avenue; (604) 731-4722; Greek

Montri's, Fourth Avenue and Trafalgar Street; (604) 738-9888; Thai

Orestes, 3116 West Broadway; (604) 732-1461; Greek

Pasparos Taverna, 132 West Third Street, North Vancouver; (604) 980-0331; Greek

Raintree, 1630 Alberni Street; (604) 688-5570; Northwest Coast

Szechuan Chongqing Restaurant, 2495 Victoria Drive; (604) 254-7434

Top of Vancouver Revolving Restaurant, Harbour Center, 555 West Hastings Street; (604) 669-2220; traditional favorites/West Coast specialties

West Vancouver Seafood & Grill, 2168 Marine Drive, West Vancouver; (604) 922-3312; seafood/grilled meats

VICTORIA

Adrienne's Tea Garden Restaurant, 5325 Cordova Bay Road; (604) 658-1515; Continental

The Bird of Paradise Pub, 4291-A Glanford Avenue; (604) 727-2568; Mediterranean/pub fare

Blethering Place, 2250 Oak Bay Avenue; (604) 598-1413; British

DINING HIGHLIGHTS: BRITISH COLUMBIA

Camille's, 45 Bastion Square; (604) 381-3433; West Coast contemporary

Chantecler Restaurant, 4509 West Saanich Road; (604) 727-3344; Continental

Chauney's, 614 Humboldt Street; (604) 385-4512; seafood

Colwood Corners Pub, 1889 Island Highway; (604) 478-1311

Cordova Seaview Inn, 5109 Cordova Bay Road; (604) 658-5227; steaks/seafood

Da Tandoor, 1010 Fort Street; (604) 384-6333; Indian

Four Mile House, 199 Island Highway; (604) 479-2514; tea room/pub/restaurant in historic roadhouse

The French Connection, 512 Simcoe Street; (604) 385-7014; French

Grand Central Cafe, 555 Johnson Street; (604) 386-4747; contemporary Cajun/Creole

Harbour House Restaurant, 607 Oswego Street; (604) 386-1244; seafood/steaks

Herald Street Caffe, 546 Herald Street; (604) 381-1441; Italian/Continental

James Bay Tea Room, 332 Menzies Street; (604) 382-8282; British

John's Place, 723 Pandora Avenue; (604) 389-0711; fresh, house-made, innovative breakfast/lunch/dinner

Kaz, 1619 Store Street; (604) 386-9121; Japanese

The Latch, 2328 Harbour Road, Sidney; (604) 656-6622; Continental/seafood in elegant historic waterfront home

The Metropolitan Diner, 1715 Government Street; (604) 381-1512; eclectic

Oak Bay Beach Hotel, 1175 Beach Road; (604) 598-4556; afternoon tea

Olde England Inn, 429 Lampson Street; (604) 388-4353; English/prime rib

The Oxford Arms Pub & Restaurant, 301 Cook Street; (604) 382-3301; international/pub fare

Periklis, 531 Yates Street; (604) 386-3313; Greek

Rebecca's, 1127 Wharf Street; (604) 380-6990; view dining

Romeo's Pizza, four locations: downtown at 760 Johnson, at 1581 Hillside, in Langford at 2945 Jacklin, and at Quadra and Mackenzie

Siam, 1314 Government Street; (604) 383-9911; Thai

Six Mile House, 494 Island Highway; (604) 478-3121; changing menu of beef/seafood/pasta

Soho Village Bistro, 1311 Gladstone Avenue; (604) 384-3344; eclectic

Spinnakers Brew Pub, 308 Catherine Street; (604) 386-BREW; self-serve brewpub/lunch/snacks/dinner

Swan's Pub, 506 Pandora Avenue; (604) 361-3310; pub fare

The Swiss Neighbourhood Restaurant; 1280 Fairfield Road; (604) 384-6446; Swiss/European

Three-eight-six Deli, 1012 Blanshard Street; (604) 386-3354; pasta/pizza/soups/desserts/takeout items

The Tudor Rose Tea Room, 253 Cook Street; (604) 382-4616; light meals/afternoon tea

WHITE ROCK

Black Forest, 3140 King George Highway; (604) 536-7950; German

APPLICATION TO LIST YOUR B&B IN *BED & BREAKFAST HOMES DIRECTORY - WEST COAST*

Name(s) _____

Mailing address _____

City/State/Zip _____
City/Province/Postal Code

Telephone _____

Best time to phone you _____

Brief description of your home and room(s) available: _____

_____

_____

_____

_____

_____

_____

_____

_____

_____

_____

There is a two-year listing fee which is equal to two times the highest (double) rate you charge for one night's lodging. (Example: If your rate is $60, listing fee is $120.) Hosts must maintain clean, comfortable accommodations and a hospitable manner toward guests. Fee is payable upon author's visit.

Signature _____

Date _____
DEADLINE: March 1, 1993

CUT HERE

From_____

_____

_____

Diane Knight
Knighttime Publications
890 Calabasas Road
Watsonville, CA 95076

- - - - - - - - - - - - - - -FOLD HERE - - - - - - - - - - - - - - -

CUT HERE

STAPLE OR TAPE

B&B TRAVELERS REPORT

Knighttime Publications would like to receive any comments you may have about your experiences while using this directory. Please report any comment, suggestion, compliment or criticism as indicated:

Name and location of B&B _____

Date of visit _____

Length of stay _____

Comments _____

_____

_____

_____

_____

_____

_____

_____

_____

_____

_____

_____

Your name _____

Address_____

City/State/Zip _____
City/Province/Postal Code

Telephone_____

CUT HERE

From _____

Diane Knight
Knighttime Publications
890 Calabasas Road
Watsonville, CA 95076

- - - - - - - - - - - - - - -FOLD HERE - - - - - - - - - - - - - - - -

CUT HERE

STAPLE OR TAPE

B&B TRAVELERS REPORT

Knighttime Publications would like to receive any comments you may have about your experiences while using this directory. Please report any comment, suggestion, compliment or criticism as indicated:

Name and location of B&B _____

Date of visit _____

Length of stay _____

Comments _____

_____

_____

_____

_____

_____

_____

_____

_____

_____

_____

_____

Your name _____

Address_____

City/State/Zip _____
City/Province/Postal Code

Telephone_____

CUT HERE

From_____

_____

_____

FIRST
CLASS
POSTAGE

Diane Knight
Knighttime Publications
890 Calabasas Road
Watsonville, CA 95076

- - - - - - - - - - - - - - -FOLD HERE - - - - - - - - - - - - - - - -

CUT HERE

STAPLE OR TAPE

ORDERING ADDITIONAL BOOKS

Please send me: (I enclose payment with order)

_____additional copies of *BED & BREAKFAST HOMES DI-RECTORY - WEST COAST* (7th edition) at **$12.95** each. Include **$2.00** postage and handling for first copy, plus **$1.00** for each additional copy to the same address. *California residents add current sales tax.*

Canadian residents, please send payment in U.S. funds using the above pricing.

Name _____

Address_____

City/State/Zip _____
City/Province/Postal Code

Send as a gift to: (Use extra paper for additional gifts)

Name _____

Address_____

City/State/Zip _____
City/Province/Postal Code

Gift card should read: _____

Mail this form with payment to:

KNIGHTTIME PUBLICATIONS
890 Calabasas Road
Watsonville, CA 95076